The
Kardashians

ALSO BY JERRY OPPENHEIMER

RFK Jr.: Robert F. Kennedy Jr. and the Dark Side of the Dream

*Crazy Rich: Power, Scandal, and Tragedy Inside
the Johnson & Johnson Dynasty*

*The Other Mrs. Kennedy: Ethel Skakel Kennedy:
An American Drama of Power, Privilege, and Politics*

*State of a Union: Inside the Complex Marriage
of Bill and Hillary Clinton*

Just Desserts: Martha Stewart—The Unauthorized Biography

*Front Row: Anna Wintour—
The Cool Life and Hot Times of Vogue's Editor in Chief*

*House of Hilton: From Conrad to Paris:
A Drama of Wealth, Power, and Privilege*

Toy Monster: The Big, Bad World of Mattel

Madoff with the Money

Seinfeld: The Making of an American Icon

Barbara Walters: An Unauthorized Biography

Idol: Rock Hudson: The True Story of an American Film Hero
(with Jack Vitek)

The Kardashians

AN AMERICAN DRAMA

Jerry Oppenheimer

St. Martin's Press
New York

www.stmartins.com

The Library of Congress Cataloging-in-Publication Data is available upon request.

ISBN 978-1-250-08714-0 (hardcover)
ISBN 978-1-250-08716-4 (ebook)

Our books may be purchased in bulk for promotional, educational, or business use. Please contact your local bookseller or the Macmillan Corporate and Premium Sales Department at 1-800-221-7945, extension 5442, or by email at MacmillanSpecialMarkets@macmillan.com.

10 9 8 7 6 5 4 3 2 1

For Caroline, Trixie, Ruggles, Toby, Jesse, Louise,
Julien and Max, and in memory of Cukes

CONTENTS

PART III: THE "MISCREANTS"

SOME OF THE CAST OF CHARACTERS

ROBERT GEORGE KARDASHIAN
O.J. Simpson's friend and "mouthpiece," he became a born-again Christian because of a horrific family scandal, and his later life spun out of control through misplaced loyalty, disastrous choices in women, and failed businesses.

KRISTEN "KRIS" HOUGHTON KARDASHIAN JENNER
From dysfunctional blue-collar roots with little more than a high school diploma, her sole ambition in life, with her single mother as her enabler, was to find and marry a rich man. She was later branded an adulteress and "momager."

THOMAS ARTHUR "TOMMY" KARDASHIAN

Older brother of Robert, he would follow in their father's footsteps running the family's meatpacking business, but would get caught in a corruption scandal that would forever impact his life.

PASTOR KENN GULLIKSEN

Helped to convert Bob Dylan to born-again Christianity, Gulliksen did the same for Robert Kardashian, and became a close confidant, officiating at Kardashian's marriage to Kris, and watching as their marriage fell apart.

CESAR SANUDO

A professional golfer from Mexico, he met and fell in love with seventeen-year-old Kris, but caught her with Kardashian, and soon after ending it with her Sanudo discovered his valuable gold coin collection was missing.

PRISCILLA PRESLEY

Kardashian desperately wanted to wed the ex-wife of Elvis, but the "King" continued to dominate, and she ended it with Kardashian, which is when he married Kris Houghton, who he thought was too young and unsophisticated.

DENICE SHAKARIAN HALICKI

Blond, buxom third cousin and fiancé of Robert Kardashian, who retained him to help in an estate battle. They fell in love but their relationship ended when he cheated on her.

JONI MIGDAL

A confidante from childhood and Robert Kardashian's lover for a time, she was present when he first met Kris and asked for her telephone number. Later, her attorney daughter was O.J. Simpson's murder trial "babysitter."

BARBARA WALTERS

She got the first TV post-trial sit-down with Kardashian, but she broke her promises about how the interview would be conducted, and he lied to her about how the trial impacted his life.

LARRY KRAINES

Multimillionaire close friend of Kardashian since high school, and known as "Uncle Larry" to the Kardashian kids, he caught Kris cheating with her lover in his Beverly Hills mansion, and warned his furious pal.

JOAN ZIMMERMAN

Close school chum of Kris, Joan saw big changes in her when, in eleventh grade, Kris began pursuing older men and was seeking them out at a resort that reportedly catered to mobsters.

CINDY SPALLINO

Bonded with Kris Houghton when they were training to become stewardesses, and saw how desperate she was to marry Kardashian, and how jealous she was of Priscilla Presley, for whom he had dropped Kris.

ROBERT HOUGHTON

Kris's alcoholic, abusive biological father, he abandoned the family when she was seven, and later took up with a number of younger women. He was killed when his Porsche crashed into a truck on his way to marry again.

O. J. SIMPSON

Football hero, actor, and acquitted murderer, he was Robert Kardashian's hero, and he defended Simpson when he was accused of murdering his wife, Nicole Brown, and her friend, Ron Goldman, in the "trial of the century."

CAITLYN MARIE JENNER (AKA BRUCE JENNER)

Olympic gold medal winner, he married Kris Kardashian even before the ink was dry on her Kardashian divorce papers. She claimed she didn't know he was always a woman trapped in a man's body during their years of marriage. In January 2017, he had gender reassignment surgery.

Prominently featured, too, are the leading featured players in the long-running Kardashian drama. The cast of characters could not be complete without the theatrics and spectacle of Kim Kardashian West and her siblings: Kourtney, Khloé, Rob, Kendall Jenner, and Kylie Jenner.

PROLOGUE

Shortly after the O. J. Simpson murder trial concluded with a shocking acquittal on racial lines in October 1995—considered to be one of the grossest miscarriages of justice in the twentieth century—O.J.'s longtime friend and legal "dream team" defender Robert George Kardashian attended a small gathering of confidants who were born-again Christians like him and offered them an eerie story about a curious prediction that had suddenly come true.

After regaling everyone with insider stories about what would become known as the trial of the century, Kardashian revealed that a Christian prophetess—a religious woman who foretells the future—had once held his hand and made a curious prophecy.

"She prophesied that one day my name, the Kardashian name, would be known around the world," he told his rapt friends.

Kardashian went on to disclose that he had long forgotten the odd prediction, but that the prophetess's words had come rushing back to him as he stood before a microphone in the lobby of a Century City office building for a press conference announced by O. J. Simpson's lead attorney, Robert Shapiro. It was shortly after five P.M. on the day of the infamous white Ford Bronco police chase. Shapiro had asked Kardashian—the press would later refer to them as "the two Bobs"—to read to the assembled media throng the letter the on-the-run accused murderer had penned and left in Kardashian's Encino home before he fled in the Bronco with their mutual friend Al "A. C." Cowlings at the wheel, and "the Juice" in the backseat with a loaded pistol aimed at himself.

Like other contemporary historic events, such as the Kennedy assassination, O.J.'s run of his life was filmed and televised. Millions of viewers around the country were mesmerized, watching the police chase, and thousands of Angelenos stood alongside L.A. freeways and on overpasses cheering as the Bronco raced past, followed by a swarm of LAPD black-and-white cruisers.

Usually shy about public speaking back then, Kardashian initially resisted Shapiro's entreaty to read O.J.'s words, but soon acceded.

The date was June 17, 1994.

An international army of reporters, who had descended on Los Angeles to cover the breaking news story about the vicious murders of O.J.'s beautiful wife, Nicole, and her young friend, Ronald Goldman, with the football great as the prime suspect, listened intently and took notes as Kardashian slowly and precisely read O.J.'s letter.

"I have nothing to do with Nicole's murder." Kardashian solemnly and confidently began reading his friend's plea and conceivable suicide note. "I loved her, always have and always will . . . Peace and love, O.J.," he concluded.

It took Kardashian six minutes to go through the entire bizarre missive. He did it like a pro, surprising even himself.

Six minutes was all it took for Robert Kardashian's life to become an American moment.

And when he was finished, the press mob barked at him to identify himself. "Who's the bloody mouthpiece?" shouted a journo for a Fleet Street red top.

To the assembled scribes, Kardashian was an unknown, just another Beverly Hills type in an expensive designer suit with fashionably wide lapels, and with a funny-looking white streak in his well-coiffed hair.

Obediently, he said his name was Kardashian, Robert Kardashian.

"Spell it," the reporters shouted, and he did. "K-A-R-D-A-S-H-I-A-N."

On TV screens across the country, the super popped up under his frozen face. It read: "Robert Kardashian, Simpson Friend."

At that moment, for the first time—on live television and in press accounts transmitted around the world—the Kardashian name, virtually in an instant, had become known, just as the prophetess had prophesied long before.

Fast-forward to the spring of 2016.

A born-again Christian woman with the joyous name Happy Rue recalled Kardashian's revelation about the prophecy at that small gathering at the home of his close friend and religious counselor, Pastor Kenn Gulliksen, some two decades earlier. Rue was the widow of Brent Rue, an evangelical minister who had been Gulliksen's associate pastor at his charismatic evangelical Vineyard church for two years, and there had closely bonded with the church's Elder, Robert Kardashian.

"My husband and Robert got along so well," she recalled. "They both had an incredible sense of humor. Brent was kind of a fun-loving guy who was quick with his humor, and Robert was, too, and they played on each other."

The Rues also got to know the pretty former junior flight attendant Kris Houghton even before Kardashian had married her.

"When Robert first hooked up with Kris and they became kind of an item, he called up Kenn and his wife, Joanie, and me and my husband, to come over for dinner. He was so anxious to introduce us to her, and Kris cooked up a big Mexican feast there at Robert's Beverly Hills house." Happy Rue had never forgotten. "Kris was delightful, and Robert was so excited by Kris, really bedazzled by her. And I remember we were all holding hands and praying over Kris's meal, and I've thought many times about what happened to all of us over the years, and about Kris's history of infidelity with Robert, and how she really broke his heart."

MOTHER OF FOUR AND COUGAR extraordinaire, Kris thought she had found the perfect spot in the late eighties to have afternoon assignations with her hunky twenty-three-year-old boy-toy lover, Todd Waterman. She knew the layout well. Kris had accompanied husband Robert to the Beverly Hills mansion of close friends Larry and Joyce Kraines a million times for socializing and as A-list guests at the Kraineses' elegantly done soirees, where Kris was always considered the belle of the ball. Robert and Larry had bonded in tenth grade at Susan Miller Dorsey High School, class of 1962, in Los Angeles, and had remained close confidants ever since.

"Robert and I and our families spent New Year's Eve together forever it seemed," Larry Kraines fondly recalled, reminiscing about their friendship years later.

At first it was Robert and whomever he was dating at the time, along with Larry and Joyce Kraines, and O. J. Simpson and his first wife, Marguerite. Then it was Robert and Kris and O.J. and Nicole with the Kraineses.

"We all did the New Year's holiday for years," said Larry, heir to an auto accessories fortune. "We went together on Thanksgiving trips, and we skied every Thanksgiving at Vail. Robert had a guy who he knew who rented a whole house to us in Vail, and we did that for years, usually during the spring break. My daughter and son went to the same school, Buckley, with the older girls, Kourtney and Kim, who were close friends. Before Vail we'd go to Park City, back in the days when Khloé was three. I had a plane and we took all the kids up.

"My relationship with those girls and Kris and Robert goes back decades," continued Kraines. "At their weddings today the Kardashian kids all run up and hug and kiss me. They still call me 'Uncle Larry.' "

It was Joyce Kraines, then pregnant, who threw Kris a fancy wedding shower when she became engaged to Robert in 1978, and she was one of Kris's bridesmaids.

With that kind of loving and long relationship, there was absolutely no reason for Larry and Joyce to question Kris's motivation and agenda when she innocently asked permission to drop by on her own when no one was at home and use their professional gym to do her workouts in the lower level of the Kraineses' gorgeous circa 1929 Spanish-style Beverly Hills mansion.

She said she especially wanted to use their sun bed in hopes the ultraviolet rays would cure a bothersome and unsightly case of psoriasis she had. A Beverly Hills physician had advised her to spend time in a sun bed "every other day," but it was her idea to combine treatment with sexual pleasure.

To Kris's friends the Kraineses, her request was a reasonable one, not a problem.

Larry and Joyce trusted Kris implicitly.

One afternoon, however, Larry arrived home early and was in for a shocking surprise when he "sort of got caught in the middle" of discovering his best friend Robert's wife, Kris—who he thought he knew well after a decade of closeness—"with her boyfriend downstairs in my house, doing their thing, and she got caught, and this was going on, on Robert."

The Kraineses' housekeeper had told the master of the house that Kris had been coming over to "do the sun bed, and then it went further, that this guy Todd Waterman was there working out with her," Larry Kraines recounted. "What the housekeeper said was that they were doing something bad, that it was very quiet down there in the gym."

When confronted, Kraines had never forgotten, "Kris said, 'Oh, he's just my friend and we just came over.' Kris is very quick on her feet, and she's been quick on her feet her whole life."

Kraines knew by then that Kris had the ability to come up with an answer, an excuse, or an alibi in any situation with the best of them. And he immediately surmised that she "absolutely" knew his hectic work schedule and had started using his absence from his home to secure a creative meeting place for her clandestine afternoon playdates with her lover.

"Kris would come over two or three times a week to work out. She'd use the sun bed, and basically this was an escape to meet the guy and do whatever," asserted Kraines. "I knew something was up—Kris knew it, and I knew it. I saw guilt in her face. We talked about it, and I told her, 'No, what you're doing isn't very good.' I said, 'Kris, this is wrong.' I called her on it. I said, 'Stop this, and not in my house. Robert's my best friend.'"

Larry and Joyce Kraines had suspected before Kris was caught that there was trouble in the Kardashian marriage.

"I knew things were rocky because Kris was close to my wife, Joyce," said Kraines.

But Kris didn't directly confide in her.

"Kris was always very smart that way, smart and street smart," observed Kraines. "She really didn't want to embarrass herself by saying something stupid like admitting cheating. On the other hand, we knew there were problems, and by then Robert knew there was a problem.

"Robert actually brought it up, and he told me that he knew Kris was cheating on him, and he told me, 'I know who the guy is,' and he asked me, 'Do you know anything about it?' I said, 'A little bit,' and I told him that the guy came over and was with Kris downstairs when she was in the sun bed.

"Robert says, 'Yeah, well, you know that's all bullshit.' I know Robert was following the guy around, and Robert told me that he once pulled up next to him and threatened him to stay away from Kris. I remember telling him, 'You had better be careful. You can't just do stuff like that.' "

Kris later told Larry and Joyce that she "regretted" what she had done in their home.

But she continued the affair.

Years later Kris would make the odd claim that she was a "good girl," and strangely attributed to the devil her desire to have an affair.

In her 2011 memoir, *Kris Jenner . . . and All Things Kardashian*—in which she takes many liberties with the truth—she wrote: "I felt on some level like Satan had just taken over my body and said, '*You're mine.*' "

By then, shrewd operator Kris Houghton Kardashian Jenner was already known as the "momager"—a self-proclaimed sobriquet, meaning mom of her kids and manager of their lucrative careers—who had taken her and her vapid children's well-plotted trials and tribulations to the world via reality television and, in the process, built the Kardashian Inc. brand, making them all a fortune.

Their timing was spot-on, their debut in reality television coming as the Facebook generation and social media was exploding. Online, on TV, in the supermarket tabloids, on the covers of the celebrity weeklies, and even in the mainstream media, their banal lives were documented twenty-four/seven; the Kardashians would be loved, ridiculed, and despised around the world by millions, making them even more millions in the process.

Long dead by that point—and likely rolling over in his grave; esophageal cancer had taken him at the age of fifty-nine—was the contemporary patriarch of the Kardashian tribe, Robert, dubbed the "mouthpiece," who first made the Kardashian name famous by defending his bosom buddy O. J. Simpson in one of U.S. history's most famous murder trials.

And what may be the final act in the long-running Kardashian family drama starred Kris's second husband, father of two more of her children, the gold medal–winning Olympian Bruce Jenner—an attention getter like the others—who for years felt he was a societal "misfit"—a woman trapped in the body of a man, in his case a very athletic man. He famously rectified his problem in 2015 by coming out blazing on national television as the glamorous transgender woman Ms. Caitlyn Marie Jenner, soon with her own well-publicized reality TV show, and with a new calling: defender of the transgender community.

Here, then, is the untold and often shocking story of the Momager, the Mouthpiece, the Misfit, and their supporting cast of characters, told for the first time by the people who knew them best.

PART I

The "Momager"

ONE

Stay Classy, San Diego

Forget about the big homes, the designer clothes, the fancy cars, the private jets, the millions of dollars' worth of diamond jewelry famously stolen from daughter Kim in Paris in 2016, the celebrity lifestyle, and the immense riches. Nouveau riche Kris Houghton Kardashian Jenner's predominate family roots are buried deep in the poor, mostly unschooled Deep South, and the simple blue-collar Midwestern folk of nineteenth- and early twentieth-century heartland America. Hillary Clinton might have used the term "deplorables" to describe them.

Kristen Mary Houghton, the future ambitious momager of the Kardashian-Jenner clan, who came into the world on November 5, 1955, was essentially brought up by her down-home, domineering, all-business maternal grandmother, Lou Ethel Wyatt Campbell Fairbanks.

She was Kris's "hero" and "most instrumental" in her upbringing.

Kris's mother, Mary Jo Campbell Houghton Shannon, was Kris's "pillar of strength," but in a far different way.

There was, however, little or no paternal influence. Kris's father, Robert True Houghton, was an alcoholic who abandoned the family when Kris was seven and her sister, Karen, was four.

Lou Ethel would have very little fame, unlike her granddaughter and great-granddaughters, a bit of fortune with a small business, and a troubled time with men. She was born in Jackson, Missouri—scene of two fatal cholera epidemics that struck in the nineteenth century—ten days before Halloween in 1913. She was the only child of native Mississippian Walter Wyatt, said to be a physician's son, and Mary Wyatt, known as "Tiny."

Hope, Arkansas, where Lou Ethel reportedly was raised, was famous as the birthplace of William Jefferson Clinton, governor of Arkansas and president of the United States. Like Lou Ethel, Clinton's mother, Virginia Clinton Kelley, had man trouble, too, and had four marriages. Lou Ethel would have at least two.

Her first husband was one Gordon Lowe Campbell, a native of tiny Tulsa and Sapulpa, Oklahoma, a burg called Mounds, in Creek County, a tiny dot on the map that never had a population of much over a thousand—and that was only when the oil boom struck Oklahoma during the Roaring Twenties. But the poor Campbells never had a gusher, let alone a trickle of the black gold.

Their town was once called Eufaula, but in the late 1800s the whole place—lock, stock, and barrel—was moved five miles away—why is unclear—and was oddly renamed Mounds, because of the nearby twin hills, and not because of the popular coconut candy bar that came in two chocolate mounds but still hadn't as yet been invented.

No one known to be famous had ever come out of Mounds.

On September 4, 1932, with the Great Depression ravaging the nation, Lou Ethel married Campbell, and two years later, in October 1934, she had her one and only known child, a daughter.

The Campbells called her Mary Jo—a good old down-home name.

"M.J.," as she also was known, was the future mother of the momager Kris and the future maternal grandmother of Kourtney, Kim, Khloé, and Rob, from Kris's first marriage, to Robert Kardashian, and Kendall and Kylie, from her second, to Bruce Jenner.

But the Lou Ethel Wyatt–Gordon Campbell union bit the dust sometime after Mary Jo's birth: Lou Ethel discovered that Gordon was allegedly cheating on her—cheating being a familiar theme in Kris Jenner's biography—so her grandmother packed her bags and, with Mary Jo in tow, left Kris's maternal grandfather.

About six years after M.J. came into the world, and not long before the Japanese attack on Pearl Harbor and the U.S. entry into World War II, her philandering father remarried, taking as his wife one Juanita Ethel Patton, a Missouri telephone operator and a Baptist. They had a daughter, Carolyn Sue.

Gordon Campbell died at the age of forty-two in 1951, according to an obituary.

When Lou Ethel left him, she had hightailed it to sunny Southern California, and the lively military and tourist town of San Diego—home in contemporary pop culture to the fictional goofy TV news anchorman Ron Burgundy, whose ironic signature sign-off was "Stay classy, San Diego."

There, Lou Ethel, who was business-minded, got a job supposedly doing some sort of accounting at San Diego's sprawling U.S. Navy and Marine Corps base.

As Kris later described it, her "very strong-willed and stubborn" grandmother had the "gumption to leave," deciding "she didn't need a man in her life."

Many years later Lou Ethel's granddaughter, Kris, would make it onto Wikipedia's long list of famous San Diegans, among many of her other unexpected and very surprising achievements.

Despite Kris's claim, Lou Ethel found that she did, indeed, need a man in her life, and married another blue-collar fellow, by the name of James Edwin Fairbanks, originally from Arcola City, Illinois, birthplace

in the late nineteenth century of John Barton Gruelle, creator of Raggedy Ann and Raggedy Andy.

In San Diego, Kris's step-grandfather, Jim Fairbanks, was a menial-
labor truck driver who hauled panes of glass for San Diego Glass and
Paint, and was, as Kris later described, "pure working-class Middle
America." In other words, he was a mensch, at least compared to Lou
Ethel's philandering first husband.

Fairbanks became the male figure in Kris's life, and Lou Ethel was
the matriarch.

Kris's mother, Mary Jo, and Kris herself would both follow in Lou
Ethel's footsteps, each having at least two marriages and marital problems. A couple of Kris's daughters would, too.

In that family, history definitely repeated itself.

Mary Jo, tall and slender, was a very attractive girl, and Lou Ethel
apparently saw money-making potential in her looks, so when M.J. was
fifteen, she was enrolled in a San Diego charm school called Fashional-
ity, where hairdos, makeup, posture, and hemlines were taught. A representative of the school often traveled around lecturing to women's
groups, such as the Chula Vista Woman's Club. Mary Jo later claimed
that she had done some modeling, but there's nothing that could be
found by the author in the public domain to support such an assertion.

Known for her hype, exaggeration, and image-creation, Kris would
later compare her mother's looks and fashion sense to none other than
one of America's most glamorous first ladies, Jacqueline Kennedy, claiming that Mary Jo always looked like she was wearing "some fabulous
Chanel ensemble."

Like her mother, who married an adulterer the first time around,
Mary Jo also clearly didn't make the greatest choices in men, and married at least two who were alcoholics.

The first, Robert True Houghton (pronounced Ho-ton), was the biological father of Kris and her younger sister, Karen.

Mary Jo knew Bob Houghton, three years her senior, when they both
attended Herbert Hoover High School in San Diego—he was in the

class of 1949, she in the class of 1952—and he always thought she was the prettiest girl in school. But it wasn't until later that they became an item. He was then working as an aeronautical draftsman in the aerospace field—Kris described him as an "engineer"—employed at San Diego's big airplane manufacturing company, Convair.

Mary Jo and Bob were married in the white-bread Eisenhower era of the early 1950s—but the Houghtons were nothing like the fictional middle-class Andersons of *Father Knows Best* TV fame, the fifties program that exemplified happy, middle-class, morally upright American family life.

The Houghtons were more the Andersons' dysfunctional next-door neighbors.

Bob and Mary Jo were living in a working-class section of San Diego called Point Loma, a seaside community and home to several military installations, when Kris was born, a month after her mother's twenty-first birthday. If one believes in the Zodiac signs of astrology, Kris turned out to be a true Scorpio, good and bad—sexual, secretive, manipulative, independent, resourceful, and dynamic, she was all of them and more.

Her father was tall, handsome, and slim with striking very dark brown, almost pitch-black eyes, which his daughter Kris would inherit, and which would be the only good DNA of his that was handed down to her, except for an aggressive ability he had to pitch and sell anything to anybody. Because of her eyes, people who knew Kris would say she looked like Natalie Wood. Her first husband, Robert Kardashian, especially was mesmerized by them, but other men would be, too.

Three years after Kris was born, Mary Jo gave birth to another girl, who the Houghtons named Karen. (Kris would later carry on the tradition of naming her own daughters with the first letter *K*, but it had nothing to do with the name Kardashian, as would be claimed.)

In 2013, Mary Jo gave a curious and very superficial interview to a fashion writer for *The Daily Beast*. It took place in the children's clothing boutique she owned in La Jolla, where a large framed photo of her famous—and infamous—granddaughter Kim Kardashian hung on the wall, appropriately enough behind the cash register, for customers to ogle.

M.J. offered some biographical data about herself and her children and grandchildren, but oddly never once mentioned that she had been married to Bob Houghton, father of her two daughters, Kris and Karen, and paternal grandfather of Kim and her Kardashian siblings, and with whom Mary Jo had lived for a decade, stormy though their union may have been.

Instead, under the headline "Keeping Up with Granny Kardashian: Meet Mary Jo Shannon," she questionably claimed, and it was duly reported, that she "married her high school sweetheart at the age of eighteen," not identified by her, and that "they divorced after two months." That marriage would have taken place around the time she graduated from Herbert Hoover High School. Two years later, she said, she had Kris. She said she then "remarried twice"—no names mentioned—and remained with the last guy, one Harry Shannon, "for forty years," until his death. Depending on who's keeping score, the momager's mom may have had three or four husbands based on the statistics she offered, but she made no mention of the man who actually fathered her famous daughter.

As a close family source who read the story later observed, "What M.J. says is *really* strange. It just doesn't compute."

In any case, the year Kris was born, the number one album in the United States was *Love Me or Leave Me,* an Academy Award–nominated Doris Day soundtrack from the romance film of the same name.

In 1962, when Kris was seven and Karen four, Bob Houghton and Mary Jo split after a decade of rocky marriage with much bickering and fighting regarding his drinking and verbal abusiveness. They didn't love each other anymore, and he decided to leave, just like in the lyrics of that Doris Day number.

Mary Jo filed for divorce in San Diego in October 1963, citing "extreme cruelty," and received custody of her two daughters, and their father severed all contact.

As Kris later stated, "The divorce was tough for me and had lasting effects."

Kris and Karen would not reunite again with their father until more than a decade later, when Kris, about eighteen, was living with a golf pro, the Mexican-born Cesar Sanudo, and was being chased by the Armenian American lawyer Robert Kardashian.

Bob Houghton had by then returned to San Diego from Los Angeles, where he had moved after the divorce, and was living with a woman by the name of Leslie Johnson Leach.

The two couples, Kris's father and his girlfriend, Leslie, about a decade his junior, and Kris, a dozen years younger than her lover, Sanudo, would actually double date, and Kris would be witness for the first time to her father's drunken rages and abusiveness.

Houghton was an irresponsible alcoholic who didn't even carry insurance on his classic red-orange Porsche coupe. He would later die after drinking and then driving that sports car, slamming into a truck head-on and leaving his passenger, the mother of two young boys he had planned to take as his second wife, almost a cripple. But all of that was far in the future.

Several years after Houghton had walked out on Kris's mother, Mary Jo, she had a new man in her life.

His name was Harry Shannon.

Like Bob Houghton, Harry was an alcoholic.

M.J. could certainly pick 'em.

During the three years they dated on and off before marrying, Shannon showed his hard-drinking persona. Once, in the middle of the night, for example, he showed up banging on Mary Jo's bedroom window and her front door, waking her daughters, causing a major commotion in his effort to see her, and frightening Kris, then about ten, and Karen, about seven. Neighbors were said to have complained, and probably wished that that rowdy bunch next door would move.

Mary Jo finally put her foot down and ordered Shannon to sober up if he wanted to get serious with her, or get lost. She used the old "my way or the highway" to force him to stop drinking if he wanted her, and he actually did quit.

Harry's mantra, according to Kris, was: "If you want something bad enough, and are willing to change your life for it, you can do anything."

Like her mother, Kris would have the ability to manipulate and influence men, as her future would hold.

Harry Shannon was a character and a hustler, hawking yachts at one point, and even had gotten into the abalone—that's a fish—processing business at another point, but lost a bankroll when a partner took off with it. Unstoppable, and always able to find a way to make a buck, Shannon turned up for a time across from SeaWorld, in San Diego, as the proprietor of a used-car rental business called Ugly Duckling Rent-A-Car, and still later he was known in the San Diego automobile dealers' trade as the guy who pinstriped new cars. He also found a moneymaking calling installing television antennas, crawling up on people's roofs like Spider-Man.

The lovebirds tied the knot in style in June 1968 in beautiful and romantic Puerto Vallarta, on Mexico's Pacific coast.

They were, Kris later pointed out, "just like" Elizabeth Taylor and Richard Burton (also an alcoholic), who put Puerto Vallarta on the map as a sublime and very private getaway for the rich and famous and lovers of all persuasions.

Burton and Taylor, each married to someone else, established a love nest there called Casa Kimberly, which was the name of a villa owned by the director John Huston. Years later, Casa Kimberly and Puerto Vallarta held such fond memories for Mary Jo that when Kris gave birth to her second child on October 21, 1980, it was M.J. who suggested that the baby be named Kimberly—as in Casa Kimberly, in honor of the clandestine Burton-Taylor hideaway in Puerto Vallarta littered with Burton's liquor bottles, where infant Kimberly "Kim" Noel Kardashian's grandmother and the newborn's grandfather took the vows of holy matrimony. Kris however, would later claim that she named Kim after a girlfriend named Kimberly.

In any case, Harry made Mary Jo an honest woman by marrying her.

In her memoir, Kris Jenner boasted about what a great guy the once liquored-up, high-energy salesman Harry Shannon was, who she now called "Dad." After developing what was said to be a staph infection in the hospital following an auto accident, Shannon, in his mid-seventies, died in 2003, the same year Robert Kardashian passed away.

While Harry Shannon was trying to find the right moneymaking proposition back in the early 1960s, he and Mary Jo and the kids, Kris and Karen, moved like Okies from one Southern California location to another. Kris was unhappy, later revealing, "I never again wanted to be in the position of being completely powerless to do something about a situation I didn't want to be in."

They finally settled down, moving around the mid-1960s to a relatively new development of cookie-cutter single homes, duplexes, and apartments called University City in the San Diego community of Clairemont.

Financially, Kris's family was in better shape and seemingly more stable. Stepfather Harry Shannon was bringing in money, and Kris's maternal grandmother, Lou Ethel Fairbanks, had opened a small business called the Candelabra, selling candles and other decorations in La Jolla, with her husband, the truck driver, helping her out on his off-time. Kris and Karen's mom, Mary Jo, was working a variety of jobs— she had even purchased a flashy Ford Thunderbird convertible, circa 1956, and much later opened her own candle shop, Candles of La Jolla, located next to a waffle shop. Still later, she was the proprietor of a small children's clothing store in La Jolla, but by then her daughter Kris was a high-living housewife of Beverly Hills, married to Robert Kardashian.

TWO

School Days

Schooling was never a big priority for Kris Houghton, as schooling had never been of great importance for her forebears up to and including her maternal grandmother and her mother, neither of whom ever went beyond high school. Two of Kris's daughters, Kim and Khloé, would follow the same path, but Kourtney would attend and get a degree from the University of Arizona, a noted party school, and Kris's troubled son, Rob, would follow, somewhat, in his father's footsteps and attend USC, graduating in 2009 from the Marshall School of Business. He was later reportedly caught lying when he tweeted that he had been accepted at a law school.

In Kris's three-hundred-page memoir, she sums up her twelve years of public school education in very few words; to wit: "I went to school, I got good grades, I had lots of friends."

But shining a spotlight on that important period of her life reveals much about the persona of the budding momager.

At the age of twelve, in seventh grade at Marston Middle School, located on Clairemont Drive, in Clairemont, fresh-faced, congenial Kris Houghton had volunteered to work as an office aide, telling one of the ladies there that she planned to be either a schoolteacher or a secretary when she grew up, and that she believed being around the school office would be good experience for her.

But she may have had another reason for volunteering: by working in the office, she was able to skip gym class, which she hated.

Kris had a vivacious personality even back then and could easily charm people and make them feel comfortable, so she anointed herself the school office's unofficial greeter, welcoming anxious parents and helping nervous new students in the school, which served seventh, eighth, and ninth graders.

One such case involved Marla Tafelski, an electronics salesman's daughter, who arrived with her mother to register at Marston for the first time in the middle of her ninth-grade year, in 1969, when Kris was about fourteen.

"It was so embarrassing because I was with my mom and my siblings and Kris was in the office and she was just super nice and introduced herself, and she volunteered to take me around the school and introduce me to people," Marla recalled years later. "I met her friends and she showed me different areas of the school, and after that we just became super-good friends. She probably had an insight that I was feeling pretty uncomfortable. I was feeling lost and she just made me feel welcome."

In looks and style the two girls were very different. Marla was "more earthy"—jeans, boots, a peasant top—and Kris was "*always* more nicely dressed. I was more casual, she was *always* dressed up more—more adult-looking."

Marla saw that Kris was "very social, with a huge smile and friendly with everybody," and they all seemed to like her. The two began hanging out "a lot" at each other's homes, just the two of them. While Marla had made a few other friends, none were "as close" as Kris Houghton, and their friendship seemed like it would go on forever.

They listened to music—Marla was more "hardcore rock 'n' roll," Kris "was more into the pop stuff."

They talked about boys, went to the movies, just hung out.

Kris's home was just like Marla's, she recalled, and just like most of the others in University City—"your typical house in a development, and nicely decorated."

And whenever Marla was there, she remembered clearly, Kris's mother, Mary Jo, was there, too.

"To me, she always seemed to be home, was kind of petite but with really *big* dark brown hair, and she always dressed *really* fancy with high heels and tight pants, and a frilly blouse. Compared to other mothers I knew back then, Kris's was more dressy, and just really kept herself up," Marla noted.

Sometimes a man would be present, "very stern-looking with glasses, wasn't real friendly, and just a not real acknowledging-of-my-presence type," Marla remembered. Kris never introduced him to Marla, and Marla never really knew what his role was in the house, "whether he was Kris's father, or stepfather, or what. But he wasn't a grandfather."

In those adolescent days, friendships come and go like teenage acne, while some people remain friends for a lifetime. In Marla and Kris's case, their bond began to unravel, and Kris began to drift away about seven or eight months into their relationship.

"I kind of thought that we were best pals," said Marla, looking back years later. "But I just felt I was getting further and further out of the loop, and at the time I was feeling hurt, I guess, because I thought I was more special to her, and then I realized I was just one of kind of many people in her life. She was so much more extroverted and *so* popular, and maybe I wanted more intimacy. I think we both realized we weren't each other's type after all."

Marla had a sister, Vicki, two years her junior, who became close friends for about two years at Marston with Karen Houghton, Kris's younger sister by three years.

Vicki had gotten to know Kris when she was chums with Marla and thought Kris was pretty, but nowhere near as pretty as Karen. "Karen was just *beautiful*," recalled Vicki. "Of the two sisters, Karen was the prettier one. She was just *really* pretty with long, dark hair, and big, dark eyes, and was really sweet."

Karen was in seventh grade and Vicki in eighth when they became friends, and they did the usual young teen girl stuff—go to the movies, parties, and hang out at Karen and Kris's house, because, as Vicki recalled, no adults were ever at home in the afternoon after school. Like Kris, Karen always dressed smartly. "Her attire was very up-to-date, and she was very cool," said Vicki.

One of her fondest memories of Kris's younger sister is the day the two of them, along with two other friends of Vicki's, decided to crash a fortieth birthday party that the father of one of the two girls was having.

"They were all drinking and having fun and partying, and we decided to sing for all of them at their party—give them a little concert, and we just had a blast, and one of the songs we sang for them was 'Benny and the Jets.' That's like my favorite memory of Karen. She was just very perky, very fun."

Years later, Vicki began hearing stories that Karen had had a troubled life, that Karen had a drinking problem, and that Karen and Kris had been feuding, all of which would become fodder for the tabloids, gossip columns, and the celebrity weeklies.

"I'd watch the Kardashians on TV, and kind of pay attention to see if they ever mentioned Karen. She was such a nice person."

ANOTHER GIRL WHO BONDED MORE closely than Marla Tafelski with Kris Houghton at Marston and stayed friends with her through much of high school until there was a drastic change in Kris was Joan Zimmerman.

The Zimmermans had moved to University City in 1966 from New Mexico, where Joan's father had been editor of a trade magazine dealing with nuclear weapons. His new job, in public relations for a company that built nuclear power plants, brought him to San Diego and the family into a home in University City, close to where Kris lived, and in walking distance to Marston, which is how the two met—walking to school.

"It wasn't an affluent area by any means," said Joan. "We all lived pretty much the same kind of lifestyle. But Kris's house was newer, and was one-story, and was more contemporary than the rest of the homes, and had more modern things."

Joan had never forgotten the shag carpeting that seemed to be everywhere in Kris's house, "and we used to have to rake it before we left. We'd go there after school and we had to get this carpet rake out and rake the carpet so that it looked fresh and neat. None of the rest of us had shag carpeting," she recalled, laughing about it years later. "There were four or five of us that were girlfriends, and we just laughed and had fun, and it was just very pure and very innocent."

Of Kris's tight-knit circle, Joan was the favorite and soon bonded with Kris's grandmother, Lou Ethel Fairbanks, and her husband, who ran the little candle shop in La Jolla. And Kris and Joan began working there. "It was my very first job," said Joan, "and the grandma just kind of mentored us and helped us to learn how to work in a store."

The shop, she recalled, was "tony and very quaint," and sold ordinary candles and also some fine gifts—candelabras, ceramics, candle stands, a lot of glass items. "All nice stuff. There was so much tourist traffic that would come through, so we did a lot of packaging and mailed things for people. Her grandmother had so much patience in teaching us the art of packing so things would not get broken. There were so many good things that came from that period. Looking back now, it was really impressionable on my life."

It's Joan's memory that Kris's grandmother was running things, while Kris's mother was rarely around, or somewhere in the background, unlike how it was when Marla Tafelski was palling around with Kris and Mary Jo always seemed to be a presence.

"I knew there was a mom," Joan said, "and I know she had rules in the house for Kris, but she *never* interacted with us. When she was there, we had to be quiet. We'd go there after school when she wasn't there. The family was just very private.

Joan had the impression from Kris that her mother "wasn't around all the time, but Mom's in charge of things—just not interacting. It does seem weird. I didn't want to say it was odd, but it *was* different from anybody else that I knew. Kris's home life was just very private and not approachable. I later realized I never really knew her mother at all. Kris's grandmother, though, was very nice and gentle and generous."

Later, however, Joan would come to realize that Mary Jo Shannon had much influence on her daughter in terms of men and how to meet them.

Besides Joan and Kris working in her grandmother's shop, Lou Ethel and Jim Fairbanks began inviting Joan to accompany them, Kris, and sometimes her sister, Karen—who seemed mostly always in the background—on overnight camping trips to a place called Butterfield Country, which was a blue-collar RV and mobile home park and resort about sixty miles from San Diego.

The grandparents had a house trailer for getaways, and once at the destination, Kris and Joan rode little motorbikes and hiked in the woods. "Sometimes her sister, Karen, would come along and maybe bring a friend, but Kris and I would go our separate way. I *never* had to bring anything on those trips. They took care of me, and I was a friend tagging along. The grandma was awesome and she took a genuine interest in us."

Back at Kris's house, Joan often hung out in her chum's room, and found it to be decorated much differently than her own.

"Where I had pictures of the Monkees"—a Beatles-like sixties American rock band with a British member, Davy Jones—"stuck up on my wall, Kris didn't have *any* of that. She would have had a poster of the Eiffel Tower. Everything about her room was *very* neat, and *very* tidy, and it was *definitely* feminine. *Everything* always felt like it was in its place.

"My other friends had incense burners and stereos and bongs; Kris didn't have any of that. She had cosmetics and perfumes and all that kind of personal stuff. It was a straightforward girly room."

Aside from Kris's room, her look and style was different from the other girls in her small circle.

As Joan observed, "Kris always had flair, good manners, and was always well-groomed. She had really good hair, and good skin, where a lot of us were fighting acne. I don't remember issues with her like that. She just had good traits, and it didn't seem she had to work at it.

"Back then you didn't accessorize. We all wore bell-bottoms and went barefoot. But looking back, Kris dressed like someone who was older than the rest of us. She would wear scarves and jewelry. She had a definite sense of style.

"Back then, I would not have been surprised if she had gone into some fashion and design career path. She had the flair for that. She seemed absolutely more mature than the rest of us."

In her own mind, she was a princess.

KRIS AND JOAN BEGAN TENTH grade at Clairemont High School, which later earned a very special pedigree.

Life there was the basis for the 1982 teen hippie-dippie screen classic *Fast Times at Ridgemont High,* starring such young, new stars as Sean Penn, Jennifer Jason Leigh, and Judge Reinhold.

Ironically, one of the film's coproducers was music industry power broker Irving Azoff, chairman of MCA Records in the 1980s, and through the years personal manager of Christina Aguilera, the Eagles, Van Halen, and many other music legends and monster hit-makers and moneymakers. The irony was that Azoff also would become a close friend and business associate of Robert Kardashian, and Azoff's much younger socialite wife, Shelli Azoff, would become one of Kris's best friends and party buddies after Kris married Kardashian and became a charter member of the platinum Beverly Hills wives club.

Fast Times characters included a surfer pothead, Jeff Spicoli, famously played by Penn. And Leigh had even taken a job at a pizza parlor in Sherman Oaks, the heart of Valley Girl country, to get into her character.

But Joan Zimmerman says life for her and Kris at Clairemont was nothing like the big-screen story of the school when they matriculated there, a decade earlier, in the class of 1973.

The late sixties and early seventies was an entirely different era, one of turmoil abroad in the land, with anti–Vietnam War protests, with the controversial election of Richard Nixon and the corruption scandals that brought down Vice President Spiro Agnew and the Watergate scandal that ended Nixon's presidency. And it was a nation still recovering from the late-sixties assassinations of the Reverend Martin Luther King Jr. and Senator Robert F. Kennedy.

"But Clairemont wasn't a school that had a lot of protesting," Joan Zimmerman recalled. "You saw bumper stickers on cars that said, 'Don't Blame Me. I Voted for McGovern,'" a reference to Senator George McGovern, the failed Democratic presidential nominee in 1972.

There were a few Spicoli types, who smoked pot, but it wasn't quite as extreme as the *Fast Times* story portrayed life there a decade later. As Joan noted, "There were folks who had vans out front in the morning and would tap into a keg and go to class, and the whole hippie thing was an influence as well, but none of us got into trouble with any of that."

As for smoking dope, dropping acid, or even getting high on a six-pack or a bottle of cheap wine with her friends, Kris was always squeaky-clean, Joan said.

"She had a discipline, I will say that. She had a very good discipline about *everything*, like keeping her room clean and tidy, being very well-composed, never getting into any trouble, or even *testing* the limits. Nothing ever happened to actually make me mad at Kris. She was never confrontational with anyone. That just wasn't her style. She would just disappear. If something started to get heated, you'd look around and she just wouldn't be there. She'd be gone.

"Kris didn't have any boyfriends that I can remember, and we did things socially in a group back in high school," continued Joan. "We went to dances at the YMCA, ball games, we'd hang out at the theater, we'd go to the beach. It was our parents thinking that we were safe in numbers."

Kris's only interest, even back then, was the opportunity to make money.

"Sometimes if we had days off from school or on weekends, Kris and I would work in her grandmother's candle store and get paid whatever the minimum wage was then," recalled Joan Zimmerman. "With her grandmother, she would always give us opportunities to work and let us run with it or not. And so we did."

While Kris claimed in her book that she got good grades in school, Joan asserted diplomatically, "I had a couple of other friends who were exceptional. I wouldn't put Kris in that category."

When Kris turned sixteen, her stepfather, Harry Shannon, gave her the dream Sweet Sixteen present of every teenage girl—a new car right off the lot, a red Mazda RX-2, which she still boasted about years later in her memoir. Oddly, though, Joan Zimmerman had no memory of Kris having such a flashy car. "I remember when Kris got of age they bought her a car, and I remember thinking, wow, that was really a big deal. But I don't remember that it was anything special. I think I would have remembered a brand-new red Mazda."

By senior year at Clairemont, Joan had started going to school half days because she had enough credits to graduate and was working the rest of the time, so she saw less of Kris. "And I had a boyfriend, a guy who played baseball, so my time was spent following the team around."

After she graduated, she worked for a few years, then enlisted in the Air Force, and lost track of Kris. A marriage, a divorce, and a second marriage followed.

It wasn't until years later that she heard people talking about a new reality TV show, tuned in to it, and was shocked to see her old friend Kris as the momager of the whole deal.

"I just couldn't believe it," she said. "It is strange to think I knew somebody when they were young and pure and innocent, and there she was, and I thought, 'Who puts themselves out there like that?' I was surprised that she would do that. It's just so foreign to me. And I didn't see any *real* talent in any of her kids, and thought, 'Why are they celebrities like they are?' I think most people are puzzled by it, but somehow they gravitate to it, and I guess that's why the Kardashians are so successful."

BY THE TIME KRIS was a senior at Clairemont, and while other girls in her class were excitedly planning for the senior prom and possibly college, she had ruled out any further schooling and was already looking for a man.

Even then, the future momager's mantra was "dreaming big, working hard, and setting goals." Very aware of her mother's and grandmother's dysfunctional marriages and hurtful relationships with men, number one on Kris's agenda was to find a good one, and one who could give the girl with the princess mentality everything she felt she deserved and desired in life.

With her mother as her enabler, she had set her sights on finding a rich guy.

Looking back years later, her then-close pal Joan Zimmerman observed, "The way I knew Kris, she was a good person, and then something happened. She changed and we weren't seeing much of each other. She was pursuing something else. I don't want to use a bad term, but I think her mom was kind of pimping her out."

Zimmerman acknowledges she wasn't literally suggesting that Mary Jo Shannon was a procurer for her favorite daughter, only that she was likely tutoring her on how to find a man with money, and pointing her in the right direction of where to find one.

In that same era, other mothers of certain young women like Kris

Houghton, who later would become rich, famous and, in some instances, infamous, took the same track—pushing their daughters toward men with big cars, big homes, and big bank accounts.

When later married to Robert Kardashian, Kris became close friends with the Los Angeles socialite Kathy Richards Hilton, whose daughters, hard-partying "celebutantes" Paris and Nicky, were best pals and schoolmates with Kris's narcissistic, spoiled, and glammed-up daughter, Kim.

Kathy Hilton's mother, the overbearing, ambitious Kathleen Mary Dugan Avanzino Richards Catain Fenton (she had four marriages, all hellish unions because of her outrageous behavior) had groomed her to marry a wealthy scion.

Known as Big Kathy, her constant mantra to Little Kathy and her sisters, Kyle and Kim, was "Marry rich men," and they did. She had even taught Kathy how to please a man sexually. Kathy, for instance, tied the knot with Rick Hilton, the wealthy grandson of billionaire Hilton Hotels czar and playboy Conrad Hilton. Her sister the child star and dysfunctional reality TV actress Kim Richards had a short-lived marriage to the son of the billionaire oil man Marvin Davis, goaded into it, once again, by her mother. And Kyle, featured on *The Real Housewives of Beverly Hills* with Kim, would also marry into money; her husband was an executive with the Hilton family's booming Beverly Hills real estate firm.

And years later, Kris Kardashian's daughter Kim, with her mother's backing and blessing, would emulate with great business planning that which first made Paris Hilton a world-famous reality TV star and all-around international vixen. Like Paris, Kim made a sex tape. Like the Hiltons, who were behind the project, Kris was, too. "There was a whole business plan, a marketing approach, a publicity strategy on how to deal with the blowback," claimed a close Kardashian associate. "Kris didn't need a Wharton School degree. She had savvy street smarts."

As Kris's former brother-in-law Tom Kardashian, who was a "pretty close friend for years" of Rick Hilton, and was a member of the same tony L.A. country club, noted in 2015, "Kris was driven just like Kathy Hilton."

But long before either Kathy Hilton or Kris Kardashian Jenner there was the original momager.

Her name was Jolie Gabor, a driven, ambitious Hungarian Jewish mother who dictated that her glamorous daughters, Eva, Magda, and Zsa Zsa become famous, make lots of money, and, when possible, marry rich men. In the case of the blond bombshell Zsa Zsa, she became a movie and TV star, dated many men, and one of her wealthy and powerful husbands was none other than Hilton family patriarch, Conrad Hilton, the billionaire founder of the worldwide hotel chain. Among the others were Jack Ryan, the eccentric Mattel toy company executive who invented the Barbie doll, and the British actor George Sanders, who later committed suicide.

And according to a close Kardashian family source, "Kris always *idolized* Jolie Gabor. She read all the gossip and tabloid stories about her and her daughters and how they made a fortune and became known worldwide, mainly for being famous for being famous. I remember Kris swore up and down that she could do the same with her own daughters, Kim and the rest of them, and make them and herself all rich and famous just like the Gabors."

Others who knew Kris well, like Larry Kraines and his wife, Joyce, didn't think that Kris was just blowing smoke when she boasted about the things she could do and accomplish. As Larry said, looking back to the early days when he got to know Kris as his best friend Robert's wife, "She was personable, smart, witty, and *always* thought she could be more than what she was. She always *wanted* to be more. She always said to us openly—I can do that TV show, I could be one of those announcers, I could do this, I could do that."

Even back then, people who knew Kris believed her secret ambition always was to have her own television program.

Kris Houghton grew up with similar Gabor and Hilton rules. Even in high school, primed by Mary Jo, Kris was already a shallow opportunist, focused on marrying rich. Most girls her age, as she would later observe, "were thinking about the prom. I was thinking *fuck the prom. I want to get married and have six kids.* I felt like life would start when I got that done."

Some years later, with two marriages under her Gucci belt, she would have six kids, and much, much more.

By the time Kris had turned sixteen, her friend Joan Zimmerman recalled, "Kris and her mom were involved in social activities that the rest of us weren't involved in, like Kris going out to [the posh resort] La Costa, and getting invited to events out there. I kind of felt that was her mom's doing. Kris was absolutely more mature than the rest of us. I don't ever remember her having any interest in high school boys at all, and no crushes. Guys liked her. They would always try to get a date with her, but she wasn't interested. She was probably starting to get opportunities elsewhere [to meet older, moneyed men]."

Kurt Harding was one of those Clairemont boys who would have liked to have dated Kris.

"But I guess she was just kind of out of my league," he said, looking back years later. He viewed her back in high school as "kind of stand-offish, wasn't friendly except to maybe the in-crowd, and kept to herself with the guys." He had heard the chatter that Kris's mother "kept her busy at golf tournaments and things like that so she would meet a rich guy rather than let her hang around with the high school boys."

In her memoir, Kris claimed it was her stepfather, Harry Shannon, and an uncle who sparked her interest in golf, and noted that she had "grown up going to [as she called it] the La Costa Country Club . . . and I thought those big golf events were so glamorous and exciting."

THREE

Meeting the "Mob"

Rancho La Costa, in nearby Carlsbad, with its legendary golf courses where the pros played, its tennis courts, its spa and fitness facilities, and chic poolside cafés, was as good a starting place as any for a girl with a plan to troll for an eligible man.

Back in the day, the luxurious San Diego North County resort was a high roller's paradise and hangout, and an always-dolled-up teenage Kris Houghton, who looked, dressed, and acted older—she easily could have passed for her early twenties, friends recall, and was known to tell men that she was twenty-one or twenty-two—could be quite an attraction, along with all the other man-hunters who spent time there, hoping to meet a future husband or snag a generous sugar daddy. Tennis stars, golf pros—Kris's favorite—Hollywood celebrities, wealthy businessmen, and even mafiosi, as *The New York Times* once pointed out, were attracted to this playground for the rich and famous, and all the action that could be had there.

It wasn't the kind of place that one would expect a watchful, thoughtful, concerned mother in the early 1970s to permit her very desirable, sexually mature teenage daughter to spend time meeting and mingling. But there she was, with Mary Jo Shannon's good housekeeping seal of approval, socializing with men who were much older, which were Kris's type. As she already knew back in high school when she rejected teenage boy suitors, "I always saw myself as being with an adult."

Rancho La Costa had been developed in the early 1960s by Merv Adelson, a successful Las Vegas and Hollywood entrepreneur with longstanding reputed organized crime connections. One of his close colleagues in the La Costa venture was the notorious gangster Morris Barney "Moe" Dalitz, known as "the Godfather of Las Vegas."

A couple of years after Kris got her June 1973 high school diploma and was finally through forever with her formal education—"school wasn't my thing . . . I wanted to get out into the world," as she later acknowledged—La Costa was described in an eye-opening 1975 *Penthouse* magazine investigative article as "The Hundred-Million-Dollar Resort with Criminal Clientele."

The shadowy moneymen behind the resort filed a $522 million libel suit, asserting there were no organized crime connections. The case went on for years, eventually settling with no money changing hands. However, eyewitness testimony claimed that known mob-connected types were often partying guests at the swinging resort during the Adelson-Dalitz era, so it's certainly possible, if not probable, that beguiling Kris Houghton innocently mingled with one or more of those dapper, flashy mobbed-up big spenders.

Adelson, who was also cofounder and former chairman of Lorimar, which gave the TV world such hits as *Dallas* and *Knots Landing*, told *Vanity Fair* in 2013 that he had "enjoyed a very close relationship" with Moe Dalitz, but added that in all the years they were pals and business associates, "we never discussed anything criminal."

Adelson, who married Barbara Walters, the third of her short-lived marriages, died at eighty-five in 2015. Since the Adelson-Dalitz days, the ritzy resort has gone through a number of owners and transformations, and in 2013 the La Costa Resort and Spa was sold to Omni Hotels and Resorts.

Whether Kris met any promising men during her La Costa adventures is not known—what happened at La Costa clearly stayed at La Costa—but she certainly fancied the vibe. It was her kind of showy scene, one she'd enjoy later as the flashy Beverly Hills wife of her first husband, Robert Kardashian, and the mother of their children. By coincidence, her then father-in-law, Arthur Kardashian, who was in the notorious meatpacking business and had reputed underworld connections, had enjoyed golf, too, and used to play at La Costa. He had once even scored a hole in one there, playing in a foursome with three other Armenian-American businessmen, with the last names Markarian, Agbasian, and Mazgedian.

IN KRIS'S SENIOR YEAR back at Clairemont High, there was more change in her life when she bonded with cute, sassy Debbie Kathleen Mungle, who was a year older, a member of the class of 1972, and one of the eight high-spirited 1971–72 varsity cheerleaders—"No. 1 in spirit, bounce and enthusiasm!" Kris and Debbie instantly became bosom buddies—she was Kris's new best friend. The two were inseparable, hanging out together every day. To Kris, Debbie had "great style and was always," as she would later boast, "so much fun." They would remain friends for years.

Hanging out with Debbie, Kris had all but abandoned her long-loyal small circle of pals, including her close chum Joan Zimmerman. To Kris, Debbie had the kind of pizzazz and sophistication that she felt her old friends lacked. Petite, dark-haired, and always well turned out, she seemed to have it all. As Zimmerman recalled, "Debbie fixed herself up to be more mature than a high school girl. She was a year ahead of us, so she was out of high school and we were still there, so she seemed very worldly."

And Mungle's worldliness manifested itself in a manner that shocked Joan Zimmerman when time for her senior prom rolled around.

"Debbie was very attractive and I had a boyfriend that I thought I was going to the prom with," Joan had never forgotten. "And then Debbie Mungle decided she wanted to go to the prom with him, and he took her, not me. I remember her clearly from that experience, and I knew Debbie and Kris were *really* good friends."

Like Kris, Debbie also had a sister named Karen. Debbie's father, Charles, was an engineer who worked for General Atomics & Hydranautics. More important, however, and of keen interest to Kris, was the fact that Debbie's perky mom, Beverley, was part of the glamorous professional golf world.

For Kris, a budding golf groupie who liked the game but liked the players more, her close relationship with Mrs. Mungle and her daughter was like scoring a hole in one. Moreover, Kris had the full support of Mary Jo and her stepfather, Harry—both of whom loved golf and the golf lifestyle.

Their liberal parenting style was a blessing to Kris because "when I ran off to golf tournaments with my girlfriend Debbie," Kris's folks told her just to have lots of fun, no questions asked. Kris later remarked that her parents "weren't strict," that they realized that she had always been an "independent" sort of girl, and noted that they "just followed that old philosophy that if your kids want to do something, they're going to do it with or without your blessing. So that is what I did."

Years later, her own girls would follow that philosophy, also with their mother's approval.

Beverley Mungle, who Kris had come to love almost like a second mother, was secretary, assistant, and business manager for a professional golfer by the name of Phil Rodgers, who had had five big wins on the PGA Tour in the 1960s and was once described on the cover of a 1963 issue of *Sports Illustrated* as "The Brashest Man in Golf." Known as an "arrogant" critic of other players' swings, a duffer with a hot temper, who had "notorious brushes" with the rules, he was popular on the tour and palled around with such icons as Jack Nicklaus, and had taken a liking to a personable and good-looking up-and-comer by the name of Cesar Sanudo.

Sanudo would play an important part in Kris's post–high school, early adult life. He'd be her lover, but their relationship would raise questions about her character and morals.

Kris left her formal education for the last time in June 1973 when she got her diploma from Clairemont High School.

Other than the standard photo in the *Calumet* yearbook showing an average-looking teenager with a big smile on her face, her dark brown hair parted in the middle, which was the style of the times, there are few, if any, other mentions of Kris Houghton. There was nothing to show her involvement in any school activities, clubs, or honors, and that's mainly because she didn't participate, wasn't much of a student, and was anxious to just get the hell out.

YEARS LATER, AFTER SHE HAD become rich and famous as a reality TV star and pop culture phenomenon with her brood, a British-owned Los Angeles–based news and picture agency that specialized in celebrity stories released a purported high school picture said to be of Kris as a cheerleader, which received media attention. DailyMail.com, the popular U.S. news and features Web site, an arm of London's *Daily Mail* tabloid newspaper, greeted the photo with the headline: "Flashback to 1973! Kris Jenner Pumps Her Pom-poms as a Chieftains Cheerleader in Clairemont High School Yearbook."

Along with that photo, the July 2013 story reported, "Her daytime talk show *Kris* premiered on Fox Monday. But back in 1973, Kris Jenner was just an ordinary Chieftans cheerleader, attending Clairemont High School . . . The 57-year-old momager, then known as Kristen Houghton, can be seen as a grinning teen in a series of just-released b&w yearbook snaps." *The Huffington Post* also picked up the story.

In fact, Kristen Houghton was never a cheerleader at Clairemont, according to a 1973 classmate, Cheryl Wallace Weatherford. She would know because she *was* one of the eight members of the 1972–73 varsity squad, and also one of the six members of the 1971–72 junior varsity cheer group. Kris belonged to neither team.

Weatherford, a cute blonde back then at Clairemont High, who married one of the captains of the 1973 football team, clearly recalled that Kris "was not a member of our eight-member cheer squad. Kristen tried out for cheerleader a couple of times but never made the cut for JV or varsity."

To her small circle of friends, it came as a surprise that Kris hadn't been accepted in the cheer squad because she was thought of as perky and cute and perfect cheerleader material. Kris believed she hadn't made the squad because her butt was too flat.

"She said she envied the black girls with big, round asses, and wished she had one like them," recalled a chum. "Now when I see that enormous backside on Kim Kardashian, I have to wonder whether that had anything to do with the fact that Kris really wished she had a bigger ass when she was back in high school so she could become a cheerleader."

BURIED IN THE BACK OF her high school yearbook, Kris Houghton—in what is the only known time she ever described what she would have liked to do with her life—wrote: "Brooks. Merchandising. Buyer."

A career as a buyer seemed an appropriate job choice for Kris back then since she had experience working in her grandmother's candle shop, but even more, she was, by the age of seventeen, a fashion-conscious shopaholic. Next to finding a rich husband, her passion was shopping for fashion. As a high school pal recalled, "She'd be at the malls buying, returning, buying, returning, always going for the latest styles. The term 'fashionista,' I guess, would fit. But her taste level was just so-so, and not really sophisticated."

Still, years later she and her daughters would prove to be the world's great merchandisers in the early decades of the twenty-first century, generating tens of millions of dollars hawking themselves, and building enormous fame and infamy—all of it with absolutely no discernable talent except for self-promotion and chutzpah. And the major media and an enormous swath of the public, from Wichita to Warsaw, bought in to their schtick.

Kris's mention of "Brooks" in the yearbook presumably referred to the Brooks Institute, offering photography, business, and arts courses, with the motto, "Passion. Vision. Excellence." However, there is no indication that Kris Houghton ever matriculated there.

Instead, right after high school graduation, she, along with her pal Debbie Mungle, flew to Hawaii, where Kris met her first known lover—on a golf course.

FOUR

Hole in One

Kris Houghton was just seventeen, but she became PGA Tour pro Cesar Sanudo's teenage queen. It was love at first sight, at least for him.

Kris wasn't quite as young as Priscilla Beaulieu, who was fourteen when she first spent time with future husband Elvis Presley (and would later be Robert Kardashian's girlfriend), or Nicole Brown, who O. J. Simpson pursued when she was a virginal eighteen. But at seventeen, fresh-faced and fresh out of senior year, Kris Houghton was still a veritable child when she became romantically involved with a man more than a decade her senior.

A rising golf star, Cesar was about twenty-eight, and had fallen hard for Kris, who already appeared to know the fine art of deceiving and seducing men.

"When my dad first started dating Kris she lied about her age," asserted Amber Carrillo, Cesar's daughter, years later. "He told me she told him she was twenty-one, but she was only seventeen, or just about ready to turn eighteen. He said she fabricated things and didn't really talk about where she came from, about who her real father was, details like that.

"And from my understanding, she was being groomed at home when she met my father. She wanted to be mature and be a golf groupie and try to find a man who had money, that whole thing of just climb the ladder, try to find somebody who was going to get her where she needed to go, wherever that was."

Carrillo, born in August 1970, was her father's love child with his high school sweetheart. They had never married, and the girlfriend mostly raised Amber, but Kris often babysat for Amber when she became involved with the child's father.

Cesar was the first man with whom Kris would have a live-in relationship, wasting no time after getting out of school. She eventually cheated on him, leaving him devastated. It would be the first but not the last time she played around on someone to whom she was married or romantically involved with.

CESAR SANUDO HAD A COLORFUL HISTORY. He was a poor Mexican boy, one of four brothers and a sister, whose father had abandoned them (as Kris's biological father had done). The children's mother struggled financially to raise them and also was responsible for caring for her own dying mother.

The down-and-out Sanudos were living in the impoverished Mexican border town of Tijuana, where, at age eleven in 1954, Cesar was looking for a way out of poverty, and a way to make some money to help out his family. According to an account he gave later in life, he somehow found himself wandering onto the manicured grounds of the Tijuana Country Club, located just five miles from the U.S.-Mexico border and fifteen miles from the San Diego area, where his future teenage lover, Kris Houghton, would be born a year later.

The Tijuana club had been the setting for two major golf tournaments, the Agua Caliente Open and the Tijuana Open Invitational, drawing big-name players on the PGA Tour, vying for big money. One doesn't think of Tijuana, with its long history of wild bars, sleazy dance halls, violence, and vice, as having an actual formal and proper country club, but it had been there since before the Great Depression, attracting moneyed Mexicans and high rollers from close-by San Diego.

Scoping out the fancy club and sleek course, Cesar ran into someone who suggested that the strong, handsome, personable kid should think about applying for a job as a caddie, and told him that caddies made good money and met the right kind of people. He soon got the job.

A lefty, he also quickly learned how to play the game with a set of right-handed clubs that someone had given him. One of the players he caddied for would later become one of his best friends on and off the green, the golf legend Lee Trevino, known as "Super Mex" and "Merry Mex," who also came up the hard way, raised on the outskirts of Dallas, the family living in a run-down shack. Like Cesar, he started out as a caddie, when he was just eight.

As the *San Diego Union-Tribune* once pointed out about Sanudo, "Such was the improbable indoctrination into a game that would make Sanudo a professional champion and a friend to presidents and celebrities," among them Richard Nixon, Gerald Ford, George H. W. Bush. He also dined and joked with the likes of Bob Hope and Clint Eastwood.

He met them on golf courses while playing in high-stakes tournaments. And that's how he met the Houghton girl.

The setting was the 1973 Hawaiian Open.

Kris was soon to become the kept nubile mistress of a golf celebrity. Her dream of being with a mature man with power and money who fell for her was already coming true.

The Hawaiian trip had been a graduation gift from Debbie Mungle's mother. The pro golfer Phil Rodgers, for whom Beverley Mungle worked, was their escort to Hawaii. "Debbie and I had been to many golf tournaments with Phil," said Kris. She recalled Rodgers, almost two decades older, telling her and Debbie, "You'll stay at the hotel and it will be lots of fun."

But, in 2015, seventy-eight-year-old Rodgers maintained that Kris's account involving him was "not true." He said that he had been telephoned by "the person who wrote the book [Kris Jenner's memoir], and I said, 'No, I don't know anything about any of this. I don't think it happened.'"

In her book, Kris identified her new lover as being "tall, dark-haired, funny, and successful, and he represented this glamorous world of golf. Maybe I was just a golf groupie."

But she didn't use Cesar Sanudo's real name, instead calling him "Anthony," presumably to avoid legal problems for herself and her publisher by using his real name.

While none of her friends interviewed for this book could recall her ever seriously dating or being involved with any boys in high school, Kris had a different story, noting that Anthony "made all the boys I'd hung out with in high school seem like, well, boys," and describing him as "my first grown-up, non–high school boyfriend."

In 1973, when he met Kris at the Hawaiian Open, Cesar was a hot-blooded and smitten pro golfer and envisioned the two of them spending the rest of their lives together. He would be sadly mistaken.

Sanudo's daughter came to believe that the desirable seventeen-year-old had actually seduced her earnest twenty-eight-year-old father, rather than the other way around.

"He never went into detail how they met, but I do know that she was a groupie who was following the golf scene," Amber said. "She was in Hawaii, and my dad was there. I don't know if it was meant to be that way."

Kris, however, contended in her book, "Anthony courted me."

Since Cesar was a popular San Diego celebrity golfer, it's believed by the Sanudo family and Cesar's friends that the handsome golf star had long been on golf groupie Kris Houghton's man-hunting radar by the time she met him in Hawaii.

Cesar, in fact, soon became a project for her whole family. Kris's stepfather, Harry Shannon, and his brother, both golf nuts, were said to have promoted a tournament at San Diego's public Torrey Pines golf course, where Cesar often played, and where Kris's mother and Shannon even maintained the scoreboard on the eighteenth hole. As Kris asserted, her mother and stepfather "actually came to love Anthony, as did my grandmother. In my family, if the matriarch says something is okay, then it is okay. And everyone falls in line."

The bottom line: They saw Cesar Sanudo as a good catch for Kris, at least for the moment.

Soon after Cesar and Kris became an item, the very ambitious teen began accompanying him on lavish golf trips to tournaments around the world—Europe, the Far East, Latin America.

One of Cesar's close friends, the professional golfer Jack Spradlin, who was seven years younger and viewed Cesar as his mentor, believed that Cesar was bowled over by Kris mainly because she was young and, therefore, considered hot—attractive arm candy for an older man in the public eye. Moreover, she "took a liking to him, and, God, she was like seventeen or eighteen," Spradlin noted. "I thought she was like twenty or twenty-one. But her looks weren't anything that blew me away.

"She was attractive, but she wasn't like, *oh my gosh* attractive. But she was much younger, and to him it was like, wow, I've got a nice young girl on my arm, so how much better can it be? And they both lived in San Diego, too, so how much better can that be? But I think he truly loved her. Cesar wasn't a womanizer. He was pretty much a one-girl guy."

Spradlin believed he met Kris for the first time around 1974, some months before he got on the Tour, and not long after Cesar became involved with her.

"They were heating up, and Cesar was taking her on tour with him," he recalls. "She was traveling with him. I didn't go to Europe, but I went to Mexico City when she was there with him.

"I was with her and Cesar so much that I didn't think, 'Oh, there's Kris again.' She was just part of the picture.

"I'm sure Kris saw Cesar as Mr. Moneybags; then look at her future track record, look at her success."

At seventeen and eighteen, as Cesar Sanudo's girl, Kris was mixing with some of the top money-winners in golf and their glamorous women, and she was socializing with wealthy men who enjoyed being in the circle of professional athletes. One such multimillionaire was Cesar's first sponsor, the Southern California industrialist George T. Straza.

The head of a company called Jet Air Inc., a major U.S. defense and space program contractor, in El Cajon, with such clients as Rolls-Royce and Pratt & Whitney, the big money was rolling in, and Straza, who was politically well-connected, was living like royalty with a spectacular estate in Rancho Santa Fe, where he threw parties and fund-raisers.

"I was at his house for a party with Cesar and Kris," recalled Spradlin. "George, who was phenomenal, just pretty much doled out money to Cesar for him to play. I remember he had little displays with gold ducats built into the walls of the house. I thought, 'Oh my God, this is the greatest house I've ever been in,' and so did Kris." During the course of their close relationship, Straza is said to have given Cesar tens of thousands of dollars in gold pieces, which the golfer was socking away. When it disappeared, Cesar would suspect Kris.

The wealthy Straza owned the kind of luxury yacht that even Aristotle Onassis would have envied. "Kris was on the yacht with us," said Spradlin, "and I remember she's really excited and she's going, 'Wow, this is great! I can't believe I'm on this huge yacht. I'm so happy! This is the life! This is the life I want!'"

AFTER DATING BESOTTED CESAR Sanudo for a time, Kris Houghton took the relationship up a notch and moved in with him.

And so did her friend Debbie Mungle.

They were like a real-life *Three's Company*, the popular mid-1970s and early 80s TV sitcom, about two desirable young women and a cute guy living together, with a lot of sexual innuendo, starring, when it first aired, John Ritter, Joyce DeWitt, and Suzanne Somers.

However, Spradlin, who asked Mungle out but was rejected, doesn't think there was any hanky-panky involving the threesome of Cesar, Kris, and Debbie, even though it was the swinging seventies, and anything went. "If there was something happening I would have known," Spradlin asserted, "but there was never a mention. Cesar was not that type of guy."

With his early winnings, Cesar had purchased a modest town house condominium in Point Loma, close to the Pacific, in San Diego. By coincidence, Point Loma was the same district where Kris had lived as a child, which she thought of as "a really tony area of San Diego."

But Cesar's was a plain and simple two-story place with two bedrooms, two bathrooms, a family room, and a kitchen. "It was not fancy at all," said Spradlin, who spent much time there when he and Cesar weren't on tour. For Cesar back then, it was just a layover place to crash and chill, but it was far more luxurious than his childhood abode down in Tijuana.

While Cesar's home wasn't the kind of palace in which Kris envisioned herself living—she wanted a mansion something like the one Cesar's sponsor, George Straza, occupied—she and Debbie happily took over the place and practically made it their own.

"Debbie and I convinced Anthony," Kris wrote in her book, "to let us live in the town house . . . free of charge, of course. I have to admit, we were little con artists. We told Anthony that since he was on his way to being a *truly* big-time golfer, he needed us to live in his house and watch his plants and take care of things for him. So while Anthony was on the road, Debbie and I lived in his house. I was able to save money by continuing to work at my mom and grandmother's candle stores, as well as a little dress shop in La Jolla."

"I was," the future momager boasted, "already multitasking."

The two girls took full advantage of Cesar's hospitality.

Kris put in her own private phone line, and the two were throwing parties and entertaining friends while he was away.

Cesar's brother Carlos Sanudo, who had been to one of Kris's bashes, recalled how she came on to male guests. "Whenever a bunch of us would be partying over at Cesar's condo while he was out on the road," he claimed, "Kris would hit on any number of guys. She even made a move on me."

But all that would seem quite innocent and inconsequential compared to what Kris eventually did in the house: cheat on Cesar. And she cheated on him with Robert Kardashian.

Kris wasn't as serious about Cesar as Cesar was about her. She was just taking advantage of the situation, while he already was contemplating marriage.

As she would observe years later, "The Anthony thing seemed serious, but I think I loved the lifestyle more than the man."

But he considered her responsible and even thought that one day she would make a good wife and mother. As a result he had her look after his little daughter.

Amber was only about four years old when her father became involved with Kris Houghton, but she would hear much about her from her dad and Sanudo family members through the years, none of it nice.

But Amber does have a pleasant, distant memory of her father's teenage lover who sometimes babysat for her.

"I lived with my mother about twenty-five minutes from where my dad's condo was, so Kris would pick me up quite often, so I'd be at his house to see him when he came home from the Tour, because when he was traveling I didn't see much of him," Amber said, looking back. "From what I remember of her, she was always very sweet to me. A couple of times when I would go to sleep she would lay with me and tickle my forehead. Those were the kind of intimate things that she would do. I never remember her being mean to me, and my mom said she was nice. She would save my mom the trouble of having to drive me down there to my dad's. She was happy to pick me up."

. . .

IT HAD BEEN OVER a decade since Kris's alcoholic father, Bob Houghton, had packed his bags and left the family, severing all ties when he
divorced Mary Jo. By the time Kris was involved with Sanudo, her
father was living with Leslie Johnson Leach, who was fourteen years his
junior and had already been twice divorced.

"I kind of knew he was an alcoholic, but I didn't want to face it,"
Leach said, looking back years later. "He would just get really, really
drunk, mostly on beer, and then he would attack verbally. I never saw
him attack anyone physically, but they were *nasty, nasty* verbal attacks."

In late 1973 or early 1974, Houghton and his girlfriend moved back
to San Diego because he wanted to be closer to his daughters.

"Kris was involved with the professional golfer Cesar Sanudo, so we
used to go out with them," said Leslie Leach. "We used to go and have
dinner with them, and they came over for dinner. It was very nice, and
Cesar was a lovely guy."

For Kris's age, then about eighteen, she seemed very mature, or at
least played at being mature.

As Leach observed years later, "Kris was good at *acting* mature. She
knew all the things to do and say. But I'm not sure it was *truly* who she
was, or because she'd been hanging around the golf scene for so long
she kind of knew what they were all about, and how to play the role."

Leslie also had trouble coming to terms with Sanudo's relationship
with Kris, and noticed that Kris's father looked the other way.

"I liked Cesar, but I also thought, *whoa*, Kris was only a teenager, so
much younger than him," she said. "I did get the feeling that Cesar really
did care about her, even though there was a tremendous age difference.
But once she started screwing him over that changed."

What threw Leslie off balance and took her completely by surprise
was Kris's extracurricular social activities.

"She always came across to me as being an *incredible* social climber.
And she and her girlfriend—all I ever knew about was Kris and her one

friend; I never saw her with any other girlfriends—would dress up *fit to kill* and they would go out to a golf course wherever there was a tournament *anywhere* and follow the pro golfers around, and I remember thinking, now this is *pretty* wild.

"Her one girlfriend [probably Debbie Mungle] had this *big* crush on Lee Trevino, so they were going out to the golf tournaments, and that was their primary socializing.

"They would say to each other, 'Well, let's get dressed up and let's go be social.' And they would dress up and they would go."

Knowing teenage girls, Leslie thought that "maybe" there was a sexual connotation to the code words "go be social," but she knew it clearly did mean "Let's go, and let's party, let's link up with some golfers, let's see what they are up to. Let's see what it leads to. I think that it was really open-ended. They were definitely headed in the direction of party time."

Bob Houghton watched Kris's socializing with her girlfriend and their golf groupie activities but said little.

"He definitely was concerned," Leach said. "I think he was surprised because he hadn't seen Kris in so long, and I think he was surprised that she was running around the way she was at her age."

But in Kris Jenner's memoir, she painted a brief but glowing picture of her father. She made no mention of his alcoholism and abusive behavior. Instead, she stated, "My dad was a lot of fun. He liked to have a good time. He was very social."

Vicky Kron Thomsen thought so, too.

Not long after Leslie Johnson Leach broke up with Kris's father because of his excessive drinking and emotional and verbal abuse, he came on to Vicky around September 1974 when both were filling their tanks at a service station in the San Diego neighborhood of Pacific Beach.

She was a well-educated one-time model who at the time had been divorced for two years from a Lutheran minister's hard-drinking, rebellious son, and had two boys, ages four and ten. Vicky was a slender, very pretty five-foot-three, thirty-one-year-old brunette with big brown eyes. And like Leslie Leach, Vicky was about a decade younger than Bob

Houghton. People who knew her thought she looked like Natalie Wood, just as Robert Kardashian thought Kris did.

It was just a short time after they met that Houghton moved in with Vicky, and about six months into their relationship they decided to tie the knot on Easter weekend, 1975, by the Pacific in Rosarito Beach in Mexico.

En route in his fast Porsche, they stopped for dinner and drinks at a restaurant in Baja California, Mexico, and Houghton got soused on margaritas. Back on the road, Vicky fell asleep and the inebriated Houghton tried to concentrate on the dark, twisting road high above the coastline, and, just outside the village of San Vicente, he hit a sudden curve and slammed head-on into a truck carrying vegetables. Vicky, in critical condition, had to be pulled from the wreckage but survived. The truck driver was killed instantly. Houghton, forty-two, died shortly afterward.

In her 2011 memoir, Kris Jenner remembered being called by Houghton's father, True Houghton, her paternal grandfather, with whom she was said to have had little contact, informing her that her father had died in the crash. "I screamed, dropped the phone, and was just crying, crying, crying, hysterically crying."

But Kris never contacted Vicky Thomsen, nor did any other member of her family, including Houghton's ex-wife, Mary Jo, to offer their condolences and sympathy.

"They knew about me," said Vicky. "They also chose to ignore me."

Only one Houghton family member came to visit her when she was convalescing—Houghton's father. Vicky claimed that he had had a few drinks and before he left tried to kiss her and fondle her breasts. She ordered him to leave.

As for Kris's father, Vicky called him "irresponsible, and looking back on that relationship and that horrible accident I feel that I was *saved* from getting involved in a *very* dysfunctional family—the Kardashians. I can't imagine being a part of their ballyhoo that's been going on for so many years. I can't stand them."

FIVE

Enter Kardashian

Soon after Kris Houghton turned nineteen, Cesar Sanudo popped the question and gave her a diamond ring, and she said yes.

"They were definitely engaged," Cesar's brother Rudy confirmed.

In 2015, he still had a photo he had taken of young Kris back then at his house when she would hang out with him and his girlfriend, Marcia, as they waited for Cesar to come home from the Tour. "She always looked great, and you know what, to be honest, she still looks the same," he observed.

One of the first people Cesar told about the engagement was his pal Jack Spradlin.

"He was madly in love with this girl and really wanted to marry her," he recalled. "Cesar was overjoyed that she said yes."

Kris later acknowledged Cesar's proposal, noting that she had been having "so much fun" with him that she believed saying yes to his proposal was "the right thing to do," but then came to realize, "I didn't love Anthony . . . I was too young to be engaged to anyone."

But there was more to Kris's loss of interest in Cesar than their age difference.

Another man, with more to offer this ambitious, striving young woman, was about to enter her life.

His name was Robert George Kardashian. Beverly Hills and all the luxe that went with it was beckoning to shallow Kris Houghton, seemingly always hungry for more and greater riches and lots of expensive things. With Kardashian, she saw a chance to have it all.

Kris Houghton had met her first known lover at a golf tournament. She'd meet her second known lover, the one she'd eventually marry, at a racetrack.

It happened at the Del Mar Thoroughbred Club, the track to the stars, about twenty miles north of San Diego.

Her mother, who had introduced her to the high-roller scene at the tony and then reputedly mobbed-up La Costa resort, had also opened her eyes to the fashionable racetrack scene that attracted moneyed L.A. bettors for thoroughbred events like the Bing Crosby Stakes and the Del Mar Debutante.

One of the biggest and poshest in the world, Del Mar opened near the end of the Great Depression, built by some of Golden Age Hollywood's greatest stars: Pat O'Brien, Oliver Hardy (of Laurel and Hardy fame), Gary Cooper, and the crooner Bing Crosby, among others.

To covetous Kris, "going to Del Mar was exciting because it was such an example of wealth and high society," she observed in her book. "The clothes were amazing and the fashion was over-the-top . . . I jumped at the chance to go to Del Mar with my mom."

Del Mar's slogan had long been "Where the Turf Meets the Surf."

For this story, it's where Kris Houghton, in her late teens, meets thirty-year-old Robert Kardashian, Armenian-American lawyer, budding entrepreneur, and self-styled Beverly Hills bon vivant and Rodeo Drive boulevardier.

Kris herself would later call this chance encounter of the future patriarch and future matriarch of the contemporary Kardashian dynasty
"fateful."

It happened on a sparkling La-La Land Saturday afternoon in the
summer of 1974 when Cesar was traveling on the Tour. Dressed to the
nines as usual, exhibitionistic Kris was trying to draw attention to herself with a Hollywood glamour-girl look—dressed all in white, with a
big flamboyant hat and Marilyn Monroe–style sunglasses. But around
her neck was a chain, the gold pendant on which was inscribed with the
sophomoric novelty-shop exclamation "OH, SHIT."

Still, she recalled, "I looked pretty cute. I was on my game that day."

She had come to the track with her constant sidekick, Debbie Mungle, and Kris had just placed a two-dollar bet when a guy she thought
looked like Tony Orlando hit on her, using the stale line, "You look exactly like a girl I used to go out with. . . . Where do you live? What's
your name?"

He had slicked-back hair and a bushy mustache and sported a designer jacket and sharply creased slacks, probably from one of the
fashion-conscious haberdashers he favored on Rodeo Drive, in Beverly
Hills, where he lived and often hung out. For a day at the races, his dapper outfit was topped off with a pair of platform shoes. At just five-foot-
nine, if that, Robert Kardashian would always wear expensive Italian
shoes that made him look taller. His Gucci loafers, for instance, always
had two-inch lifts.

His favorite pair of shoes back then, his pride and joy, however, was
a collectible he had picked up at a celebrity auction and wore on special
occasions: Elton John's white patent-leather loafers with obvious lifts in
a big square heel, according to her friend.

Between Kris's outfit and Kardashian's getup, both clearly savored
drawing attention to themselves.

Robert had come to the track with his older brother by four years,
Tommy. They and their older sister, Barbara, were the three grown
children of swarthy Armenian-American businessman Arthur Thomas

Kardashian and blond, blue-eyed Helen Jean Kardashian, a popular, well-respected, and relatively affluent couple in Los Angeles's tight-knit and provincial Armenian community. While Robert had graduated from the University of San Diego School of Law and was in a small Los Angeles practice, Tom had followed in his father's footsteps, who had followed in his father's footsteps, and joined the Kardashian family's relatively successful business, Great Western Packing, one of the several largest Los Angeles meatpacking operations, serving supermarkets in Southern California. Safeway, Ralphs, all the big ones bought Kardashian meat.

Years later, Tom recalled that when Robert spotted Kris for the first time at Del Mar he didn't remark about whether she looked hot, or how fashionably she was dressed. "He and I never used to say things like that," he remembered. "When you're single and you're both in your thirties, you didn't have to say that. He ran into her, got her phone number, and they followed up. They did hook up pretty quickly after that."

In her memoir, Kris said she gave Kardashian her name, even spelling it for him, and made fun of his juvenile pickup line, but *refused* to give him her telephone number—the phone at her boyfriend, Cesar's, house. The last thing she needed was for Cesar to find out she was seeing other men. The next thing Kris claims happened was that Kardashian telephoned her, saying, "My friend Joni Migdal works for the telephone company. She just looked up your records and saw that you have a brand-new number and she gave it to me."

But in 2016, Migdal, who, like many interviewed for this book had never before spoken publicly about their Kardashian connection, gave an entirely different account. She emphatically denied she had ever worked for the phone company, and she didn't have a friend who worked there. At the time, Migdal said she was a teacher with a double master's degree in administration and was in charge of the gifted students' program in the Culver City School District in Los Angeles County. So Kris's phone company assertion was from out of left field. "I don't know why she said I worked for the phone company," stated Migdal. "I never asked her why, but it wasn't true."

Migdal, who had been Robert Kardashian's best girl friend since they were kids and was later a close confidant and, for a time, his lover, said the telephone number exchange had actually happened later at the Riviera Country Club in Los Angeles, where Kris had gone with Debbie Mungle to watch Cesar play in the Los Angeles Open.

After Robert Kardashian saw Kris for the first time at Del Mar and was smitten, he couldn't wait to share the exciting news with Joni. "He said, 'I saw the most beautiful girl I've ever seen and I want to see her again, and I want her phone number.' I said, 'Well, do whatever you need to do.' And he said, 'No, no, no—she has a boyfriend who's a pro golfer.' I said, 'Okay, what do you want me to do?' Robert said, 'He's playing golf at Riviera Country Club, and I assume she's going to be there. Let's you and I go together and I want you to meet her and get her phone number for me.' I said, 'If it's really important to you, we'll do it,' so we went to Riviera.

"Kris was watching her boyfriend play golf," continued Migdal. "We walked up to her and started talking, and she said to me, 'Oh, if you ever come to San Diego, I'd love to see you. Here's my phone number.' She believed that Robert and I were boyfriend and girlfriend. But I gave her number to him. He was standing right there. Robert knew she was living with the golfer, but he started to woo her. He was totally determined to get her, to win her over and away from Cesar. He was a man on a mission. Robert was *very* comfortable around women, confident but not overpowering. He could be very charming."

Larry Kraines, one of Kardashian's closest friends along with Joni—all three had been classmates at Dorsey High School in Los Angeles—said that Robert had given him the impression that he had first met Kris when she was working as a stewardess.

"He called me and he was excited that he met this gal on an American Airlines flight and told me, 'She's a lot of fun.'" Shortly afterward,

Kraines and his wife, Joyce, went out to dinner with Kardashian and Kris, "and we all hit it off. Kris realized how close I was to Robert, so I remember Kris saying to Joyce something like, 'I just love him. I would love to be his wife.'

"Kris had an eye for this guy, and that was what it was going to be. I think Kris loved Robert right from the get-go. He was fun. He was personable. He was quick, smart, and Kris needed that stimulation because I got the impression she was that way, too—very much so, although people maybe didn't get it about her at that point.

"People like Kris just don't become smart overnight," observed Kraines. "They don't become ambitious overnight. They aren't visionaries overnight. But Kris had had that in her genes *forever*. And she was good at it—not just good; she was *great* at it. She's very clever. She learned how to put herself with the right group of people. She was a sharp young gal with lots of personality and funny as shit. She was the belle of the ball."

The most off-the-wall and bizarrely false recounting of the merger of Kris Houghton and Robert Kardashian came from none other than their adult daughters, Kourtney, Kim, and Khloé. "Our mom and dad first met in San Diego. She was seventeen and working as a flight attendant. He was eleven years older and studying law," they stated as fact in a bestselling fan magazine–style, ghostwritten 2010 book, *Kardashian Konfidential*, published by St. Martin's Press, the publisher of this book.

Joni Migdal recalled that Robert "thought Kris looked like Natalie Wood, but that was just in the eye of the beholder. I didn't think she looked like Natalie Wood. I thought she was pretty, but if he thought she was *beautiful* and *looked* like Natalie Wood, that was the most important thing to me because I was his best friend. But was she *the* most beautiful girl he'd ever seen? I don't know. But if he thought she was— she was. That's it."

Migdal didn't pass any judgment on Kris's looks or personality at the time, and she could never have imagined in those still-innocent days in the early 1970s that her pal and the cute teenage girl whose number he so desperately wanted would eventually marry, igniting an unending and turbulent drama played out in private and in public.

"My relationship with Kris was a respectful one in that she knew that Robert and I were very good friends," said Migdal. "But Kris was almost uncomfortable—not with me, but with the relationship between Robert and me, and she wanted to have that kind of relationship with him. She wanted to be that person—the buddy, his confidant, not just a pretty object."

BY THE TIME OF Kris Houghton and Robert Kardashian's second face-to-face meeting at the Riviera Country Club, she had been in the golf world with Cesar Sanudo long enough to have emulated the fashion style of the other players' glamorous girlfriends and well-coiffed wives— wearing the same kind of little sweaters, spiffy golf shoes, and Ray-Ban sunglasses and carrying the Gucci bags that they all sported. And she and Debbie, courtesy of Cesar, had VIP passes just like all the other pros' women. With the golf get-up and the free passes, she was convinced, "I looked like I had been out on tour for ages."

For Kris, it seemed to be all about fantasy, image, and lifestyle. And now, with Robert Kardashian in the wings, she saw her chance to move on up to the big time.

Since there were always plenty of gorgeous women in the Beverly Hills world Robert Kardashian inhabited, one had to wonder why he was so enthralled with the teenage Kris Houghton, who, while fresh-faced and cute in a common sort of way, was no total knockout in the looks department.

A close friend, however, would later suggest a reason: "He always kept his eye on having his life 'look right.' Well, Kris looked right, like the kind of girl he should marry."

Moreover, he was a family-oriented kind of guy—some say even a mama's boy—and he wanted a big family to carry on the Kardashian name. And that wish would *definitely* come true, in a manner he never could have imagined in a million years.

For Kardashian, however, Kris Houghton was a perfect match because, as she knew back in high school, she wanted to get married and have lots of kids.

But with Kris and the other women in Kardashian's life through the years—and he would be with some real beauties, literally and figuratively—he would have a number of troubled and curious relationships. He wouldn't always make the best choices in women, or in marriage. Kris Houghton would be the first of three such questionable choices.

IN THE LATE SPRING OF 1975, with nineteen-year-old Kris planning to accompany her fiancé, Cesar Sanudo, to the British Open—he had received an invitation, but there's no official record of him actually competing—she got yet another call from her frustrated suitor, once again pleading with her to get together.

But this time Robert Kardashian threw out some bait that he hoped would finally lure her in.

His news was that he and his brother, Tom, had just bought a new house, to be their bachelor pad, in fashionable Beverly Hills, with O. J. Simpson as a frequent guest. The one-time football great was considered "the black Kardashian brother," recalled a friend from that time. While Robert and Tom's place was in a far less ritzy section—few if any of the area properties were gated—their house on Deep Canyon Drive, north of Sunset Boulevard and south of Mulholland, did possess the iconic 90210 zip code, giving it some seductive allure.

To Kris it sounded like nirvana, especially compared to her lover Cesar Sanudo's boring condo. To be clear, the Kardashian boys' new abode was no Hollywood movie mogul's estate—far from it—but it did have the requisite La-La Land swimming pool and tennis court, and

Tom, an astute businessman who had an accounting degree from USC, had been able to negotiate a good price of several hundred thousand dollars, considered a steal back in the day. They had even retained a popular Beverly Hills interior decorator, Judy Wilder Briskin, to give the place some panache.

"They were very conservative in the decorating," recalled Joni Migdal. "It was decorated almost in a Ralph Lauren kind of look. And was very well done, very tasteful. Robert always had *very* good taste. At that time, Tommy was the flashy one and Robert was the quiet one—almost like the little brother. He *was* the little brother who looked up to Tommy."

But that would all change.

Well paid at the time, working as general manager of his family's meatpacking business, Tom Kardashian noted years later, "I had enough money so I could buy a house in Beverly Hills, and I always felt it was good if my brother and I could make such an investment. I paid for two-thirds and he paid for one-third."

Before they partnered on buying Deep Canyon, Robert had moved into a home Tommy had on Hidden Valley Road, just south of Mulholland, and Tommy made baby brother Robert stay in the servant's quarters over the garage while he took the master bedroom suite for himself. "Tommy treated Robert like a little brother who was never going to do any good or be important. And he treated him that way *for years*," asserted Migdal. Larry Kraines recalled that when Tommy was wheeling around town in a slick Corvette, Robert was driving a lowly Chevy Corvair, a high school graduation gift.

At the time Robert was doing pretty well, too, working in the law offices of two shrewd Armenian-American attorneys and entrepreneurs, John Bedrosian and Richard Eamer. Besides handling routine client business matters, Kardashian was always looking to make investments in some of his entrepreneurial clients' business deals. At least one, a music tip sheet called *Radio & Records*, would have a big payoff when they sold it to the tune of about $12 million, split between the brothers and the fellow who came up with the idea, a law firm client of Robert's.

Excited about his new Beverly Hills address, Robert called Kris on her private phone at Cesar Sanudo's to invite her to be his date at the housewarming party he and his brother were planning. Having gone in circles attempting to get her to go out with him, he demanded a quick and positive answer.

But he had no need to be concerned. The idea of a guy who seemed to have big money—underscored by owning a home in 90210—was a veritable turn-on for the materialistic Miss Houghton.

Kris gave him an immediate yes.

And then she took off with Cesar for Great Britain and the British Open.

It was right then and there that Cesar decided they should get married.

In her book, Kris claimed that a fellow golfer, who she indicated was a friend of Cesar's, the champion player Tom Watson, and his wife, Linda, had suggested that the wedding be held on the grounds of the home they had rented while he played in the legendary tournament.

" 'How much fun would that be!' " Kris quoted the Watsons as saying, with Cesar agreeing that it was a " 'great idea.' "

But queried in 2015 about the scene painted by Kris in her memoir, Linda Watson, long since divorced from Tom, said it never happened.

"I have a great memory, and that information is just off the charts," she asserted. "When we were at the British Open, Tom and I were there for one reason, to win. We would never have endeavored to host or allow the hosting of a wedding when he was playing in the Open. None of that happened."

She said that, yes, they knew Cesar, "but not well," and added, "The chances that I would have even offered this to a total stranger [Kris] when all we cared about is winning would never have happened."

It didn't matter in the end because Kris had no intention of tying the knot with her golf pro; she had been stringing him along. She used as her excuse for not marrying him in Merry Olde England the fact that her family wasn't there to bear witness.

In fact, she claimed in her book that when Kardashian had called and invited her to his housewarming party she had told him about "my plan to break up with Anthony . . . and told him, yes, I would be his date to his big, important party."

When the day of the bash rolled around, Robert Kardashian was at LAX expecting to greet Kris with "two dozen red roses," she later claimed. But she never showed; she was still across the pond with Cesar. She further stated that Kardashian was so disappointed that he "walked to his car alone and cried all the way home."

At the party, she professed, Kardashian "looked like a fool" because he "didn't have a girlfriend, he didn't have a date . . . and I had blown him off." She said she called him the next day to say she was sorry and "I could hear him crying on the other end of the line."

If anything, she made Kardashian, who would one day be the father of four of her six chidren, seem like the ultimate wimp.

As a close friend of Kardashian's, a prominent Los Angeles attorney who also knew Kris well and had read her book (twice) because he was "so shocked" by what she had written that "I had to take another run-through," declared, "She is so full of shit, it's un-fucking-believable. If Bob was around he would have sued her and her publisher. He's probably turning over in his grave."

SIX

An Affair to Remember

Kris Kardashian Jenner claimed in her book—published when she was still married to second husband Bruce Jenner—that her relationship with the pseudonymous "Anthony"—Cesar Sanudo—ended when she discovered that *he* had cheated on her.

Like Robert Kardashian, Sanudo is dead, so her account was once again one-sided, and there are always two sides to every story. In this instance, the other side of the story came from the late golf pro's family and his friends.

And they all contended in candid interviews in 2015 that Kris's declaration that Cesar was a philanderer was false.

In fact, it was Kris, they assert, who had played around on Cesar, that she was the cheater.

It had all started coming to a head sometime in 1975 when Kris was back from her trip to England with Cesar. She was still putting him off about marriage, knowing full well that she never really had any intention of becoming his wife. She wanted more than what he had to offer. She wanted Beverly Hills and everything that came with that glitzy, one-percent lifestyle. Robert Kardashian could offer her that.

By then she had come to realize that Cesar Sanudo wasn't the well-heeled sugar daddy she probably thought he was when she first mesmerized him at the Hawaiian Open.

Initially, she was captivated by the handsome charmer who intro-duced her to the glamorous, international world of professional golf, played rounds with several commanders-in-chief, and broke bread with golf-crazy Hollywood celebrities.

As Cesar's close friend Jack Spradlin observed, "Kris met those guys with Cesar. It was exactly the kind of scene she was looking for."

But Sanudo, to Kris's displeasure, was never a big-money winner, and when he wasn't playing he didn't pursue the kind of high-life pleasures she desired or bestow upon her the luxury goods she wanted. While he played in some 250 events in the fourteen years that he was on the PGA Tour, Sanudo's career total earnings between 1970 and 1989 amounted to a mere $159,973.15.

According to Spradlin, "Kris saw a far better financial opportunity with Kardashian than with Cesar."

After "blowing off" Robert for so long with tantalizing telephone chat but no action, Kris finally decided to get involved with him, on the sly, and behind Cesar's back, while he was on the road.

She called it "our big, long-awaited first date," which ended up in the bedroom she shared with her fiancé, Sanudo.

Known many years later for airing her family's scandalous lives on their reality TV show, which kept addicted viewers, the weekly tabloids, celebrity magazines, and gossip columns coming back for more, Kris did the same for readers of her book, telling her titillating but very ques-tionable version of what happened that night.

Kris was probably hoping for a romantic and very expensive dinner at Chasen's, with drinks later at the Polo Lounge or the swinging Luau, Robert's usual haunt in Beverly Hills. Instead, their first date involved nothing more than a movie, popcorn, and sodas. Beneath his patina of sophistication, Kardashian was basically a down-to-earth guy with pretty simple tastes.

In any case, they did wind up back at Cesar's house, and Kris Houghton turned out to be one hell of a hot first date.

"We made our way upstairs. We were messing around and heading in the direction of some major hanky-panky when we heard the front door open. *Anthony was home!*"

They were, as she noted in millennial parlance, "so busted," and added, "Thank God we had our clothes on."

Others would later contradict her assertion that they were, in fact, still dressed based on Cesar's furious recounting of events.

At the front door, he angrily confronted his cheating fiancée and her new love. According to Kris's rendition, he grabbed Robert by his expensive Gucci sweater. " 'Don't touch the sweater!' " Robert screamed, she claimed. " 'It's my brother's!' "

But Cesar "didn't give a damn . . . and ripped it . . . ruining it." It was at that point, Kris stated, that she realized "Robert was not a fighter. . . . Robert just broke away and went hauling down the street, running for his life. . . . He had probably never been in a fight in his life before that night."

But Kris's published account was far different from what Cesar Sanudo had told family members and friends about what transpired that night.

Jack Spradlin recalled that his furious, cuckolded pal had always maintained to everyone, "I was out of town and I came home and I caught Kris and Kardashian *in bed.*"

In a jealous rage, he had "thrown them both out of the house." At one point, he even bragged that he had actually tossed Kardashian out of a second-floor window, an exaggeration made by an outraged lover.

Another of Cesar's golf buddies recalled getting a telephone call from him at three in the morning on the night of the explosion.

"He was so crazed and upset I thought something had happened, like an accident, but he told me, and I've never forgotten the words, 'I found that bitch in bed with a sleazy Armenian. I could have killed the motherfucker.' I never heard such language from Cesar because he was a pretty clean-cut guy. He called her a whore and a slut and kept using the C-word and everything else in the book. I thought he was going to burst a blood vessel. I really felt sorry for Cesar because he was a really great guy, and she was lucky to be with him, and she just fucked him over."

Kris later maintained that it was *she* who had actually ended it with Cesar, declaring that *he* had cheated on *her*. She based that on a hotel receipt she said she had mysteriously gotten in the mail and phone calls she had received from "a young woman . . . looking for Anthony. . . . He wasn't returning her phone calls. She was pissed, which is why she called me."

He denied that he was seeing anyone else, but Kris told him, " 'I'm out of here.' "

She had found her excuse to end it with him and to start up with well-heeled Robert Kardashian.

LOOKING BACK YEARS LATER, Cesar Sanudo's daughter, Amber Carrillo, was still saddened and upset by how her father had been treated, and angry about how Kris had turned the story around in her favor.

"I know my dad was pretty adamant that he had caught Kris in his bed with Robert Kardashian, and that he had kicked her out of the condo, and that they had broken up at that point. She says in her book that my dad took her back, but he says that he kicked her out immediately, and for good. My dad was very, very hurt by what Kris did to him, by her cheating. He was pretty messed up about it for a long, long time."

In fact, Kris Houghton's carrying on and her claim that Cesar cheated had angered the whole Sanudo clan and his close friends.

"Cesar *never* cheated on Kris," Jack Spradlin maintained. "She said it to make *herself* look good! With Kardashian, she went for it—that he was going to make her life so much better. But if you looked at Cesar and you looked at Kardashian and you gave them both a million dollars and the same Beverly Hills house, you'd go after Cesar because he was a much nicer guy, and far better looking than Robert Kardashian."

Amber's uncle, Rudy Sanudo, was still boiling years later about Kris's shabby treatment of his brother.

"That bitch was a snake," he declared in 2015. "My brother thought their relationship was serious. He thought they were going to get married until he caught her with Kardashian."

A few days after nineteen-year-old Kris Houghton accused her fiancé of cheating on her and then stormed out of the condo they shared, she immediately drove to her mother's for consolation and advice. Then, she called the new man in her life and made arrangements to be picked up at LAX.

Waiting at the curb, thirty-one-year-old Robert Kardashian was at the wheel of Kris's kind of car, a spiffy Mercedes-Benz, painted green, a color that literally and figuratively screamed money. Riding shotgun with him was his best friend, law firm client, and partner in some small business enterprises, the handsome, rugged twenty-eight-year-old black NFL celebrity player Orenthal James "O. J." Simpson, who Kris would get to know well socially and, as some would later claim, intimately.

As she stated years later in her memoir, "I absolutely loved O. J."

Having left Cesar, Kris had finally arrived at the Beverly Hills address of the house that Robert Kardashian owned with his brother, Tom. She was knocked out by how luxurious it was and instantly concluded that these two boys were "stylin,'" as she later put it in the jargon of the black rappers with whom she and her daughters often partied after they all became famous. They were definitely "living *the life*." And the brothers Kardashian, she deemed, were "two of the most eligible bachelors in Beverly Hills."

Years later she'd reminisce about that first visit to the Kardashians' chic manse with the very special 90210 zip code, which would later become her home (just as Cesar Sanudo's mundane condo became hers for the duration of their relationship).

"I rushed into the guest room and closed the door and called my mother and whispered, 'You're *not* going to believe this place! This is incredible . . . a tennis court. A swimming pool. And Mercedeses and Rollses in all different colors!' "

Mary Jo Shannon, who had trained her daughter well regarding men and the finer things in life, was down with it.

MEANWHILE, BACK IN SAN DIEGO, the first thing furious and distraught Cesar Sanudo noticed after booting Kris out was that his thirty-thousand-dollar cache of gold—mostly coins gifted to him over the years by his millionaire sponsor, George Straza—was mysteriously missing from its hiding place in his Point Loma condo.

"My dad had gold bullion, gold coins, and one day, a couple of weeks after Kris left, my dad went to look for them and they were gone," asserted Amber Carrillo. "Sometime later he said he had run into Kris's mom and he saw that she was wearing a bracelet that had gold coins on it, and my dad thought they were from his collection. How much of that is true, though, I really don't know."

Amber's uncle Rudy also believed that Kris was the culprit, but that was only based on what his brother Cesar had told him. "To top the whole thing off when she left Cesar," Rudy Sanudo maintained, "she took those gold coins he was saving with her, too. At least that's what Cesar told me, but I never saw the gold."

Jack Spradlin had long heard from Cesar that he owned thousands of dollars in gold coins, but also had never actually seen the collection. "But I heard Kris took them," he said. "On more than one occasion, Cesar said he called Kris and asked for the money [the missing gold coins] to be returned."

Still, one has to wonder whether his anger at being cheated on by Kris had led him to wrongly accuse her.

THE LAST TIME JACK SPRADLIN saw Kris before he spotted her in a TV infomercial with her future second husband, Bruce Jenner, pitching workout gear, was aboard an airliner bound for San Diego from Dallas.

She was then working as a flight attendant, serving the well-heeled in first class, naturally.

"I was in coach and she was walking down the aisle of the American Airlines plane and she goes, '*Jack*, how ya doin'?' And I go, 'Kris, it's good to see you,' " Spradlin had never forgotten.

"She says, 'I'm doing well, how's Cesar?' And I said, 'Cesar's doing really, really well, thanks. He's actually engaged to be married to a really nice girl,' and she goes, 'No kidding, gosh, good for him. Come up to first class and I want to introduce you to my boyfriend.'

"So I went up to the front of the plane and she introduced me and said, 'This is Robert Kardashian.' "

When he stood up, Spradlin noticed how much shorter he was. "And that's why he probably was so standoffish to me, because I remember Kris said, 'This is a friend of Cesar's who he plays the Tour with.'

"I thought, this guy's a weasel."

CESAR SANUDO EVENTUALLY FOUND love again with Jacqui Schenz, a cute, petite cocktail waitress with a teaching degree, who was nine years his junior, and just a few years older than Kris.

"He told me he had a girlfriend before me and that her name was Kris and that she really cheated on him and brought some guy, or guys into his condo when he was out traveling, and that she was kind of baby-sitting the house," she said in 2016. "And the one statement he said to me that I'll never forget was, 'Don't you *ever* do that to me!' I said, 'Well, that isn't my plan.' " He told her, " 'I don't want to talk about her ever again,' and I went, 'Okay.' "

They tied the knot in April 1978. She was twenty-six and he was thirty-five. Three months later, in July, Kris Houghton would marry Robert Kardashian.

During Jacqui's marriage she gave birth to two sons, and one of them, the firstborn, was given the name Anthony—curiously, the pseudonym Kris had used for Cesar in her book, and members of Jacqui's and Cesar's family had wondered whether that was purposeful on Kris's part, because, as one of them asserted, "She was a total bitch who would actually do something like that."

Jacqui's marriage to Cesar ended in divorce in 1987; Kris's with Kardashian would end in 1991. While Jacqui says hers was an amicable split, the Kardashian final breakup was far from that.

IN 2007, WHEN *KEEPING UP with the Kardashians* debuted, all the dark memories that Cesar Sanudo had of Kris Houghton Kardashian Jenner came flooding back, according to his daughter, Amber.

"Oh, yeah, when the Kardashians came on the scene as far as the show, my dad started watching it, and he always had things to say about it, how she fabricated things. He didn't like the way she portrayed her daughters, that she was more interested about making money than caring about the kids. He was upset about that."

But what really infuriated him, she said, was the interracial vibe that ran through the show.

"My dad would say, 'Why would Kris let her kids date black men?' I said, 'Dad, this is not the 1920s. Come on, you have to get that fifties and sixties mentality about race out of your head, it's not where it is today.'

"But that racial mixing angered him. And that's why he used to say that Kris was sexually involved with O.J. How real that is, and did my dad witness it, I don't think so. He said he was pretty sure that she was seeing O.J. along with Kardashian, that she had an affair with O.J., too. How true that is I don't know. He thought more or less that Kris would be with O.J., and I always had to correct him. I said, 'Dad, this is not the Middle Ages.' I said, 'Dad, you're a Mexican. Let's be real here. You can't say that people didn't stereotype you when you were younger. So you can't say that about Kris's situation.' "

On August 28, 2011, just around the time Kris Jenner's memoir was published, Cesar Sanudo, suffering a number of health problems, died. He was sixty-seven.

SEVEN

Coffee, Tea, or Me?

Kris Jenner claimed that she had actually turned down Robert Kardashian's first proposal of marriage made just "three weeks" after they had finally gotten together following her inglorious breakup with Cesar Sanudo.

She asserted that Kardashian was "devastated" when she told him "no," and that he felt she was "slamming his character" by rejecting him. She maintained that she rebuffed his proposal because she had just ended that "crazy thing" with Sanudo and supposedly wanted some space.

And out of the blue, the way she tells it, she decided to become a flight attendant for American Airlines.

Her whole account was laughably outlandish—a truth-stretcher, if not an outright fabrication—for there were other genuine, far more serious reasons why she was forced to table her longtime dream of marriage to a well-to-do man-about-town with a Beverly Hills address and instead assume the dreary labors of a lowly stewardess trainee, living in a drab, barracks-like corporate dormitory for six weeks with strangers near the Dallas–Fort Worth Airport.

The truth is Kardashian had ended it with Kris, not the other way around. And he gave her the brush-off because he had become romantically involved with someone else.

Moreover, he felt that Kris was still too young for marriage, at least at that moment in time, and didn't have enough worldly experience, despite her affair with Sanudo, which had started when she was just seventeen, and that Kardashian himself had helped break up.

It was while Kris was learning to schlep a drinks cart up and down a narrow aisle above the clouds that Robert Kardashian was on cloud nine, having put Kris mostly out of mind and fallen hard for another woman, and not just any woman, but rather a gorgeous divorcée with a daughter and an internationally known pedigree.

To Kris's deep regret and extreme jealousy, the man of her current dreams was suddenly head over heels in love with the ex-wife of "the King," Elvis Presley.

As Kris noted in her book, "When I flew away, he began dating someone else right away: *Priscilla Presley.*"

The begrudging italics are Kris's.

As she so crudely put it, "Payback is a bitch."

While Robert Kardashian wasn't a kiss-and-tell kind of guy and stayed below the radar in the years before he became O. J. Simpson's well-known mouthpiece, he couldn't wait to tell his friends that he was involved with the former Mrs. Presley, a big-time romantic and sexual trophy for him.

"He calls me and he says, 'Do you want to have dinner? I have a new date.' I said, 'Yeah, who's that?' He says, 'Priscilla Presley.' I said, 'Yeah, go fuck yourself. What are you talking about, *Priscilla Presley*?' He says, 'No, seriously, we met, we hooked up!' So, we went and had dinner, and Priscilla couldn't have been sweeter, couldn't have been nicer," recalled Larry Kraines, one of Kardashian's closest friends.

Kraines, his wife, Joyce—his second marriage—and Robert and Priscilla became an instant fun foursome.

"We went to football games, Sunday football games regularly. We went to dinner. She was such a normal person, you'd never know who the hell she was—that she had been Elvis fucking Presley's wife," Kraines said, still seemingly awed years later.

Priscilla's father was an ex–Air Force guy like Kraines's dad, and he loved playing with CB—Citizen Band—radio, so Larry Kraines sent him a present: a state-of-the-art CB rig, one of the many products of his company, Kraco. "Priscilla graciously thanked me," said Kraines proudly. "She was very gracious, very polite. You'd never know who the fuck she was."

ACCORDING TO JACK SPRADLIN and members of the Sanudo clan, it was Cesar Sanudo who had actually helped Kris get the stewardess job. "This was while they were still together, and Cesar knew someone at American Airlines," Spradlin said. "She didn't have money and she needed a job. She felt she could travel around and still be with Cesar. But all of a sudden they were no longer an item."

But in her book, Kris gave no credit to Sanudo for helping her get the job, crediting only herself, asserting that applying to be a stewardess was a way to "take control of my life."

It helped for Kris to have a sponsor like Sanudo because the airlines back then had been doing very little hiring, and reportedly only one out of a hundred who applied got jobs as flight attendants. Still, she had to have several interviews, meet the height and weight requirements, and undergo drug testing before being accepted into the training program.

The sixties through the seventies were the golden decades of the stewardess—"When they were uniformly young, single, slim, attractive, and female. A good smile (all teeth, no gums) and some ability as a conversationalist were further prerequisites," according to the writer Bruce

Handy, in *Vanity Fair*. And Kris Houghton, who another flight attendant remembers was "stunningly beautiful, like a tall Natalie Wood, who turned heads everywhere she went," fit the profile perfectly. "[F]lying was an adventure in and of itself at a time," observed Handy, "when the average woman got married at the age of twenty and when opportunities outside the home were limited to teaching, nursing, and the secretarial pool."

There's an old joke, however, that underscores the vibe of the era: A stewardess enters the cockpit of a commercial plane and asks the pilot, "Coffee, tea, or me?" The pilot says, "Whichever is easier to make."

For a young, sexually experienced stunner like Kris with no formal education beyond high school, it was the perfect job, at least until she could convince Robert Kardashian to really pop the question.

At the American Airlines training center in Texas, twenty-year-old, five-foot-six Kris bonded with twenty-three-year-old Cindy Spallino, also a gorgeous five-foot-six brunette with brown eyes, much like Kris's look. Unlike Kris, with just a high school diploma, Cindy was a very bright UCLA graduate with a degree in physiology who had spent some time doing medical research and had worked for a while as a paralegal for a gilt-edge Century City law firm, but decided to become a stewardess as a way to "shake up my life."

Cindy arrived at the flight attendant training school in February 1976, a week after Kris. And they soon became bosom buddies, a friendship that would endure for years.

And she found Kris in an entirely different state of mind regarding Robert Kardashian than the scenario painted years later by Kris in her memoir, which she expected readers to take at face value and believe.

It was clear to Cindy that Kris was "desperate" to marry Kardashian— "I *knew* she wanted to marry him, but I also knew from her that Priscilla Presley was there in the background." Cindy also was aware from Kris that Kardashian thought she was too young to take a chance on her to be his wife and the mother of his children, because he wanted a big family.

"Kris talked nonstop about Robert when we were in training," Cindy said. "She told me he was very funny, very charming, very classy, just rock solid, but she never mentioned his looks, never mentioned that he was handsome, or sexy."

Nor did she disclose anything about her relationship with Cesar Sanudo and how it had scandalously ended when he had caught her with Kardashian. "She was probably too embarrassed to reveal that," Cindy believed. "But she told me she was immediately drawn to Robert. She didn't use the word 'attracted.' But she used the word 'drawn.'"

And even though Kardashian was involved with Priscilla Presley, Kris was constantly calling him long-distance.

"We didn't have phones in our rooms, and *the* phone was a pay phone in the hall, and Kris would call Robert *every* night, feeding quarters into the phone," Cindy recalled.

Kris's biggest concern, was Elvis's ex-wife. "Kris would just say, 'He's seeing her. He's awfully close to her. I really don't know the nature of the relationship.' But she was *very* concerned. She was more threatened by it in terms of their potential future together. She felt that even if they weren't together, if Priscilla was free, Robert would choose to go there. She just felt Priscilla Presley was a potential threat to any future Kris would have with Robert. And Kris knew that if Robert could have a life with Priscilla that he would choose that over her."

The other issue that caused Kardashian to cool it with Kris, Cindy understood, was Kris's age. While Kardashian was sexually attracted to Kris, he thought she was too young—almost a dozen years younger—to get serious enough about to marry, at least then, and especially with Priscilla Presley in the picture.

"Kris said that Robert had been taking it too slow with her," recalled Cindy. "Kris was twenty, twenty-one, and her youth was part of the problem with Robert. Kris told me, 'He's taking it so slow, *too* slow,' and I said, 'Kris, you're only twenty, twenty-one, you're in airline school, you haven't lived as much as he has.' We had this conversation, Kris and I, that 'maybe Robert feels that you need to live a little bit more before you're ready to settle down.' But she thought she *was* ready."

It was also clear to Cindy that Robert Kardashian represented a whole new way of life for Kris—a moneyed way of life, one that she desperately wanted.

"Kris's mom was a single mom who, until she remarried, struggled to support the family, and Kris knew what that meant," observed Cindy. "And Kris never wanted to struggle like her mom struggled. Kris wanted financial security. She knew that she was beautiful enough to have that, that wealthy men were very drawn to her, so that the dating pool included financial security for her. She liked nice things in life, and wanted them. She wanted romance and she knew she could be wined and dined. Cesar had done it, Robert had done it, and she *loved* that."

While the only man she ever talked about to Cindy was Robert Kardashian, with whom she wanted marriage and lots of kids, other men desired her, too.

When the opportunity arose, Kris would accept a dinner date with an attractive, well-heeled stranger on a plane.

"We didn't have any money," said Cindy, "so if somebody wanted to take us out to dinner, it was just fine. Men would definitely flirt with you, men would ask you out. But I never felt, for lack of a better word, *icky*. I always felt in control, and I think Kris did, too."

Cindy didn't think Kris's dinner dates ever went further than a free meal, pleasant talk, and maybe some flirting. She didn't view Kris as a slutty Rachel Jones or Trudy Baker of *Coffee, Tea, or Me?* infamy. Nor did she believe Kris had ever joined the mile-high club.

But she noted: "*All* men were drawn to Kris because she was so beautiful. Wealthy men who could have their pick of women were attracted and drawn to her. But so were poor men, so were pilots, so were other flight attendants. They were attracted to her, and wanted to get to know her. 'Hitting on her' is not a word that I would use, but probably they did. Men would flirt with her. I saw that, oh, yes. I would walk through an airport with her and heads would turn because she was *totally* stunning, and photographs did not do her justice. Men were attracted to her *always*."

After Kris and Cindy finished their month and a half of training and got their wings as flight attendants, they were based together in New York. Kris moved in with a group of stewardesses in a small two-bedroom apartment on the Upper East Side of Manhattan near Spanish Harlem, and Cindy moved in with a group of stews in Midtown.

Because of their friendship, however, they volunteered to fly the same flights together, but Kris flew back to L.A. as often as she could in order to try to win back Kardashian from Priscilla Presley.

EIGHT

Kardashian and Presley

At twenty-eight, Priscilla Presley came out of her famous and tumultuous Graceland union a relatively wealthy woman, with shared custody with the King of Elvis's only child, Lisa Marie. She reportedly had a brief affair with the British photographer Terry O'Neill. Priscilla met him when he came into Bis & Beau, a Beverly Hills boutique she had invested in. O'Neill, actress Faye Dunaway's future husband, later criticized the way Priscilla dressed as a "fashion disaster," but was turned on by her sexuality, which was underscored by her kinky master bedroom, with a four-poster bed, special dimmed lighting, and a mirrored ceiling—definitely Elvis's Las Vegas style.

Their relationship lasted about sixty days.

Then, as one observer noted, Priscilla was on the hunt "for a replacement" and "settled" at the time for Robert Kardashian.

Having come from a headline-making marriage to one of the most idolized rock 'n' rollers of his time, some wondered what Priscilla saw in the somewhat nerdy-looking Kardashian.

"She liked him because he had a magnetic personality," observed Joni Migdal. "Robert wasn't particularly attractive, but he was funny, personable, and very nice. Priscilla liked that about him.

"Elvis was Robert's music idol. He *loved* Elvis," continued Migdal. "Robert and I knew all the words of Elvis's songs, and we would drive around with the top down singing our heads off, just knowing every word, and that was in the early 1970s [before he met Priscilla]. Then Robert started dating Priscilla and that made him *very* happy. He wanted to marry her and have children with her. That was definitely his hope, his plan."

And that was Kris's biggest fear when she was in stewardess training, and later when she was flying the friendly skies.

The Robert Kardashian–Priscilla Presley love connection actually began with Robert's older brother, Tommy, around 1975.

He had been dating a woman for a couple of years whose close friend was Joan Esposito, a pretty blond former Miss Missouri beauty queen, who was the ex-wife of Joe Esposito, Elvis's longtime road manager and charter member of the King's so-called Memphis Mafia.

When the woman Tom Kardashian had been dating ended it to marry another man, she graciously introduced him to Joan, divorced, with two young daughters. The ex–Mrs. Esposito had abandoned Memphis and Graceland and was then living in Los Angeles and working as an assistant to Susan Stafford, a devout born-again Christian and Hollywood insider, who had been the original hostess and letter-turner on the popular TV game show *Wheel of Fortune*, before Vanna White and Pat Sajak became the longtime talent.

As Esposito's wife, the future Mrs. Tom Kardashian was a trusted and close member of Elvis's posse, the one who Elvis had assigned to escort teenage Priscilla Beaulieu from Germany, where she had been living with her military family, to Graceland for a Christmas visit with the

King. But the plan fell through at the last minute and Priscilla flew alone. But Joan soon became a mentor to, and close confidant of, Priscilla, and was her advisor regarding her Presley wedding plans and was Priscilla's maid of honor. Priscilla would later write in her 1985 bestselling memoir, *Elvis and Me*, that the ceremony had gone off without a hitch because of her "good friend" Joan, who was "great that way. Joanie knew all the social graces along with the proper etiquette."

From Joan, Tom Kardashian learned the scandalous reason why her marriage to Esposito had fallen apart, and why Priscilla's to Elvis had, too.

"Elvis didn't want the women around, so Joan and Priscilla wouldn't be allowed to go on all the tours," revealed Kardashian in 2015. "Elvis was far and away the biggest woman-getter in the world. He *was* the King, and all these women were at his beck and call. Joe [Esposito] also had girls in all these places, and Joan didn't believe that he would cheat on her, but it was inevitable. Elvis kept Priscilla and Joan and the other wives away from what was going on, and that's why the relationships failed."

The way Tom Kardashian told it, Robert and Priscilla's meeting came about "because Robert knew that Joan and Priscilla were close, and there'd be times the four of us would go out, and then they kind of went out on their own."

But Migdal, who later got to know both Priscilla and her sister, Michelle, remembers a different scenario.

"Tommy met Joanie Esposito, but he *really* wanted to date Priscilla. But when Tommy and Priscilla finally met, it was Priscilla who decided—'Well, why don't we double date and I'll just go out with your brother.'"

Some members of the very private and low-key wider Kardashian family were appalled when they learned that Robert had become romantically involved with Priscilla Presley. To them, it was like he was involved with scandalous royalty, and that he'd end up plastered all over the tabloids. And there was more than a hint of jealousy and envy in the family, too.

One of those was one of Robert's cousins, Joan Agajanian, daughter of the auto-racing impresario J. C. Agajanian of Indianapolis 500 fame, and sister of Robert and Tommy's closest cousin, the motor sports attorney, promoter, and race car owner Cary J. C. Agajanian. Joan claimed the only reason Priscilla went out with Robert was because "she had no one else to go out with." She and Priscilla met at a trendy Beverly Hills health club, and the two bonded. Priscilla came to view her as her mentor on how to become a Beverly Hills socialite. "She'd never been anywhere. She knew nothing. . . . I don't think she was demure," Agajanian once told a Priscilla biographer. "I think she was intimidated by anyone who was socially adequate. She was socially inadequate to the point of pain, of just shutting up. But she's a very smart girl. Street smart."

When Robert and Priscilla became an item, Tom Kardashian was a bit jealous.

"Pissed doesn't even cover Tommy's reaction when Bob won the Presley prize," observed a longtime friend of both brothers. "It caused sibling tensions, the old brotherly rivalry."

Looking back to that time in 2015, however, Tom Kardashian, happily married to the former Joan Esposito for going on four decades, had long ago resigned himself to the fact that Priscilla had chosen his brother over him. He thought she could be too controlling.

"Priscilla really changed a lot of my brother's thinking of how he should dress, how he should even drive, and what he should do—and she changed him easily because she was so attractive, and so she had a lot of influence on him," he maintained. "She could tell him something and he would listen. But I also realized that the women in my brother's life were strong, and he listened to Kris, and to some of the other girls he was involved with, or he would play second fiddle to them."

In her book, Kris noted that Robert was "instantly smitten" with Elvis's ex, and Priscilla "apparently was smitten with him."

All that was true.

What wasn't true was Kris's assertion that Kardashian and Presley "quickly moved in together."

In fact, they never actually lived in the same house during their year-long, sometimes rocky relationship. Some believed it was because Robert's best friend, O. J. Simpson, then playing for the Buffalo Bills, often camped out and partied at the Kardashian brothers' Beverly Hills bachelor pad—friends called them "the Three Musketeers," especially when the Juice was on the outs with his wife of twelve years, Marguerite Whitely Simpson, mother of three of his children, Arnelle, Jason, and Aaren.

Still, Robert Kardashian and Priscilla Presley were having some great times together while stewardess Kris Houghton literally stewed, believing she had forever lost him to Elvis's ex.

Of Priscilla, Kris enviously observed, "She was *gorgeous*, of course, petite and perfect . . . I would see pictures of her and just die . . . [but] deep in my heart I was still hoping that Robert would end up being the guy for me."

A couple of times when Robert was out and about with Priscilla they were spotted by the paparazzi, and photos of them appeared once or twice in one of the weekly supermarket tabloids, causing Kris to "avoid the *National Enquirer*," her favorite form of weekly reading matter at the time. Back then she lived vicariously, buried in the tabloids, reading about celebrities and their glamorous and scandalous lives.

Meanwhile, it was a Sisyphean task for Kardashian to convince Priscilla to marry him, which he desperately wanted. But he was up against the King, who still loomed large in Priscilla and Lisa Marie's lives. At one point, Kardashian complained to a friend that while he was making love to Priscilla, she would get incoherent phone calls from Elvis "and she would put the receiver on the pillow between them and let him listen."

Larry Kraines recalls Kardashian telling him that Priscilla was "terrific and nice, 'but this guy Elvis doesn't stop controlling her,' didn't want her going with anybody because they had Lisa Marie, and Elvis was very involved in that. Robert was very bothered by all of that. So one thing led to another and I guess Robert just felt that he couldn't take the pressure that Elvis was putting on Priscilla, and he basically broke it off and said, 'This isn't going to work,' and that was that."

But Kardashian's friends were hearing only one side of the story.

In fact, it was Priscilla who would eventually end it with Kardashian, and one of the reasons was that Robert had begun trying to control her just as Elvis had done, and that infuriated her.

One example was when he pushed her into preparing a dinner for him—and then complained to her that she was a lousy cook. With Elvis, the best she could put together was a simple breakfast. Robert was now hoping to turn Priscilla into his version of a domesticated "Armenian housewife," Migdal said.

"Priscilla once tried to make dinner for Robert because he kept asking her," said Migdal. "He wanted her to be more of a housewife. So Priscilla said that one night she cooked asparagus, and she made this, and she made that, and we both laughed about it because he was very picky about what he ate, and she went out of her *way* to make it perfect for him, and he *hated* it. He did *not* like it. She said that after that meal he never suggested that she make dinner for him again."

Priscilla was hurt and insulted.

But there was little time left in their relationship for any more Kardashian domesticity tests, because Priscilla was honest with him and made it clear that marriage wasn't in the cards.

She told him, "Look, I'm not going to marry anyone until Elvis dies."

And that was the end for Robert Kardashian with Priscilla Presley.

IN 1976, AMERICA'S BICENTENNIAL YEAR, a few odd coincidences occurred involving some of the principals in the Kardashian drama.

Kris Houghton, based in New York for American Airlines, heard from Robert that he and Priscilla had broken up. She was joyous. And Kardashian's pal O. J. Simpson had gotten hired by ABC Sports to be one of the Summer Olympics commentators in Montreal, where a young athlete by the name of Bruce Jenner was on the U.S. team, competing in the decathlon.

Kardashian and O.J. made plans to go to Montreal for the games with a stopover in New York, and Robert asked Kris to meet them and pick up where they had left off before Priscilla had come into his life. The threesome—Kris, Kardashian, and O.J.—checked into a suite at the Plaza Hotel, shopped, dined, and partied at Studio 54. As Kris stated when she saw Kardashian again, "I could feel everything around me changing so fast."

And when Jenner won the gold medal, all of America, including Kardashian and O.J., was excited, except for Kris.

"Who's Bruce Jenner?" she asked.

Meanwhile, back at Graceland, Elvis and his live-in girlfriend Linda Thompson, a former Miss Tennessee, snuggling together in the King's bed, were also watching the Summer Olympics and "were pretty closely following" Jenner's progress, she recalled.

As Thompson has never forgotten, "Bruce was on the final lap of his last race, the tenth event, and as he crossed the finish line to win the Olympic gold medal, distinguishing himself as the 'world's greatest athlete,' Elvis and I were exuberant. . . . We were also commenting on what an amazing specimen of a man Bruce Jenner was.

"Elvis remarked, 'Damn, if that guy is not handsome! I'm not gay, but damn, he's good-looking.'

"I quite agreed and teasingly said, 'Wow! He is gorgeous. I'm going to marry that guy someday!'

"Elvis replied, 'Yeah, sure, honey, over my dead body.'"

When Elvis died of an apparent heart attack on the toilet in his bathroom at Graceland in August 1977 at just forty-two—addicted to drugs, his body bloated from junk food and generally in horrifically poor health—it was Linda Thompson who discovered him. Joan Esposito, then engaged to Tom Kardashian, would be at Priscilla's side through her mourning (and Linda Thompson's), and Joan's ex, Joe Esposito, would be one of the King's pallbearers.

Kardashian had started seeing Kris again, with her hopes high that they would be married.

They were having dinner with Robert's friends the Kraineses when they heard the news that the King had died, a death that shocked the entire world. But Kris, who knew that Priscilla wasn't going to commit to marry until after Elvis's passing, was again concerned that she'd lose Robert to the Presley widow. That concern was magnified ten times when Kardashian immediately got up from the table and placed a private call to Priscilla. In her memoir, Kris said she worried for some months whether Robert and Priscilla Presley would get back together.

But virtually to the day of the first anniversary of Presley's death her worries ended. She and Robert would be married.

Linda Thompson's prediction to Elvis that she would marry Jenner one day came true, too—they would be wed in January 1981.

And Kris Houghton Kardashian, a decade later, in 1991, would marry Jenner, even before her and Robert Kardashian's signatures were dry on their divorce papers.

PART II

The "Mouthpiece"

NINE

A Corrupt Family Business

It was just less than eight miles from the Kardashian family home-stead in the upper-middle-class development of View Park–Windsor Hills, in Los Angeles, to the city of Vernon. But the two locations were a world apart.

One was where Arthur Thomas Kardashian and his wife, the former Helen Jean Arakelian, comfortably resided and where their children, Robert, Tommy, and Barbara grew up. The other was a foul-smelling, industrial hellhole, four miles south of downtown L.A., where the Kardashians made their money.

It was in Vernon—California's tiniest city, a 5.2-square-mile quagmire of grimy warehouses, factories that specialized in mixing toxic paint, a rendering plant that boiled dead pets into animal feed and grease—where the Kardashian family's successful meatpacking business, Great Western Packing, was located, at 3377 East Vernon Avenue.

As Tom Kardashian recalls, "Most all of my friends hated to go down there, and they still talk about what the city of Vernon smelled like. If you didn't grow up around cattle with the smell, you wouldn't understand, but if you did grow up around cattle on a daily basis like I did, it's like being a doctor and doing surgery."

While tens of thousands of people labored in Vernon by day, the city was deserted by nightfall, except for less than a hundred who actually resided there in a few dozen low-rent, city-owned apartments and houses—a "dreary municipal oddity" where there were no parks, stores, schools, or any other form of civilization, except for four restaurants that were shuttered by late afternoon.

Members of certain families had corruptly run the city since the early years of the twentieth century, causing *Forbes* to once call Vernon a "benign dictatorship," creating "spoils for a few and a toxic stench for everyone else."

One of Vernon's major business enterprises for years had been meatpacking, and by the mid-seventies about a dozen permeated the hellish little city, run mostly by Jews and Armenians like the Kardashians, who fought one another for business.

Great Western Packing had been founded by Robert Kardashian's grandfather, Tatos Saghatel Kardashian—better known as Tom—and his brothers. They were together in many other businesses—hog ranches and rubbish and garbage collection. One of Tatos Kardashian's first jobs when he came to Southern California from the old country was driving a truck for Angela's Furniture Company for ten dollars a week. After a time, he talked a banker into trusting him enough to loan him some money so he could buy his own truck, and he started a trash-hauling business, "and that's how a lot of Armenian guys ended up in the rubbish business," said Tatos's grandson and his namesake, Tom Kardashian.

The sprawling Kardashian family had arrived in America from their village in Armenia in the early 1900s. It was in California where Tatos Kardashian met his future wife, Hamas Shakarian, the matriarch and the great-grandmother of the famous Kardashian siblings. Hamas's brother, Issak Shakarian, had made a fortune in the dairy business in

Downey, California. His son, Demos Shakarian, took over the business, but would earn his greatest fame as a Pentecostal evangelist who believed in miracles and healings, and in the early sixties would found a global organization for Pentecostal Christian businessmen called the Full Gospel Businessmen's Fellowship International. And curiously, his granddaughter, Denice Shakarian Halicki, a glamorous blonde, became Robert Kardashian's fiancée after his divorce from Kris. She was Robert's third cousin.

DESPITE THE VERY CLOSE family ties and successful family businesses, the entire Kardashian family was in for a devastating, scandalous blow.

In the early 1970s federal prosecutors began a top secret, wide-ranging probe of corruption in the city of Vernon's meatpacking industry. And dead center in the government's net was none other than Great Western Packing, the Kardashians' long-successful family business, then run by the new patriarch, Arthur, his brother Bob, and the junior member, Arthur's son, Tom Kardashian.

And it was Robert's brother, Tom, who would take the fall for his father and uncle. Unlike Robert, Tom grew up in the meatpacking business. When he was a kid, he'd travel with his father, Arthur, on cattle-buying trips, and he quickly learned the ins and outs of buying livestock. After graduating from Dorsey High School, in Los Angeles, he went to USC, lived at home, and majored in accounting, utilizing what he learned for the family business, which he described as "volatile. Some years we could make good money and some years we'd lose money. You couldn't do anything to prevent the losses."

Tom rose to general manager of Great Western, which advertised in Los Angeles–area newspapers in the 1970s as selling "Selected beef by professional livestock men," and he was living the high life with his kid brother, Robert, in their Beverly Hills bachelor pad, with their buddy O. J. Simpson as their regular guest, and it was always party time.

But on Tuesday, March 19, 1974, thirty-three-year-old Thomas

Arthur "Tommy" Kardashian—future uncle of Kourtney, Kim, Khloé and Rob—was arrested by the FBI on charges of either bribing or offering to bribe U.S. Department of Agriculture inspectors.

The USDA inspectors and meat graders regularly came around with their hands outstretched seeking cash in exchange for giving Kardashian meats a better grade. If a housewife thought she was buying a prime sirloin steak for the family dinner, she might have actually been taking home one of lesser quality. It was a sleazy way of doing business, but a way of life for the Kardashians' operation, and for some other meatpacking houses in the gritty little city of Vernon.

As Tom Kardashian asserted, "Believe it or not, it all started with the federal meat inspectors and the federal meat graders, and they were the ones that could coerce and hold us hostage if we didn't do certain things like give gratuities and pay those guys to just do their job."

Nevertheless, Tommy's shocking and surprise arrest has quietly and scandalously lived in Kardashian family history, a long-held family secret and a major embarrassment known only to a few.

From the time Kris married Robert Kardashian and even after he divorced her, and from the time she married and divorced Bruce Jenner, she religiously abided by the Kardashian family's *omertà*—its code of silence about criminal activity—and kept the dirty little secret that her brother-in-law Tom Kardashian was a convicted felon.

But in a series of confessional interviews for this book in 2015, seventy-five-year-old Tom Kardashian, then billing himself as a "business and professional coach," broke his long silence about his arrest, indictment, and conviction and the decades he had lived under a dark cloud as a convicted felon until a Republican president gave him a rare pardon.

Curiously, in his 2015 online résumé advertising his services in hopes of generating new clients as a business consultant, Kardashian boasted, "As President of Great Western Meatpacking Company, he grew the organization into an industry leader."

But on that horrific day back in mid-March 1974, Tom Kardashian was no family business hero, as he's never forgotten.

"The FBI took me in handcuffs out of my plant in front of all the people because I was the general manager running things. It was totally unexpected," he said, looking back to that horrific time. "I was taken to the federal building in Los Angeles and booked. And so I was held until the attorneys got me released, which was the same day.

"Then I had to go to federal court and go in front of a judge, and I ended up pleading guilty to a felony in a plea bargain, so I didn't have any jail time. I was a young man and I felt terrible. There were two other employees who were involved in the day-to-day operations, so the three of us were indicted by the federal government."

Kardashian was one of thirteen men from five meatpacking firms, including the Kardashians' family firm, indicted by a federal grand jury in Los Angeles on March 20, 1974, on charges of bribing U.S. Department of Agriculture meat graders. Eleven of the indicted were arrested the next day when Tom Kardashian was taken into custody. Five of the indicted were owners of meatpacking plants.

The charges stemmed from offers of bribes ranging from sixty dollars to three hundred dollars *per day* to federal meat graders to upgrade beef quality, allowing the meatpackers to charge more money and make more money. The Department of Agriculture graders had the responsibility to make the determination whether meat was classified as USDA Prime, Choice, Select, or lower quality.

In one case, according to the assistant United States Attorney for the central district of California at the time, Robert C. Bonner, and the FBI, a meat grader was offered a payoff of one hundred dollars a week if she would overlook tapeworm-infested beef—at a firm other than Kardashian's. Bonner stated at the time that to the best of his knowledge no contaminated meat had been shipped to any supermarkets, and that none of the meatpacking plants caught up in the raid would be shut down.

Tom Kardashian and others were charged with paying bribes ranging from sixty to one hundred dollars a day to USDA meat grader Charles Gledhill.

William A. Sullivan, then the assistant FBI director in charge of the Los Angeles office, said that those indicted could, if convicted, face maximum prison sentences of fifteen years and fines up to twenty thousand dollars for each count of bribery or offering of a bribe to a federal official.

Looking back in 2015, Tom Kardashian acknowledged, "Our company was indicted for some improprieties, but it was an industry situation, at a time when our industry was kind of corrupt. Our meat was distributed interstate, so we were a part of the federal thing, and our plant was federally inspected."

He said his lawyers had advised him to make a plea bargain deal and avoid a trial and possible imprisonment. He was placed on three years probations and fined ten-thousand dollars on November 25, 1974.

"I couldn't use the defense that this [bribing USDA graders] was an industry practice," he maintained. "A conspiracy is the same as actually doing it. It made no difference whether it was my idea, or somebody else's idea, or an industry practice. The government went after each company separately, so I couldn't use the defense that this is what was going on. Also, I was a young man, so I had to go through the advice of the attorneys on what would be the net effect on my family, and on myself personally."

Kardashian says he decided to take the fall—think Al Pacino as Michael Corleone, the Corleone family protector in *The Godfather*—even though he had no direct ownership in his family's business but had been a part of it since his childhood.

"They would have arrested my uncle, or my dad, who were shareholders, in place of me," he explained. "But I was young and figured I could take it. I knew my uncle had a bad heart and it would have been difficult on him. But I didn't realize what kind of effect the conviction really would have on me.

"It restricted me as a young business guy," he continued. "I had the stigma, meaning that I could not be on the board of any companies because I was now a felon. Once you're a felon, you're a felon. Whenever I'd go somewhere, even voting, or to be on a jury, one of the questions is—have you ever been convicted of a felony?"

He eventually got a position with a company called Public Storage and became president of one of its divisions. "But when we had to do public filings, the attorneys for Public Storage had to put a whole disclaimer that I was a felon. It was not an enjoyable thing." He also was installed as a member of the Young Presidents' organization in 1978–79. "They knew I was a felon," he noted, "and they accepted me anyway." His membership coincided with his marriage to Joan Esposito, a month after his brother, Robert, married Kris Houghton, in July 1978.

Under federal rules, Kardashian wasn't permitted to apply for a pardon for a period of ten years following his conviction. He did apply in 1984 and was rejected.

"I was told it was too soon," he said.

"But here's the deal," Kardashian continued. "Twenty years after my conviction I got a federal pardon from the president of the United States, the senior Bush, because I did a lot of community service, and I was involved in my church. After all those years, the government saw my background, and I hadn't given a bunch of money politically to make that happen. Very few people get a pardon from the president."

In fact, two days before he left office in January 1993, President George Herbert Walker Bush issued only a dozen pardons and commuted the sentences of two other men. Two of those pardoned had been contributors to Bush's reelection campaign a year earlier.

Kardashian was given a "full and unconditional pardon" for the offense of "offering gratuities to public officials."

The others pardoned by Bush included crimes ranging from bank fraud to tax evasion to drug dealing and smuggling.

Kardashian's name was buried deep in the list of Bush presidential pardons and commutations released to the media by the U.S. Department of Justice's Office of the Pardon Attorney, on January 18, 1993. Of the twelve, Kardashian's name was number eight, listed between a felon convicted in 1955 of larceny and a felon convicted in 1962 of a drug charge. Bush declined to give his reason for the Kardashian clemency.

YOU HAD TO BE A tough guy to be in the meatpacking business, and Tommy Kardashian could be a tough guy. The labor unions that Great Western Packing had to contend with—such as the then-corrupt Teamsters union—were a constant problem, like maggots infesting meat.

"There was a lot of fear in dealing with the unions," Kardashian asserted, pointing to the Teamsters, who were the truck drivers who hauled the meat, and the butchers' union, and the operating engineers' union, whose members took care of the refrigeration. Tommy's uncle, his father, Arthur's brother, Bob Kardashian, was in charge of Great Western Packing's negotiations with the union reps. But when the talks broke down and there was a strike and labor trouble, Tommy Kardashian stepped in as the company's muscle.

"I was young enough to drive through the pickets," he boasted years later. "I brought in protection—big guys who played football." Some were from his and Robert's and their friend O. J. Simpson's alma mater, the University of Southern California, Los Angeles. "I was in my early thirties. I was single. I'd get some of my ex–football player friends. That's just the way it was."

Tom's brother, Robert, patriarch of the contemporary Kardashian clan after his marriage to Kris Houghton, knew for years that his family's meatpacking business was rife with corruption, and he didn't want any part of it.

As Tom noted, "Ours was just not a good business, and I couldn't wait to get out of it. My brother saw that early on, and that's why instead of working for the company and having to work for me he just said, 'I gotta do something else.' Robert knew being in the family business there was corruption. If you were to ask me, did I know I was doing wrong, did I know it was illegal to do that, I'd have to say yes. It's not like somebody pulled something over on me. I can just imagine some of those guys who are the sons of Mafia people. They don't have much of a choice.

"But Robert didn't care about our thing, and the number two part of that was he was going to have to be number two to me, and when your older brother is telling you, 'you gotta do it this way and that way,' you know it doesn't work."

After Tom Kardashian's conviction, continued government investigations, and tightening regulations, the Kardashian family's meatpacking business became increasingly more difficult to operate and was far less profitable, so in the early 1980s Great Western Packing ended a many-decades-long and lucrative run, corrupt as it may have been at times.

"We couldn't really sell the company," said Kardashian. "It didn't bring a premium price because the whole industry was really being watched, and the government was putting extra pressure. It was hard to stay in business.

"We didn't even have a lot of land to sell off," he continued. "We were in Vernon, which wasn't a strong place where all of a sudden land values escalated. My dad decided to retire when he was, like, sixty-five, around 1982. [Arthur Kardashian, paternal grandfather of Kim, Khloé, Kourtney, and Rob, died at ninety-five, close to Christmas 2012, outliving his son, Robert, by a decade.] All I can say is the government virtually put our industry out of business."

THE CRIMINAL PART OF THE Kardashian family's meatpacking business, the one that got Tom Kardashian in serious trouble, was even evident at times in the Kardashian home.

A close high school friend of Robert Kardashian's, Phil Pennino, says he knew for certain that "Bob's father and his uncles were very powerful in L.A. County. They were heavy-duty." Having grown up in an Italian American home with Sicilian roots, Pennino could spot a goombah— an Italian who might have unsavory connections—a mile away. "One of the guys that used to come around to the Kardashian house was a gangster, an L.A. gangster, and I know Bob knew him," stated Pennino. "He used to come around to the family business, too, and I said to Bob, 'How the hell do you know this guy?' and he said, 'He and my dad blah, blah, blah.' So I knew the Kardashians knew certain connected people.

"Bob just said the family knew the [L.A. gangster] guy. He said he was a 'close friend, a part of my family,' and 'Oh, yeah, we'd make a joke of it.' We were about seventeen and we laughed at it because it was kind of cool, but we really didn't understand the full ramifications of what was going on."

Some years later, after Robert was hanging with his best friend, the football hero O. J. Simpson, they were in their favorite Beverly Hills hangout, the Luau, and were hitting on a couple of women, and Kardashian was doing his best to impress them. And out of the blue, he boasted about how he was a made member of organized crime, that he was an enforcer in the Armenian Mafia, and that his expertise was breaking the knees of those who didn't cooperate. The women seemed both impressed and frightened. While Kardashian's story was probably little more than macho braggadocio, it said something about the family and business from where he was coming.

He would later confide in his close friend Joni Migdal, whose Jewish family, the Linsks, were neighbors of the Kardashian family in View Park–Windsor Hills, that he knew of the corruption and criminality that existed in his family's business, and that he didn't want to be a part of it.

"His whole family wanted him to join that hierarchy of Armenian business people, and Robert made a conscious decision to not have any part of that business," Migdal stated. After graduating in 1966 with a degree in business administration and psychology from USC, Kardashian went straight to study law at the University of San Diego School of Law. "At that time," said Migdal, "we were having lunch almost every day, and we had a long talk when Robert was about to get his law degree about whether he was going to join his family's businesses and be the *consigliere* of that group of people, or go another route that was a more honest way of making money, and he decided to go that way."

Kardashian would join the Beverly Hills law firm of two entrepreneurial attorneys—the partnership of Richard Eamer and John Bedrosian, a first-generation Armenian-American whose parents emigrated to the United States when the Kardashians had in the early twentieth century.

Migdal firmly believed that Robert made the right decision because it was just a few years later that his brother, Tom, would be arrested and forced to make a plea bargain deal to avoid imprisonment in the Great Western Packing bribery case.

"Robert was devastated and *really* supportive of Tom," she said. "But the family was secretive about it, and they were embarrassed because they had never had anything like that happen. Robert told me about his brother's arrest even before it hit the headlines, and he was really broken up. But the whole culture of Arthur and Helen and Tommy and Robert and Barbara was just to go under the radar."

Robert Kardashian's only actual experience working for Great Western Packing occurred as a teenager in the summers when his father was hoping he'd follow in his and his brother's footsteps and one day join the family business. With that in mind, and just to give him a taste of what the business sometimes entailed, Robert was assigned the god-awful, bloody task of stunning Kardashian cattle before they went to slaughter.

"That was his summer job for a while, to use a big rubber thing like a sledgehammer, pounding the cows over the head," recalled his friend and confidant Larry Kraines. "He stunned them enough for them to go to the next process. He told me he didn't like doing it, and he didn't like the family business. It wasn't for him. But he'd go in and do it and pick up some cash."

TEN

A Kardashian Childhood

Robert G. Kardashian was born on February 22, 1944, the youngest of Arthur and Helen Kardashian's three children—the one who would make the Kardashian name famous.

Because he came into the world on George Washington's birthday, his parents had honored the nation's first president by giving their second son the middle name of George—Robert *George* Kardashian.

He was four when the family moved into the home where he and his two siblings, Tom and Barbara, would grow up—a handsome three-bedroom, five-bath, almost four-thousand-square-foot house, built in 1942, at 4908 Valley Ridge Avenue in the hilly and airy View Park–Windsor Hills development of Los Angeles, known generally as Baldwin Hills. The Kardashians had moved "up the hill" from a far more modest home in a far less fancy area of L.A. as Great Western Packing's wartime money, sometimes involving the black market sale of meat, was rolling in.

While the Kardashian family was relatively affluent and fell into the upper-middle-class bracket, Arthur and Helen had something of an immigrant mentality when it came to living large.

"My dad and mom never traveled," said Tom Kardashian, looking back. "They never went to Europe, or on boat cruises, or any of that kind of stuff. We had enough money to live well, but we didn't have an abundance of money to go out and say, 'Oh, we're going to buy an airplane,' or 'We're going to buy a boat.' We didn't have a second home. My mom and sister and my brother and myself would get away to Balboa, and my dad would go back and forth from the city on weekends." Balboa, where the Kardashians inexpensively vacationed, is a peninsula in the Pacific, part of the ritzy city of Newport Beach, south of Los Angeles.

But Robert and Tom would live far differently, owning fancy Beverly Hills homes, driving Rolls-Royces, and courting women with expensive tastes, Kris Houghton as the best example.

Because Mrs. Kardashian's sons were rambunctious and Mr. Kardashian was rarely home, always on the road buying cattle, Helen Jean Kardashian had decided to send her boys to a neighborhood military school, the California Military Academy, founded in 1906, on Angeles Vista Boulevard, within walking distance of the Kardashian home.

"It was all about discipline and respect," ex-felon Tom Kardashian said.

The Kardashian boys wore military uniforms and sported dog tags around their necks, had to report for formations, kept their shoes spit-shined, were required to respond "yes, sir" and "no, sir" when addressed, and had to salute their teachers, according to the rules established by the academy's director, Colonel Albert E. Ebright, who stressed competition among the cadets, and whose office was decorated with trophies and weapons of war. "When a boy comes here, we assume he is a good lad," was Ebright's motto. "We stress that he will be good because he wants to be. Not because he is afraid of not being good."

· · ·

HELEN KARDASHIAN WAS UNLIKE most Armenian women, who have dark hair and olive skin like her granddaughters Kourtney and Kim. Instead, she had blond hair, a light complexion, and blue eyes that gave her an angelic look, but her sisters were all dark-skinned. It was similar to the situation with Robert and Kris's third-born, Khloé, who was blond and looked nothing like her siblings or her father. But that situation would be more complicated.

Mrs. Kardashian had a toughness about her and ruled the Kardashian household with an iron fist. Larry Kraines, who often slept over at the Kardashian home on weekends after he and Robert bonded in tenth grade, has never forgotten that Helen Kardashian was an obsessive housekeeper. "Oh my God, if Robert got up at five thirty, six o'clock in the morning to go to the bathroom, Helen would clean and have his bed made up before he had a chance to get back in it. She was unbelievable, a real character."

And some who knew her said she could also be a "bitch on wheels."

She had come from a poor Armenian family, was one of four children of Arut and Annie Arakelian, and grew up in the gritty, ethnically diverse working-class Los Angeles community of San Pedro, close by the Port of Los Angeles, which had long been the home port of the U.S. Navy's battle fleet.

Helen Kardashian once told Tommy that she was "very poor growing up, but she didn't know she was poor," he recalled. "She and her sisters used to take the streetcar to get around." And before she married Arthur Kardashian, who came from a family with its hands in a lot of different businesses—such as hog farming, meatpacking, and waste management—she had worked for the StarKist company packing fish. She died at the age of ninety-one in 2008, and like her husband, Arthur, outlived their famous son, Robert.

After finishing sixth grade at the California Military Academy,

Robert was enrolled at Audubon Junior High School, down the hill in the nearby Leimert Park neighborhood.

Unlike his first wife, Kris, Robert was an academic high achiever in school, popular with his classmates, and active in organizations.

At Audubon, he was the student body president and was a member of the student council.

As Linda Matsuno-Parmenter, an Asian-American Audubon classmate who also was on the student council with Kardashian and is pictured next to him in the class of 1961 Audubon yearbook, said, looking back to that time, "Robert was just a person who got along well with *everybody*. He just had a friendly personality and no matter what group you hung out with, he was able to kind of connect with people."

His popularity increased in high school. In his class at L.A.'s Susan Miller Dorsey High School—then a third black, a third white, a third Asian, and the only all-black high school in Los Angeles in 2016—he was on the honor roll, was a member of the service boards and the Triangles service club, was "best all-around" of the "significant seniors" along with a classmate by the name of Sylvia Duran, who are pictured with their arms locked together in the *Circle 1961* class yearbook. He was a Yell King—a cheerleader with mostly girls—and he was elected student body president.

Robert was inducted into the Bishops, a cliquish social club for the school's elite "where we got our butts wacked as an initiation," recalled Kardashian classmate Tony Byler, who played football and later, like Kardashian, became an attorney. Byler married another member of Robert's class, Donna Tom, who has never forgotten how he crashed a little birthday party she was having at school with a chocolate cake she had baked. "And Bob Kardashian ate so much of it he claimed he got sick, but he might have been kidding me because he was *very* social."

For a time in high school he was going with an Armenian-American girl, Dee-Dee, a student at St. Mary's Academy, whom he had met at the Armenian Pentecostal church that his family attended every Sunday, where a Kardashian family relative was the pastor, according to Tom Kardashian. "Robert dated a lot of girls, a lot of Armenian girls, and he was not afraid to bring girls home and around our parents, where I was pretty much the opposite. I kept to myself. As the second boy in the family, he was very outgoing and had the kind of personality that created a lot of friends."

One of Robert's close high school pals, Phil Pennino, remembered Dee-Dee well. "It was a high school romance and Bob was pretty serious about her, and she was *gorgeous*. We double dated many times. Robert *always* kind of had a girlfriend."

Back then Kardashian was a big rock 'n' roll fan who especially liked the surfer music of the Beach Boys and Jan and Dean. "Bob taught me how to do the 'surfer stomp.' I was all intimidated by learning that dance, and he'd just laugh," said Pennino. When they were seniors, the two pals went stag to see the Kingston Trio, then a popular folk music group, at the Copacabana.

When Robert graduated from Dorsey, his class yearbook noted the following about him: "*As head of the Student Council this past semester, Bob Kardashian has more than proved his leadership as displayed by excellent executive ability tempered with a wonderful sense of humor, good judgment, and fairness at all times. Bob leaves Dorsey held in the high esteem of all those who know him.*"

"He was," as his brother said, "Mr. Personality. He was student body president and was all those things that came along with being a good person, a good guy, and so he had popularity from that, and that was strong for him."

Arthur and Helen Kardashian threw a big graduation party for Robert at the house, attended by many of his high school friends and members of the wider Kardashian family. And because he had done so well academically and in September was to begin his college career at the University of Southern California, his parents gave him a new black with a white interior Chevrolet Corvair, a rear-engine compact introduced by General Motors a few years earlier to compete with the new breed of inexpensive, fuel-economy foreign imports that were becoming popular with the American motorist in the early sixties.

"When he had that Corvair, he had to keep a spare fan belt in the glove box because that would always break or come off and the car wouldn't run," remembered Larry Kraines. "I'd make fun of him—'Your brother's got a Corvette, and you've got a Corvair, what the hell's with that?' " Phil Pennino recalled going on double dates with Robert in the Corvair, and there were always mechanical problems. "He told me the engine fell out a couple of years later. It was a piece of junk."

The year 1962, when Robert graduated from high school, was a dangerous time. That October the Soviet Union deployed ballistic missiles to the communist island of Cuba, just ninety miles off the coast of south Florida, in what became known as the Cuban Missile Crisis. The Russians threatened to escalate the Cold War into a possible nuclear war. And in Southeast Asia, the war in Vietnam was expanding and would end with the deaths of more than fifty thousand U.S. troops.

With all those international hot spots, a number of Kardashian's Dorsey High classmates who didn't go immediately to college and secure a deferment like him were drafted into the army, while some patriotic young men enlisted.

Robert had signed up for the draft at eighteen as required by the Selective Service, but according to Tom Kardashian, "He never did go in. He was 4F, or whatever they called it. He was kept out of the draft because he had acid reflux, and his esophagus would close up and he had a hard time swallowing."

But close friends of Robert's like Joni Migdal and Larry Kraines had trouble swallowing Tom's story.

Migdal, for one, said she was totally unaware of Robert having an issue with acid reflux back then, and was "sure" it was more likely that he "got a doctor to write something," which resulted in a medical exemption that along with school deferments kept him from being drafted and possibly sent to war.

Immediately after graduation Kraines enlisted in the California Army

National Guard's 40th Armored Division, on the advice of his ex-military father, who told him that with the Cuban Missile Crisis, and with "Vietnam ramping up," he should get his military obligation out of the way.

But, Kraines said Robert went off to USC and "did the school defer-ment thing *forever*," and he questioned Tom Kardashian's version of events. "Robert really felt strongly against what we were doing at the time in Vietnam, and he just didn't want to have any part of it. That's what made him continue his education to the degree that he did. The longer he stayed in school the safer he was."

ROBERT KARDASHIAN, WHO WAS SHORT, liked being around big ath-letes, especially football players. For a time he played quarterback for the Dorsey High "B" squad, the team for the smaller, good athletes, recalled Kraines, who played halfback on the varsity squad, the Dorsey Dons.

"Bob and I were both not of athlete size; that wasn't gifted to us," said Tom Kardashian. "And my brother was never big enough or strong enough to play football when he went to USC. We both *loved* football. Our dad used to get tickets to the USC games before we ever went to school there, and the Coliseum wasn't too far from where we lived, and we used to go to the Los Angeles Rams games, too. It was kind of a family thing to do on Sunday."

When Tom was at USC, four years before his brother, he was man-ager of the Trojans football team, and Bob took the same job when he matriculated there.

He loved being manager, idolized the players, traveled with the team, and stayed in hotels with the squad for away games, and it made him feel important.

"Bob had to be at practice every day, and part of the responsibility of the team manager was to make certain that there were forty-two play-ers on the bus, forty-two players at the training table, all the things that were required to babysit the team," said Kardashian. And he boasted,

"My brother and I had what was called lifetime passes to all the games given to us because we were four-year varsity lettermen as team managers."

Still, Joni Migdal acknowledged that, Robert, was really nothing more than a "glorified water boy," and another close observer called Robert's managerial slot "the prototypical hanger-on position." But with all that pigskin in his blood, it was no surprise to anyone who knew him well that one of Kardashian's closest adult bonds was with famous USC alumnus and Heisman Memorial Trophy winner O. J. Simpson, which underscored Robert's desire to pal around with gridiron heroes. Kardashian bonded with O.J., who was three years younger, after both were out of college.

At Dorsey High, Robert's pal Pennino was one of the school's handsomest guys—he was named the "best-looking" in his class—and one of its top athletes, playing varsity football. And he was not surprised that Kardashian would later become close to the Juice.

"I know that Bob and I were friends really because I was one of those guys," he observed, looking back years later. "Bob liked that I was a handsome guy and a football player, and Bob liked to hang with those kinds of people. He liked to be around the good-looking people—the athletes, the people who stood out, the big shots. I hate to use the word 'sycophantic,' because it's kind of extreme, but there was a bit of that in Bob. He liked those in the limelight, and he liked the limelight, he liked the glitz."

Later, Pennino followed Kardashian's life after they had gone in different directions and lost touch. This was when Kardashian was front and center in a moneyed, fast crowd and was hanging with O.J. Pennino concluded that that was Robert Kardashian's "destiny—the big houses, the Rolls-Royces, the women. He was comfortable in that social strata."

Because of his looks, athletic ability, and style, Pennino would later go into acting for a time after finishing college and serving in the army in Korea.

He studied with the powerful acting coach Harry Mastrogeorge, whose students had included stars like Robert Redford—"and I thought I was going to be one of them," said Pennino wryly, looking back at what turned out to be a rather lackluster career. However, he did appear in a couple of off-Broadway plays and was cast in a small role near the end of *Rocky II.*

On the set, Sylvester Stallone "referred to me as 'Rocky Jr.' *That* was my big claim to fame," he said, laughing at the memory.

By then, he and Kardashian rarely saw each other.

"I don't think I carried enough weight for Bob to consider me worthy to be a friend in the later years, that's my feeling," said Pennino. But, if Pennino's acting career had taken off, he speculated that they would have reconnected. "That would have been when it would have happened, absolutely. If I had become a star."

ELEVEN

Jesus and the Kardashians

Devastated by the bribery scandal that had enveloped his brother and the family meatpacking business, Robert Kardashian had sought to cleanse himself of the shame, taint, and guilt he felt by becoming a born-again Christian. He was baptized in the Holy Spirit in the Pacific Ocean surf in July 1974, during a ceremony at the Calvary Chapel Costa Mesa, home in conservative Orange County of the Jesus Movement.

"*I repent of every wrong thing I've ever done,*" he declared in the service, "*and receive the forgiveness that you offer. I surrender my life to you this day. You have made me a new creation, and I am now born again of the spirit of God. Because of you I will go to heaven when I die . . .*"

Robert prayed daily, carried a Bible everywhere, and publicly and proudly advertised his religious fervor and commitment by displaying the age-old Christian fish, a symbol that identified him as a true believer and one who had been baptized. The fish was emblazoned on a plaque on the back of his conservative black Rolls-Royce Silver Shadow for everyone to see, and after he sold it, he put another fish plaque on his next Rolls, a much flashier white Silver Shadow.

His choice of luxury cars adorned with the Christian fish symbol underscored two sides of Robert Kardashian's complex persona: the pious and the poseur.

The Calvary Chapel, where Kardashian gave himself to Jesus, was the epicenter of the Jesus Movement. Its founder, the Reverend Chuck Smith, had introduced the conservative evangelical movement to the liberal hippies of the late sixties, luring them in with the beginnings of Christian rock 'n' roll and his hip style.

Still, like traditional evangelists going back ages, Smith—known as "Papa Chuck," who preached in a Hawaiian shirt and replaced organ music with electric guitars—had predicted armageddon, the end of the world, was against sex outside of marriage, declared a war on drugs long before Nancy Reagan's "Just Say No," and denounced abortion and homosexuality, calling it a "perverted lifestyle."

Before Smith's death at eighty-six in October 2013, he declared that the 9/11 terrorist attacks were a sign of God's anger with the public's growing acceptance of homosexuality and abortion.

During his reign at Calvary Chapel, Smith had mentored a number of pastors who went on to found their own popular evangelical churches, and one of them was handsome, blond-haired Kenn Gulliksen, son of a Norwegian, who would found the hip and trendy evangelical Vineyard church, whose fast-growing membership back in the mid-1970s in the upscale enclaves of Brentwood, Beverly Hills, Santa Monica, and the San Fernando Valley included some of Hollywood's and rock 'n' roll's biggest names as adherents. Gulliksen himself became known as "Bob Dylan's pastor" after introducing the Jewish rocker to evangelical Christianity.

And charming and likable Gulliksen, a father of four, would become one of Robert Kardashian's close friends, his spiritual advisor, and the minister who would officiate at his marriage to Kris Houghton. He would also be involved in their premarital counseling, closely observe their turbulent union, and become aware of Kris's cheating and witness how devastating it would be to her husband.

While Bob never gave Gulliksen the precise reason why he had decided to become born-again, the minister believed "absolutely, unquestionably" that it was the bribery scandal in the Kardashian family that had brought Robert to the Lord.

It "was the kind of omen," said Gulliksen in 2015, "that causes people to grapple with deeper issues in life. When something like that happened to his brother, without question that would cause Bob to be humbled, and that opened his heart to the reality that he needed something more. Bob's only comment to me when we talked about his family—and this is before he met and married Kris—was that there had been family difficulties, but he never told me any of the details. He never talked about his family except about the kind of prophetic word that convinced the family to get out of Armenia."

As Tom Kardashian's bribery case was being adjudicated, Robert, freshly minted as a born-again Christian, appeared at Gulliksen's first independent Bible study held at the home of Christian rocker Chuck Girard in the town of Sun Valley, in Los Angeles's San Fernando Valley. Girard, looking back to that time, said, "It was during the O.J. murder case when I realized, 'Oh, that's that guy who came to Kenn's Bible study. It was then I made the connection."

It was because of Kardashian's hair.

Always most memorable about Kardashian's look was that very odd white streak in the front of his hair. Many thought he was making some sort of fashion statement, that he was having the white streak put in by a Beverly Hills hairstylist in order to give himself, a small man with a big ego, a signature look. It worked but it wasn't planned. The white streak had begun to appear in his late twenties because of a lack of pigmentation.

The next time Girard ran into Robert Kardashian after noticing him at his home during Gulliksen's first Bible study was at another hip nondenominational charismatic evangelical church in Los Angeles called the Hiding Place, started by "another Jesus music guy," Henry Cutrona. "One night I went there and Bob had brought his girlfriend, Priscilla Presley."

According to Girard, the Hiding Place had "just gone through kind of a revelation that people called 'name it and claim it,' where God wants everyone to be wealthy, and you just speak out with your words what you want, and God starts to bring you those things, so it was a little bit materialistic. I got to see Kardashian there, and Priscilla up close, which was kind of cool."

Priscilla Presley wasn't the only celebrity who came to services at the Hiding Place, according to Cutrona. Other stars included the actress Meg Ryan, along with fellow actors George Clooney and David Hasselhoff—all part of a congregation of about two thousand who Cutrona describes as "The kind of people who came to this church because they were the kind of people who didn't go to church."

When the Hiding Place ended its run, Kenn Gulliksen's Vineyard church was going strong, and Robert Kardashian was playing a big role. "I invited him to participate as an Elder in our church board," said the pastor. "That's how real his relationship with the Lord was, and his passion to bring people into the church. Bob was very aggressive as basically a layman evangelist, so to speak, to bring his friends into the church.

"Before he brought Kris, he would bring the women he was dating with the *genuine* hope that they would become born-again, and one, obviously, was Priscilla Presley. I walked up to Bob and gave him a hug, and he said, 'I'd like to introduce you to Priscilla,' and I said, 'Hi, Priscilla,' but I really didn't recognize who she was.

"And then someone whispered to me, '*That's* Priscilla Presley.' But that didn't really impress me, because we were surrounded by those kinds of folks. There were lots of actors and actresses, and thirty percent of the church were Jewish believers. We were in West L.A., so lots were in the business, and lots had a deep, deep love for Jesus."

But layman evangelist Robert Kardashian wasn't always successful in luring potential converts who he felt needed to be saved. Priscilla Presley, for one, later became a devoted member of another church—the controversial Church of Scientology. And Kardashian tried and failed with two other of his closest friends, Joni Migdal and O. J. Simpson, to bring them to the Lord.

"AS BOB WOULD BRING his dates to our church, he also brought all of his friends and clients, and he brought O.J.," a connection that Kenn Gulliksen had never forgotten. "And I probably spent more time at O.J.'s place on Rockingham than at Bob's house for a number of reasons."

Brought by Kardashian, O.J. first appeared at a Bible study on Easter Sunday, 1975. It was regularly led by Gulliksen at a beautiful home on Bundy Drive in Brentwood owned by a born-again Christian interior designer by the name of Beverly Trupp.

"Bob brought O.J., and he brought Bubba Smith [then playing for the Houston Oilers in the NFL], and all these other Heisman Trophy winner guys," said Gulliksen. "Bob was so committed to believing that these guys would realize there was forgiveness for their past and great purpose for the future if they had intimacy with the Lord. It was so genuine."

Unknown to the public, to his idolizing fans, and to the sportswriters who helped build his gridiron myth as one of the greatest football players ever, O.J. began coming to a Bible study every week, said Gulliksen.

"O.J. I think was really impressed with these people [big names in the entertainment industry] who attended, and O.J. always liked to be around celebrities, and liked their celebrity to rub off on him," Gulliksen perceived. "For all O.J. had accomplished, he was so *insanely* insecure."

Still, O.J.—long a textbook narcissist and a closeted sociopath at that point in time—refused to follow his pal Robert Kardashian's preaching that he be baptized in the Holy Spirit and officially become born again.

"Every week," said Gulliksen, "I would corner O.J. as often as I could and ask him, 'Why is it that you haven't invited the Lord into your life?' And he finally answered me and he said, 'I don't see any difference between Jesus and Buddha and these other guys.' That was O.J.'s answer. But he still came, I think, in deference to Bob. But also he would come sometimes on his own because there were so many people there that were friends of his—other football players, film people."

At the time, O.J., who wanted a movie career, and with fantasy dreams of even becoming a studio head after retiring from football, was already doing lucrative commercials for Hertz as the first black spokesperson for a major corporation and beginning to make cameo appearances in lightweight films.

But Gulliksen came to think of O.J. as a narcissistic jerk and viewed him as a self-loathing black man who wanted to be white.

"O.J. was his *own* God, in his *own* universe," the pastor soon concluded. "*Everything* was about O.J. There was not a time when I was with O.J.—and I'm talking hours and hours over the course of years—that *everything* he did was to get me to like him—nice things that he would do, his smiles, his 'Hi, Kenn.' And there was this odd sense that I had about him that he always wanted to be bigger and better—and that he actually wanted to be white."

Gulliksen had taken note that when O.J.'s black friends from the football world would come to the Bible studies, O.J.—who brought them there through Kardashian—wouldn't sit with them.

"O.J. was always hanging out," recalled Gulliksen, "with the rich white, Jewish, or Armenian folks."

Gulliksen's oddest encounter with Simpson was in the immediate aftermath of his daughter Aaren's tragic drowning death in the family pool, a month before her second birthday, in August 1979, a year or two before Simpson stopped attending Gulliksen's Bible studies.

"Marguerite probably called and we found out that Aaren was at the hospital, and I called O.J. and I said, 'Can Joanie and I go pray for Aaren?' and he was so detached, it was almost like I was calling him to get someone's phone number—'Yeah, sure, that's fine.' I mean there was absolutely *no* emotion. So Joanie and I immediately got in the car and zipped down to the hospital, but when we got there Aaren was dead. We wept. It was just a very sad experience."

IN THE CASE OF Joni Migdal, Robert Kardashian was so determined to have his close friend dating back to childhood become born again and join Kenn Gulliksen's Vineyard church that he delivered her to one of America's then best known Christian televangelists, Robert Schuller, whose broadcast was seen worldwide, in hopes that he would help convince her to drink the holy Kool-Aid. The setting was the immense reflective glass Crystal Cathedral, with the largest organ in the world, in Garden Grove, south of Los Angeles, in Orange County, and just twelve miles from where Kardashian was born-again, at the Calvary Chapel in Costa Mesa.

"Robert actually wanted me to convert and I'm Jewish. He was proselytizing," related Joni in 2015. "I said, 'Robert, I'm very comfortable with my religion.' I told him no. And he said, 'Well, come and talk to this person who runs the Crystal Cathedral.' Robert seriously wanted me to consider changing my religion. He wanted me to at least give it a chance. I think because he had become born again and embraced it with such a fervent focus that he wanted me to do it.

"So, he actually brought me down to talk to Robert Schuller, at the Crystal Cathedral. I told him I was Jewish, that I was happy being Jewish, and Schuller looks at Robert and says, 'Robert, leave her alone. She's one of the chosen people, why are you bothering her?' And that was the end of it."

Migdal believed that one reason for Kardashian's push to have her convert came around the time the two platonic friends became lovers for a brief time, long before his marriage to Kris. "Robert's parents were not happy about the fact that he would be with a Jewish woman, but if I were a born-again Christian that might be more acceptable."

That would not be surprising, because there was evidence of anti-Semitism in the Kardashian clan of Robert's parents' generation and the earlier one.

Tom Kardashian notes that Jewish competitors in the meatpacking business made life difficult for the Kardashian family business, Great Western Packing.

"You gotta understand that when my grandfather and my parents grew up in what's called Boyle Heights [once an immigrant-ethnic area of Los Angeles], that was a section of town that was mostly Jewish, and nobody trusted anybody. And there was maybe only two gentile [meat-packing] companies, and the Jewish guys, even though we got along with them, they were competitors and you might say they were friendly, but they weren't. Those Jews were extremely competitive. They would tell you one thing and do another."

Earlier, in the late forties, Robert and Tom's grandfather, Tatos Kardashian, then the family patriarch who dominated the Kardashian household, had helped sponsor and pledged to build a temple in Los Angeles for an Armenian faith healer and mystic, twenty-year-old robed and bearded Avak Hagopian. For a time Kardashian had actually teamed up with another financial backer of the mystic, one Clem Davies, an avowed anti-Semite, whose books included such titles as *The Racial Streams of Mankind*, *What Is Anglo-Israel?*, and *Pre-Adamic Races*. He was known as a member of the Christian Identity Movement, using strange interpretations of biblical scripture to "prove" white superiority and to demonize Jews.

The anti-Semitic hate that Davies spewed seemingly didn't conflict with Tatos Kardashian's old-world Armenian views of Jews. The hate-monger and the businessman appeared to get along swimmingly.

Fast-forward to 2015, when the Kardashian sisters—Kourtney, Kim, and Khloé—and their entourage visited their paternal forebears' homeland and were greeted by throngs as the world's most famous Armenians. The trip was featured on their reality show and received enormous publicity. But unmentioned on the show was the fact that anti-Semitism was still alive and well in the homeland of their fore-bears. An Anti-Defamation League poll revealed that 58 percent of Armenians harbored anti-Semitic views, and in recent years there had been acts of vandalism against Armenia's small Jewish population.

A December 2014 article on Armenian anti-Semitism by Dr. Alexander Murinson, a professor at the Begin-Sadat Center for Strategic Studies, reported that "Horrifically, many Armenians have taken to addressing Jews as 'ocar,' the Armenian word for soap . . . an underhanded reference to the Nazi practice of turning corpses of the victims of their extermination camps into soap."

ROBERT KARDASHIAN WAS FROM a different time and place and had little or no prejudices. Some of his best friends were Jewish. And as a born-again Christian, he was well-known for his generosity. To Kenn Gulliksen's Vineyard church, he usually tithed 10 percent of his income, and he often opened his own home in Beverly Hills for religious fellowship gatherings.

"Sometimes we had an all-day men's retreat just to talk about a topic like dealing with sexuality," said Gulliksen. "The new believers, the young men who had just accepted the Lord into their lives, would meet in Bob's big family room. One Saturday, we had an especially large group, about seventy, and I started off by saying that now that you're all here, the first part of this meeting will be about circumcising the new believers, and I pulled out a big knife.

"Everyone in the room froze, but Bob doubled over. He enjoyed that. He thought it was pretty funny."

COMPARED TO KARDASHIAN'S RELIGIOUS FERVOR, junior flight attendant Kris Houghton's religiosity involved little more than lighting a candle at Saint Patrick's Cathedral, in Manhattan, where she was based for American Airlines in 1976–77, and self-servingly asking God to get her a transfer to Los Angeles so she could permanently be with the guy she "thought" she loved, or so she claimed.

"I kept praying, praying, praying, and lighting candle after candle . . . and believing that something good would happen," she professed, suggesting to readers of her 2011 memoir that she possessed a religious leaning.

In fact, her prayers worked. Her requested transfer was approved.

"I fell to my knees and thanked God," she actually avowed. "I was bawling, literally crying, over this miracle."

At LAX, Robert Kardashian, in his regal black Rolls-Royce with the Christian fish insignia on the back proclaiming his born-again baptized status, picked up Kris, then twenty-one, and their romance was now in full swing, with wedding bells in the not-too-distant future. She thought of him as her "prince," and "flew" into his arms, she later gushed in her book, published two decades after her philandering-ignited hellish divorce and eight years after Kardashian's tragic and premature death. "Oh my God, oh my God. I'm finally here!" she recalled crying out to him.

In her book, Kris Houghton Kardashian Jenner would make the outlandish claim that what really attracted her most to Robert Kardashian was not his fabulous home, or his awesome Rolls-Royce, or all the money he had in the bank, or the Beverly Hills lifestyle that would be hers, but rather, as she declared, his "love of God and religion."

But Kenn Gulliksen, who became Kris's pastor when she formally hooked up with Kardashian, saw a different persona than the one she later portrayed and asked readers of her book to believe.

"I just sensed that Kris saw in Bob a kind of gold mine," the pastor who got to know her well asserted. "That was my perception. I never, ever had the impression that Kris had a relationship with the Lord that was genuine, and certainly was not as real as Bob's, and I always got the impression that her *whole* thing was more about *getting* Bob, so in that sense she didn't come across to me as having any kind of spiritual relationship.

"Kris was attractive enough to get pretty much any guy she wanted," continued Gulliksen. "But, of those guys, Bob stood out because he had a genuine love for God, and that was attractive to her. But it didn't mean she really shared it. Bob was someone she could trust and manipulate. He was a charming, rich guy who carried a Bible, and that was part of his charm for her."

At Kardashian's urging, Kris claimed, she began accompanying him to a weekly Sunday Bible study at the stately, gated Beverly Hills mansion of entertaining legend and born-again Christian Pat Boone, at the corner of Sunset Boulevard and North Beverly Drive, close to the iconic Beverly Hills Hotel.

"Pat Boone hosted, but others often led the studies, particularly our pastor, Kenn Gulliksen. Pat couldn't have been nicer, and his wife, Shirley, was so sweet," Kris stated in her memoir. "I met his daughters, too, and I was especially excited to meet his daughter Debby, who would become a popular singer just like her dad. . . . I had a wonderful time going to the meetings and I really became closer to Jesus Christ because of them."

But in October 2015, eighty-one-year-old Pat Boone firmly stated that he "barely knew" Robert Kardashian—and likely didn't know of him at all until he became synonymous with the accused murderer O. J. Simpson some two decades later, in the mid-nineties. And Boone certainly would have had no knowledge at the time of his Bible study of the pretty, young, obscure flight attendant Kris Houghton, who later claimed Kardashian was squiring her to Boone's home.

"Pat and Shirley were very generous in opening up their home to different people who led Bible studies at different times," said Kenn Gulliksen, who led a Bible study there for only two months. But Gulliksen emphasized that he had absolutely "no memory of Bob and Kris attending," and he knew both of them well.

In fact, Kardashian and Houghton, if they were there, would have been lost in the sea of famous faces—the actor Glenn Ford, the singer-actress Doris Day, Kardashian's ex-girlfriend Priscilla Presley, and a glitzy celebrity who Kris avidly followed, the Gabor sister Zsa Zsa, a precursor of the famous-for-being-famous Kardashian sisters—among many other popular celebrities who attended Boone's open houses.

The stars crowded into his big family room and turned those weekly sessions into more of a red-carpet celebrity event than a Bible study. As Gulliksen recalled, "We stopped going to the Boones' home because too many people were showing up strictly because they wanted to see what Pat Boone's house looked like on the inside."

A close colleague of Boone's and Gulliksen's, Susan Stafford, the first letter-turner on *Wheel of Fortune*, whose personal assistant, Joan Esposito, became Kris's sister-in-law when she married Tom Kardashian, was an integral part of the Boones' Bible studies. While Kris made the Boones' event sound very exclusive, Stafford says showing up there was no big deal.

"You could take anyone to Pat Boone's, and sometimes it was for sincerity, and sometimes it was for making contacts, and sometimes it was to meet guys, or girls, and some of it was because we wanted to learn," she observed, looking back years later. "It was a social event. We had a lot of people who came to follow the celebs. We knew that, but that was okay, because whatever it was, it got them in the door to believe in God, never mind Christ—and some of them didn't even believe in God."

Stafford considered Robert Kardashian "a wonderful human being who cared a great deal," but she saw Kris strictly as a "very attractive, very sexy" young woman, but who was "not" a true Christian, and "not born-again. I never saw her as a disciple."

Later, when Kris was married to Kardashian, Stafford said she heard "so much" from Tom and Joan Kardashian. "Everyone," she asserted, "knew she was playing around. Joanie would indicate, 'We have problems right here in River City' "—regarding Kris's extracurricular activities—"and just shake her head. If it's your sister-in-law you better be quiet."

Stafford said she only had respect for one thing about Kris after she became a reality TV star and momager: "She knows how to make money."

IN 2015, PASTOR KENN GULLIKSEN decided to read Kris Jenner's four-year-old memoir for the first time and was "shocked" at a number of her claims, even down to her relatively benign, if boastful, comments about meeting the Boones.

"What Kris says in her book is a real stretch," he asserted. "Pat didn't even know who Kris was."

Kris further made the claim in her book that she had "accepted Christ through those [Boone] Bible studies . . . and I became a born-again Christian."

But this Pastor Gulliksen highly doubts from what he knew then, and in view of Kris's disingenuous later life as the reality TV momager.

"After reading her book, I was grieved as Kris described her infidelity, astonished at her language, her self-centeredness, and lifestyle. I was amazed at how totally self-centered and narcissistic Kris is. I did not see that when I knew her. I was astonished that I didn't recognize this person. It's the Kris she was, but not the Kris she presented herself to be, maybe because she was trying to impress me somehow—that she was a really sweet, innocent girl that would be good for Bob. I find her to be an absolutely dishonest person, who has perverted honesty, and was trying throughout the book to validate her behavior."

He continued: "My thought was how heartbroken Bob would have been had he lived. . . . He would be devastated by the family as it exists now, and that's very sad for me as well. I pray one day Kris recognizes the counterfeit Christian as well as she recognizes a fake Gucci."

TWELVE

A Stepford Wife

Sometime in 1977, O. J. Simpson briefly reconciled with his wife, Marguerite, and moved out of the Kardashian brothers' bachelor pad on Deep Canyon Drive in Beverly Hills and back into his mansion on Rockingham Avenue, in Brentwood, all the while continuing an affair with his future second wife, the hot, blond teenage cocktail waitress Nicole Brown, who had worked at the trendy Daisy in Beverly Hills. Around the same time, Tom Kardashian, engaged to divorcée and mother of two daughters Joan Esposito sold Robert his share of Deep Canyon and bought his own house for himself and his fiancée near Sammy Davis Jr.'s Beverly Hills estate, where they became friends with the popular entertainer, who had converted to Judaism and was then married to the third of his three wives, Altovise.

Thus, with the "boys' club," as Kris Houghton called it, gone, the American Airlines junior flight attendant finally moved in with Robert, and thought it would be permanent. She thought wrong.

She also assumed that as the current lady of the house she was free to spend, or at least borrow, money from her lover. She was wrong about that, too.

When Kris moved into Casa Kardashian, she was flat broke, apparently having been unable to put away any of her modest airline salary because she was always splurging on clothes and partying. While Robert had a Mercedes and a black Rolls-Royce and was soon about to sell it and buy a white one, Kris was driving a clunker, believed to be the six-year-old red Mazda that her stepfather, Harry Shannon, had given her for her sixteenth birthday.

"Kris moved in but Robert really didn't treat her very well," recalled his close friend Joni Migdal. "Kris needed tires for her car and he wouldn't buy them for her, and I said, 'Robert, why not buy the tires?' But he was adamant and said, 'She needs to learn the value of a dollar.' I said, 'But she's driving an old car.' But he wanted her to learn about money. Even in the beginning he treated her sometimes like an Armenian housewife, which means that he needed to have power over her. Instead of giving her power, he had to be the powerful one, which I did not think was a good idea."

After they got married, though, Kris would show Robert her power, and how wantonly she could spend his money, and that would drive him crazy. Her lavish spending would become one of the many issues in what would be a very turbulent marriage. As Migdal asserted, "There would be no begging by Kris for money after they got married. She rebelled against Robert's rules and became totally extravagant."

Along with possessing the stereotypical macho-male Armenian-husband gene—the man rules the house, the woman obeys the man, or else—Kardashian had gotten totally turned on by a 1975 sci-fi thriller that he saw several times, having found the story line and philosophy so intriguing. *The Stepford Wives*, based on the bestselling novel by Ira Levin, told the frightening tale of an exclusive men's club whose sinister members turn their wives into beautiful, subservient robots who do their husband's bidding, from obsessive housework to anytime sex, all of it set in the fictional bucolic town of Stepford, Connecticut, with some scenes shot in bucolic Westport, Connecticut, then the home of the most famous real-life compulsive housewife of all, the self-styled domestic goddess Martha Stewart.

"*The Stepford Wives* had blown Robert's mind," recalled a close friend who went to see it with him the first time. "I think he always had a fantasy about being able to dominate and control women, so when he became seriously involved with Kris, he wanted her to become the ultimate Stepford Wife, and because of that film he felt that maybe his fantasy could be fulfilled. But Kris would be the one in control in the end. It totally backfired on him."

"*The Stepford Wives*," observed Joni Migdal, became "*the* model for Robert's marriage to Kris. But I always used to term that the Armenian housewife syndrome."

As a way of controlling—and even programming—high school graduate Kris's knowledge and learning during the early years of their relationship, Robert gave her self-help audiocassette tapes on a variety of subjects and instructed Kris to faithfully listen and learn from them, according to the couple's close friend, the multimillionaire businessman Larry Kraines. "In Robert's view that was to make Kris sharper, better, brighter, and he was proud to have contributed that to her. He wanted her to be the best. If there was a party and she had it, she made it the best. Because of Robert, Kris went out of her way to really make it everything to the nines."

But Kraines felt that Robert's demand underscored his early control and dominance of her. "The whole deal with the tapes," he observed, "was a little bit over the top. Kris would say, 'Oh, God, I have to finish these tapes before the week's out because we're going to talk about them.' But Robert was always making Kris smarter, teaching her. But my wife would have told me to stick those tapes up my ass."

Like the money issues, sex and religion had also become points of contention when Robert and Kris first started living together and she was still flying for American Airlines. The born-again Christian who kept a Bible on his nightstand and on his desk and carried one whenever he went out, prayed before every meal, and, as Kris later observed in her book, "wore his Christianity on his sleeve," decided that the hot, "full-on" sex they had been having while living in sin had to come to an end.

Kardashian had confided in Joni Migdal about the sticky situation, and her take was that "he wanted their relationship to be special, and he wanted her to want it as much as he did. He wanted her to love him as much as he loved her, and I would say he loved her more than she loved him. But she still was respectful."

Kris claimed that Robert had actually asked her to move out because living together and having sex out of wedlock was "not God's will."

So she moved with great reluctance and anger, getting a hand from O.J.'s compatriot and Kardashian's friend, Al Cowlings.

People in Robert's circle thought there had to be other reasons for him asking her to leave, and they had a hard time getting their heads around the fact that he would give up sleeping with her just like that because of his religious beliefs. Making it even more difficult for them to comprehend was the fact that he often boasted that Kris was wild in bed, the best sex he ever had. But he refused to talk about it, they said, looking back years later.

In any case, Kris moved into an apartment "behind a Marie Callender's pie shop" in Sherman Oaks, over the hill in Valley Girl country from Kardashian's manse in Beverly Hills, which she had already begun to feel was hers, too.

But they continued to see each other.

"We would still kiss and make out, but otherwise nothing because we were living this clean, Christian relationship," she snidely remarked.

On one visit, in her apartment complex garage, he accidentally put a dent in his glistening new white Rolls, and when he complained to her, Kris selfishly thought, *"Serves him right for kicking me out!"*

Kris, who had a high sex drive, was furious at Kardashian, Bible or no Bible. At twenty-two, she wanted frequent sex, and if Kardashian wasn't going to be the supplier, then maybe she needed to find another, as she suggested in her memoir.

If there was anyone to blame for Robert Kardashian suddenly going all celibate on Kris in the name of the Lord, it was Kenn Gulliksen.

"You know what? I'm going to plead guilty," said the pastor, looking back to that time. "Obviously, Bob was very attracted to Kris. She was beautiful, much younger, and a lot of fun, and they undoubtedly enjoyed a lot of sexual experiences together. I spoke to him and asked him whether he was living with Kris, and he said he was, and I told him, 'I can't marry you if you continue living together, or if you have to live together because of circumstance, you need to stop your sexual relationship until you marry her."

Gulliksen and his wife, Joan, were both virgins when they got married, and he was shocked that Kardashian, as an Elder of the church, who every Monday morning at six A.M. arrived without fail to pray "for people's needs," had violated the church's tenets regarding sex outside of marriage.

But after Gulliksen gently confronted Kardashian, he "immediately embraced" his pastor's request to stop living with, and having sex with, Kris Houghton, until if and when they tied the knot.

"Bob said, 'You're right. I know we shouldn't be doing this.' So, it wasn't my trying to talk him into something," asserted Gulliksen. "It was what he already knew in his heart. He had a very genuine, deep relationship with the Lord. It was real. It was honest. It informed everything he did, although he did some things that I certainly wasn't happy about, nor was he. We taught sex was for marriage, and he had had sexual relationships, and after he became a Christian he had sexual struggles.

"And if Kris couldn't hold off having sex with him, she needed to be seeing another kind of counselor. But, yes, I am the guilty one in her eyes. Kris never said anything to me about it. She only said what would ingratiate herself to me. I'm sure she didn't want me to screw up her relationship with Bob."

NOW LIVING ON HER own again in a studio apartment, unclear about her status with the man she thought she loved, and still flying for American, Kris Houghton was spending time again with her close stewardess friend and confidant, Cindy Spallino. But Robert Kardashian was always on Kris's mind.

And she especially fantasized about the rock he might put on her finger one day. In the end, her dream came true.

"We would walk the streets of Beverly Hills and we would stop at every jewelry store and look in the windows at the shiny, sparkly things," recalled Spallino. "Kris would say, 'I don't care if you're married, or not married, it's awfully hard to walk by a jewelry store and not look at all those diamonds.'

"And she saw one ring in particular and thought it was beautiful. It was a big pavé diamond, with lots of small diamonds surrounded by two bands of gold. At that point in time she was just hoping, just musing that that was the kind of ring she'd love to be given. We were just two girls walking by jewelry stores, but then on down the road it happened to be the same ring that Robert picked out for her."

Shortly after New Year's 1978, Kris had decided she finally needed to get Robert to commit to marry her, or she would move on and find another man who would treat her right and give her everything she desired. She decided to take a gamble. She'd go far away on a trip, not keep in touch with him, and hope he'd miss her so much that he'd take her back and propose.

In her memoir, Kris says that she had gotten the "ski bug," and had decided to go on what she called a "girls' trip" to "Switzerland." The term "girls' trip" had an exclusive and expensive ring to it, and so did vacationing in Switzerland. But, once again, it was pure Kris Houghton

Kardashian Jenner hype, the stretching of truth, and an outright fabrication.

In fact, she and Cindy Spallino had been offered a great discount deal by a pilot who organized cheap trips for airlines' people with little money to spend.

There was nothing exclusive or expensive about it. "It was *so* cheap," said Cindy, "including airfare, transportation to the resort, lift tickets, accommodations, breakfast every day, ski equipment—*everything*, for like $250-a person."

And moreover, while Switzerland may have had the ring of chic to Kris and her readers, a place where the rich and famous skied on the slopes in ritzy locations like Gstaad, with places to shop like Prada and Hermès for apres-ski entertainment, Kris and Cindy's actual destination was the far less tony ski resort town of St. Anton am Arlberg, which was in Austria, *not* Switzerland, as Kris had boasted. Once again in her book, Kris had embellished, if not blatantly fibbed about the facts.

And it wasn't a "girls' trip," as she had stated, suggesting a *bevy* of girls. "It was just the two of us," said Cindy Spallino, "and we didn't get to choose where we were going—you know, we want to go St. Moritz, but that wasn't part of the deal. But we had a lot of fun, and it was like we had this very high-end trip, but it was very simple accommodations. I had skied since I was seven. She could go up and down, but I wouldn't call her a skier."

It was while the girls were away that Kris shared "some" of what was going on with her and Robert, and about why they weren't living together. She made it sound as if her living with him had been just a temporary thing, and that it was her decision to move.

"She said, 'I was just staying with Robert, but I got my own apartment.' She didn't say the part about him not wanting to have sex with her. She just said he felt it was not a good idea for them to live together until they got married. I didn't judge that one way or another. I just figured that's how some people are comfortable. When she told me she moved out, I thought, 'Oh, that was just a temporary arrangement living with him until she secured an apartment.' But I know she really wanted it to be permanent.

"The ski trip was definitely meant to make Robert miss her," Cindy asserted. "It drove Robert crazy that she didn't call. I don't know if she even told him where we were going, or staying, and she didn't talk to him for the whole time that we were gone, which wasn't that long."

Kris's scheme and her gamble worked.

Shortly after she returned home, Robert Kardashian proposed.

He popped the question on Easter Sunday, 1978.

She says she had slept over *only* so they could go to early Easter church services. She claimed he even dropped to one knee—the clichéd Hollywood love story position—to make his proposal. " 'I love you so much and I want to spend the rest of my life with you,' " were the words she said he said.

She said "Yes!" and she claimed that he was "scared" and "quivering" and looked like he was "going to cry."

But he didn't immediately slip on her finger that ring she had been fantasizing about ever since she saw it in a Beverly Hills jewelry store window when she was strolling with her buddy Cindy Spallino.

Instead, she stated in her book that he gave her an advertisement in a fashion magazine for a "big gorgeous diamond," and told her that someday he'd get it for her, but in the meantime he'd pick up something else.

As she noted, Robert was a "frugal guy in those days," who could shell out big bucks for a Rolls-Royce but was cautious about spending "hundreds of thousands of dollars" for the kind of diamond that was on that *Vogue* page he had handed her. He also was the guy who'd declined to buy her new tires for her flivver because she needed to learn the value of a buck.

The next day he surprised her by giving her the ring that she had seen with Cindy in the jewelry store window. She said it was her wedding ring, and that he never gave her an engagement ring.

"I was literally shaking," when she saw it, she recalled. "Robert was THE ONE FOR ME," she exalted in uppercase type in her memoir.

"She called me and she was *so* excited," recalled Spallino.

It was after the ski trip and in the early days of Kris and Robert's engagement that Cindy met Kardashian for the first time, after hearing so much about him for months, and she saw him as a "warm, wonderful, welcoming guy."

By then, Cindy had known Kris going on two years, but what struck her on seeing Kris and Robert together for the first time was "how very comfortable Kris felt in that Beverly Hills setting. She was street smart and able to catch on to things quickly. Kris wasn't book smart, but she was life smart in many ways."

On one of Cindy's first visits to Kardashian's Beverly Hills home, with Kris now living in, the discussion centered on a dinner party that the man of the house wanted to have. "And Kris had *no* problem at twenty-one, twenty-two finding the correct florist, getting the right caterer, setting up the house," observed Spallino. "She didn't need anybody to tell her how to do that. How she knew how to do that I don't know. But she was a very capable hostess. She had certain life skills that I thought were remarkable for somebody her age."

And that probably was even before Robert Kardashian had begun ordering Kris to listen to the self-help audio tapes he gave her with strict instructions to learn from them, and then be tested about what she had learned. Cindy says Kris never mentioned those tapes to her.

Soon after they were engaged, Kris never worked again while married to Kardashian.

"When we got back from our ski trip, Kris had some vacation time. Then American told her she had to come back to work, and she had already missed her first trip. But at that point she just resigned," recalled Spallino.

With Kardashian hooked, Kris didn't need the airline anymore. With her man, she would now fly in first class, with a respectful flight attendant at *her* beck and call.

"Robert was a fun, generous guy," Cindy Spallino came to believe after getting to know him. "I did think Kris really did love him. You don't have four children with somebody you don't love. But she also loved *everything* that he brought to her life—he brought her an *entire* life. She knew he could provide for her, and she knew that she'd never have to worry about anything ever again. He was a big part of her escape from a blue-collar background."

THIRTEEN

Wedding Bells

In the spring of 1978, Kenn Gulliksen assigned one of his assistant pastors, Reverend Larry Myers, to perform premarital counseling with the newly engaged couple Robert Kardashian and the future Kris Kardashian.

A musician, Myers had joined Chuck Girard's Christian rock band in the spring of 1975, and through Girard, who was allowing Gulliksen to have a Bible study in his home, he met the young pastor, then in his late twenties. Myers soon began attending the Vineyard church services, and Gulliksen, impressed with his devotion and talent, invited him to become part of the church staff, where he was introduced to Kardashian during the summer of 1975.

"Bob was one of the church Elders already, was part of the corporate board, was *very* active, and was considered one of the leaders of the church," Myers said. "Bob was quite outgoing, very warm, and impressive. He was still practicing law, and he was working with, and kind of managing O.J."

Larry Myers thought it was ironic that he would wind up counseling Kris and Robert as their marriage ceremony neared because he had once suspected that Priscilla Presley would be Kardashian's bride. "Robert had dated other women before Kris, but Priscilla was the memorable one that he brought to our services," he noted. "But eventually he got involved with Kris and they developed their relationship and decided to get married."

Myers, who was performing most of the premarital counseling in the Vineyard church, had a series of six meetings, each an hour long, over several weeks with the church's Elder and his fiancée at the church's headquarters on Ventura Boulevard, in the L.A. suburb of Van Nuys.

"We just talked about all the different aspects of marriage, the different areas of responsibility, and I just tried to do as much preparation for them as possible," he said. "Kris was a very sweet, likable lady, and I didn't find their age difference strange at all because it wasn't like she was seventeen. She was in her early twenties and she was very outgoing, and with a very confident personality, as was Bob, so they seemed to make a good match.

"They were aware of what they were doing, what kind of a marriage they wanted, and how they would accomplish that," he continued. "They didn't ask many questions and just listened. I felt they were very conscientious and serious, and really wanted to have and establish a good marriage, and make a good home."

Unlike Pastor Gulliksen, who would officiate at the Kardashian-Houghton nuptials, but who had serious doubts that Kris had taken Jesus into her life and had become born-again, Myers, looking back, said he had "no doubt in my mind that Kris had embraced her faith and was serious about it, and about going forward in making a Christ-centered marriage."

But was Kris, savvy in weighing people's reactions to her, just playing up her love for Jesus to the hilt with Myers in order to impress him and Robert and make both believers in her sincerity?

Myers said he came away from the sessions feeling confident that Kris and Robert's bond would last a lifetime. But he also learned a dozen years later that it hadn't, that there had been many serious issues, and one of them was that self-proclaimed born-again Kris had cheated on her husband.

"I wasn't involved in their lives over the coming years, so I don't know how things deteriorated," Larry Myers said. "At the time we did the best we could in counseling them."

THERE WERE TWO KARDASHIAN family weddings in the summer of 1978. The first was Robert and Kris's, and a month later his brother, Tom, married the former Joan Esposito. Robert's was a glitzy affair, a full-blown Beverly Hills production with a professional cinematographer filming the proceedings. Tom's was nothing like that.

Before Kris tied the knot, Joyce, the pregnant wife of Robert's close friend Larry Kraines—who years later discovered her cheating on Robert with her lover in the lower-level gym of Kraines's Beverly Hills mansion—threw a fancy bridal shower for her at the ritzy Hotel Bel-Air.

By the time of the wedding, Robert Kardashian had long had a thing about not wanting to be alone, about always wanting to have a pretty woman in his life, so the fact that he was still a bachelor in his mid-thirties embarrassed him and caused him to worry that others viewed him as some kind of loser, or maybe even gay. All of that played into his decision to finally pop the question to Kris Houghton, after failing to convince Priscilla Presley to marry him. If Presley had accepted his proposal and they had tied the knot, Kris Houghton would have had to look elsewhere for another guy who would give her the kind of lavish life she always dreamed about.

"I don't think Robert ever really wanted to be by himself as many years as he was," observed Larry Kraines. "He liked companionship. He spoke about that frequently over the years. He was bothered that he didn't get married until late in life. He was bothered back in the day that people looked at him and his brother as maybe being a little weird because they weren't married."

Robert's parents, Arthur and Helen, didn't really care who he married, whether it was wealthy and famous Priscilla, or poor and unknown Kris. As Tom Kardashian noted, "My mom and dad were just happy that he was *finally* getting married. It wasn't about, 'Oh, you're not marrying the right person.' I'd gone long enough myself. I was thirty-seven years old, so that was a pretty late age to get married."

Robert George Kardashian and Kristen Mary Houghton's marriage occurred on July 8, 1978, at the Westwood United Methodist Church, long the setting for spectacular weddings since after Black Friday 1929 and the start of the Great Depression, when the first chapel was built. It's one of Los Angeles's most prominent and elegant houses of worship. The famous organ has more than ten thousand pipes and can play chimes and trumpets, which, according to the church's pitch for wedding business, "make glorious fanfares and send-offs."

Because Westwood United, on Wilshire Boulevard, was so elegant and prestigious, Kris had personally chosen it. She later stated that her "storybook romance" was "consummated" at its altar—above which was a stained-glass "Glory Window" depicting the life of Jesus Christ with a twenty-four-karat gold-leaf overlay.

Pastor Kenn Gulliksen, who officiated, believed the church was chosen because "it was the most beautiful, so it was like kind of starting off their marriage with a public declaration—*we belong*, and making a statement in the heart of Westwood, which is where everything happened."

As Kris noted in her memoir, published two decades after Kardashian divorced her because of her adultery, "no expense was spared" for the wedding, and she even boasted that the same florist who did business with the White House of President Richard Nixon had supplied her flowers at the church. She did not mention, though, that at the time of her spectacular nuptials the disgraced Nixon had been in exile for five years after resigning in the wake of the Watergate scandal, during which he famously proclaimed, "I am not a crook."

Kris stated that Gulliksen, "our pastor from the Bible studies at Pat Boone's house, officiated," only part of which was true; Gulliksen did marry her off, but as quoted earlier, he didn't remember Kris and Robert having ever attended, and Boone said he didn't even know Kardashian.

In any case, the wedding ceremony was one joyous event. "It was very, very beautiful—beautiful music, the most beautiful clothes, the *best* of everything," recalled the pastor.

O. J. Simpson, who would divorce his black wife a year later with eventual plans to marry blond Nicole Brown, was a groomsman, and his idolizing shadow, Al Cowlings, later the wheelman of the infamous white Ford Bronco LAPD chase, was the bearer of Kris's ring. Robert's best man was his brother, Tom, the felon, and Kris's sister, Karen, with whom she would have a cold and distant relationship, and who would have a troubled life, was the bride's maid of honor.

Along with Joyce Kraines, Kris's high school chum Debbie Mungle, who was with her in Hawaii when Kris scored a hole in one in meeting her first lover, Cesar Sanudo, and then roomed with the two of them in his town house condo, was one of the bridesmaids, as was Kris's close friend Cindy Spallino, from Kris's recent past as a junior flight attendant— the kind of life she'd never have again thanks to the love and generosity of Robert Kardashian.

None of the principals and none of the three hundred or so guests in attendance would have ever guessed at what a tumultuous and ill-fated union the bride and groom would have, or what the aftermath would be like.

As Pastor Gulliksen pointed out many years later, "It seemed to me to be a beautiful and genuine relationship. When I looked at them and the way they looked at each other and when I heard them share their vows, I was convinced their marriage would last forever. I knew Bob was astute and wasn't one who I thought would be taken by a woman. He was older, he'd been out with a lot of women, so he knew what he was doing, so I was well convinced that at least his vows were utterly genuine. As I recall, Kris's weren't very long. Bob was a man who once he was married assumed, presumed, expected his wife to be faithful to him forever."

After the ceremony, Mr. and Mrs. Robert Kardashian hosted a reception for their friends at the very exclusive Bel-Air Country Club, where the initiation fee was as much as six figures, and where high-powered captains of the entertainment industry, big-name Hollywood stars, and powerful politicians played. Years earlier the eccentric mogul Howard Hughes, who was running late for a round of golf with Katharine Hepburn, had landed his plane on the golf course's verdant green, refused to pay the parking fee, and resigned from the club.

Kris later called the reception an "elegant, beautiful affair."

And on her wedding night in bed at the Hotel Bel-Air, her groom told her that she was his " 'dream come true,' " that from the moment he first laid eyes on her at the Del Mar racetrack's two-dollar window he knew she was going to be his wife, " 'my future, my love,' " or so she claimed he said. And he may have even used the same loving words in bed with Priscilla Presley, whom he wanted to marry, but she didn't need him and what he had to offer as much as Kris Houghton did.

Kardashian, who wanted to teach young Kris the meaning of a dollar, who didn't buy her the hundred-thousand-dollar ring he showed her in the fashion magazine advertisement when he proposed, who even refused to fork over the little bit of money for four new tires for her beat-up car, had actually had her use her saved-up American Airlines mileage to fund the transportation to Europe for their honeymoon in France.

And in romantic Paris she said he set her straight about money. " 'I can give you a lot of material things. But I'm not going to give them to you all at once, because too much, too soon is not a good thing, either.' "

Her "greatest gift" besides the big house, expensive cars, and all the rest, she said, was when Kardashian gave her the first of the four children they would have together. In fact, far down the road, those kids would

be the best investment ever. Kris learned she was pregnant with Kourtney two weeks after the newlyweds returned from their honeymoon.

A MONTH LATER ROBERT flew to Honolulu, where he returned the
honor and served as his brother Tom's best man. Tom's August 1978
marriage to Joan Esposito, who was eighteen months younger, a divorced mother of two daughters, was "pretty much spur of the moment,"
Tom said. "We went together for a little over three years, and it was
time. When I proposed to her I gave her an option—'do you want to
wait and get married next year [1979], or do you want to get married this
year? If we do, then we should run off and get married in Hawaii. Everybody doesn't have to feel that they be burdened about coming at the last
minute, all that stuff.'"

He was already doing business with some people in Hawaii, and
when he told them he had decided to get married there they made the
arrangements with just three weeks' notice—plus one of his friends who
had a second home on Oahu turned it over to the newlyweds for their
stay. The ceremony was held at the Central Union Church of Honolulu,
a United Church of Christ, whose slogan was "We engage and embrace
all as we seek to embody Christ." The church's roots went back to the
time of whaling ships and missionaries in the nineteenth century. When
the Kardashians were married, Central Union was considered *the*
place to tie the knot and combine it with a Hawaiian honeymoon. His
brother and sister-in-law would celebrate their first anniversary there, too.

Unlike his brother's spectacular wedding affair, with a cast of hundreds, Tom's wedding was simple and small. As he stressed years later,
"There were no celebrities. My brother's was a bigger thing, big and
fancy with a lot of people." From the mainland came the bride's two
young daughters, and Joan's mother and sister, as did the groom's proud
parents, Arthur and Helen, and some close friends of his.

Tom and Joan's ceremony was not professionally filmed like Robert
and Kris's royal affair. Years later, when virtually everything in Kris

Houghton Kardashian Jenner's life appeared to become fodder for ratings, publicity, and cash, some frames of her betrothal to her late first husband were shown on an episode of *Keeping Up with the Kardashians.*

While the Kardashian brothers gave up their long bachelorhood a month apart, their wives, Kris and Joan, never became close. "They were totally different types," asserted Tom. "Kris was a lot younger."

He says it was his mother, Helen Kardashian, "who was the maternal person who held the family together, not that there were arguments, but when there were functions—Thanksgiving, Christmas—she'd figure how to get us all together. My mom would be more the one to do that than the two wives."

While Joan Kardashian, who once mentored and was best friends with Priscilla Presley, was most willing to bond with her new sister-in-law, Kris, who was at least a decade younger, she couldn't break the ice. As a mutual friend recalled, "It was all about Priscilla. Kris believed Robert still had a thing for her, plus she still resented how she believed Priscilla had stolen Bob away from her and how that would have meant the end of her Beverly Hills dream. It was very weird. It was like Elvis's ex-wife's ghost was haunting her."

As in-law couples—Robert and Kris, and Tom and Joan—they "didn't socialize, didn't go on trips together," Tom Kardashian said, even though both couples lived close by in Beverly Hills, and the brothers even shared the same dry cleaner. "Growing up, Bob and I had a lot of similarities," maintained Tom, "but that definitely changed when we both got married. I was doing my thing, and he wasn't telling me about his personal life."

TOM KARDASHIAN DIDN'T GO the born-again route like his brother had following Tom's 1974 bribery conviction. When he and Joan were married four years later and he adopted her two daughters, who went to Catholic school, he said they all joined Angeles Mesa Presbyterian

Church, which was in the View Park–Windsor Hills neighborhood, where the Kardashian boys and their sister had grown up. The church's purpose was to "spread the good news about the resurrection power of Jesus Christ available to all believers through the Holy Spirit."

The minister, he says, was Reverend Donn Moomaw, who had been an all-American football player at UCLA. "And so I could relate to him, and so he and I became best friends," says Kardashian, who, like his brother, idolized gridiron stars—O. J. Simpson, their bosom brother, being the best example.

In fact it was Moomaw, later pastor at the tony Bel-Air Presbyterian Church, on Mulholland Drive, which had a wealthy, celebrity-studded congregation, who would officiate at thirty-seven-year-old Simpson's 1985 marriage to pregnant twenty-five-year-old Nicole Brown.

Like O.J., Moomaw, the man of the cloth, had serious issues regarding women.

When Moomaw, who had the honor of being President Ronald Reagan's minister, was in the pulpit at Bel-Air Presbyterian, the handsome, married, six-foot-four religious leader and one-time star lineman was accused of "repeated instances of sexual contact" with five women, and sexual intercourse with at least one of them in 1993, and was forced to resign. He was then sixty-one. Church officials had kept the affair secret until the scandal was revealed in 1995. Two years after being suspended, he was back in the pulpit at a church in San Diego County.

In March 2016, the good Reverend Moomaw, still the Reagan family's minister, assisted the vicar of the Washington National Cathedral at former First Lady Nancy Reagan's private family funeral service in Santa Monica.

FOURTEEN

A Three-Thousand-Dollar Belt

The first of twenty-three-year-old Kris's brood, Kourtney, was born on April 18, 1979. If the baby had been a boy, the father wanted to give him the Armenian name Sarkis, a common Armenian handle, and the first name of an Armenian painter—still lifes, not houses—Sarkis Ordyan. Instead, Kardashian got a male dog, a Doberman, and named him Sarkis. During her first easy pregnancy Kris had gained fifty pounds, which she quickly lost, working out at a trendy Beverly Hills gym with cute buff trainers.

Kourtney's first positive act in life as an infant was to throw up on "Uncle O.J.," as the Kardashian children would later call him.

The next three would come in relatively quick succession. Kim, whose maternal grandmother, M.J., suggested she be named after Elizabeth Taylor and Richard Burton's Mexican love nest, Casa Kimberly, came into the world on October 21, 1980. But there would be questions about the birthright of number three, Khloé, born June 27, 1984, and whether

Robert Kardashian was really her biological father. By March 17, 1987, birth of number four, Rob, the patriarch's namesake, his father and mother's marriage was already beginning to crumble; their divorce was just three years away, with much hell in between.

Kris claimed that even when she was back in high school she had always dreamed about having six children, but the last two—Kendall and Kylie—who brought the final tally to her wished-for half dozen, would be fathered by her next husband, Bruce Jenner, the Olympic gold medal winner.

Kardashian, the epitome of the proud, show-off father who handed out twenty-dollar-a-pop banned Cuban cigars to his friends, bragged to everyone about how beautiful his girls, Kourtney and Kim, were as babies. For instance, Kris, a serial embellisher, would call Kim "absolutely breathtakingly beautiful . . . just stunning from the beginning." But beauty is in the eye of the beholder, and friends who actually beheld the little darlings weren't as impressed as their father was with their winsomeness. "My wife and I used to actually joke, 'It's such a shame those Kardashian baby girls are so homely, and looked like hairy little monkeys," said a longtime close Kardashian friend. "I realize it was a mean thing to say back then, but in light of where things are today with those two, I guess they have the last laugh."

With her marriage to well-to-do Robert Kardashian, Kris finally had the Beverly Hills life she had dreamed about. Her close stewardess friend back then, Cindy Spallino, witnessed and experienced her pal's fabulous, rich world firsthand.

"Our paths started to diverge after she married Robert, and that was mainly because I was a working flight attendant and I couldn't afford the fancy Beverly Hills lunches that Kris was having," said Spallino. "And I really wasn't drawn to that life—that lifestyle she adored *so* much of expensive lunches and two-hundred-dollar dinners. She *loved* that. I was living in a little apartment in Corona del Mar and she was living in Beverly Hills, a big difference.

"I think the last time I had lunch with her my share was like eighty dollars, and I couldn't afford it. That was like almost twenty percent of my salary, so I just couldn't do it. My life was now *so* different from hers. And going shopping and having lunch in expensive Beverly Hills restaurants seemed so shallow to me, and *that* was her life. She began to have children right away, but then she had a live-in nanny so she could still shop and go to expensive restaurants."

Spallino flashed back just a few years to the days Kris and she lived in expensive Manhattan on meager junior flight attendant salaries, five hundred dollars a month, sharing cramped apartments with other stewardesses, and never having enough money to go anywhere for fun except Central Park to people-watch and feed the squirrels.

But for Kris, that all changed with Kardashian.

"Kris's whole life led up to the Beverly Hills moment, and it felt right for her to be there," observed Spallino, who spent thirty-three years as a flight attendant, and loved every minute of it. "Kris was comfortable there. She was relaxed there, and she didn't seem out of place there as a small-town girl. Beverly Hills was like a world it seemed she had always been a part of, and wanted, and was happy there, and comfortable there, and she was never ill at ease there."

And her Beverly Hills extravagance as Mrs. Kardashian, wielding Mr. Kardashian's credit cards, knew no bounds, according to a female cousin. "Robert had a lot of flair and confidence, but his base was truly simple and down-to-earth. But Kris never held back on her spending. She once went out and bought a belt for three thousand dollars, and Robert was like, 'Three thousand dollars! Can you fucking believe that? Who needs a belt for three thousand dollars?' He had not let the Hollywood philosophy get to him. But she had. Kris spent wildly."

As Joni Migdal noted, "A three-thousand-dollar belt wasn't Robert's style."

Their premarital days when Kardashian refused to foot the bill for new tires for Kris's junker were long over, and Pastor Kenn Gulliksen heard his complaints about her spending.

"Almost from the beginning Bob had issues with how freely Kris spent money, and how she constantly wanted more, and that affects the people that you hang out with as well," he said. "You tend to want to get from *everybody*, not just your husband, and that was Kris. I know that Kris increasingly tried to dominate pretty much every area involving money, and would tell Bob how she wanted the house done, how he should spend. Robert was a very generous man, and that was *especially* good for Kris."

AS AN ASSOCIATE IN THE John Bedrosian and Richard Eamer law firm, Robert Kardashian was no budding Clarence Darrow. Kardashian mostly handled the routine business matters of some of the firm's clients, notarized legal papers for a modest fee, and helped entrepreneurs form small corporations that mostly involved paperwork. Until he became involved in the "Dream Team" defense of his pal the accused murderer O. J. Simpson in the mid-nineties, he had not been in a courtroom for two decades, and had never even seen the inside of a jail as an inmate's lawyer. "It's extremely depressing," he said at the time. And he'd soon drop the practice of law altogether in pursuit of making a big score in business, restoring his law license only when he became a Simpson mouthpiece.

By the time he married Kris, he was closing in on forty, soon with a growing family, a very extravagant wife, and a fancy Beverly Hills lifestyle to support. His dream was to make a killing in the business world, and he was always on the lookout for the perfect deal that would make him rich.

With O. J. Simpson as a business partner, for instance, Kardashian and the Juice opened a clothing and jeans boutique called JAG O.J. on the campus of their alma mater, USC. JAG, an Australian brand, had been founded in 1972 by Adele Palmer and quickly developed an iconic celebrity following, ranging from Mick Jagger to Jacqueline Kennedy Onassis. Kardashian, with O.J.'s moniker on the business name, hoped to cash in on the lucrative jeans boom of the seventies.

Kardashian had gotten a tip about the JAG brand from Joe Carl

Leach, his stockbroker at Bear Stearns, whose financial mentor was the firm's powerful and influential chairman, Alan "Ace" Greenberg, once romantically involved with Barbara Walters. A born-and-raised Texan from humble roots, Leach, a one-time basketball coach and biology teacher in the Lone Star State, discovered the JAG jeans brand—the first designer denim—while on a trip to Australia. Back in the states, he opened what was hailed as the first-ever jeans-only shop in Beverly Hills, and it was a roaring success.

"Joe was really an aggressive guy, and so he brought the JAG deal to Robert and to get O.J. to endorse and be a partner as well," said Tom Kardashian. "He brought my brother in because he was O.J.'s friend, and O.J. liked a lot of those different kinds of businesses. Joe Leach was kind of a mover and shaker, took a lot of chances, and my brother kind of liked that."

But for Robert Kardashian and O. J. Simpson, the boutique didn't take off as they had expected.

While the shop attracted many jeans-wearing coeds, they were more interested in meeting O.J. than in buying the merchandise, and the business closed after a few years.

"O.J. and my brother didn't bring me in to the JAG deal, and they were not successful," said Kardashian. "When you're young and you got name recognition you think you can open up something and people will come. But those businesses are usually a lot harder to operate than people think."

With O.J., whose name was the big selling point and draw, and with an investment from Joe Leach, Kardashian once again hoped to hit it big, this time in trendy, affluent Westwood Village, near the UCLA campus, with what was believed to be one of La-La Land's first frozen yogurt emporiums. It went through two names, first Joy, then Forty Carats, both under the corporate name Juice Inc. But it was another relative flop, and the store closed after several years of trying to make a go of it.

"O.J. had what we call street smarts, growing up in the underprivileged areas in San Francisco," said Tom Kardashian. "So when I first knew him he had already owned two or three Pioneer Chicken franchises, and he had already had a great relationship with the Hertz Corp. as its spokesman."

But his business involvement with Tom's brother, Robert, was never very successful.

"I knew they weren't lucrative deals," maintained Tom Kardashian.

Looking back to Kardashian's business deals with the Juice, Robert's friend the multimillionaire businessman Larry Kraines declared simply, "That was all bullshit."

With a growing list of business failures on his résumé, his financial mentor, George Mason, then the senior managing director of Bear Stearns & Company, asserted, "Some click, some don't. He's not the kind who wants to be chained to a desk and take a briefcase full of work home with him every night." And his record industry power broker pal, Irving Azoff, was once quoted in the *Los Angeles Times* as saying that Kardashian had some good ideas. "Some have and some haven't been as successful. But he's real dependable and honest and quite an entrepreneur."

One of Kardashian's clients at the Bedrosian-Eamer law firm was a creative young man by the name of Bob Wilson, who had a great idea but no money to launch it. According to Tom Kardashian, Wilson was a program director at radio station KDAY, in Los Angeles, and his brainstorm was to produce a pop music tip sheet aimed at radio broadcasting executives, record companies, and disc jockeys, so they would be current on the latest, hottest tunes people were listening to, week by week.

"My brother came to me and said Bob Wilson needed some backing and some business acumen, and Robert and I always discussed business stuff," said Kardashian. "Bob Wilson was a young guy with no money. My brother *and* Bob Wilson were very much the creative side, but didn't have the business acumen, and I had already gone through all kinds of business stuff"—not to mention a federal charge of bribery in 1974 for which he had copped a plea and was a convicted felon—"so my brother and I put up the money."

While Kardashian declined to reveal how much he and Robert invested, he said it was "a lot less" than a million dollars. And during the first year of operations, Wilson ran things without getting a salary. "We let Wilson think he didn't have to worry about the money side," noted Kardashian.

Whatever the investment, the Kardashians and Wilson would make a bundle when they sold their shares in the very successful trade publication, *Radio & Records*, known as *R&R* in the industry, and they became multimillionaires—on the low end of the millionaire scale, but enough to live large.

"It was," Tom Kardashian said, "a matter of luck and timing. But timing is luck."

The Kardashian brothers got others to "buy into the concept"—people in the record business. One of those was Azoff, a kingmaker, who Tom Kardashian boasts was "one of my brother's close friends, a really successful record guy because he represented the right guys early on, like the Eagles, Chicago, and then he became a promoter, and my brother did a *lot* with Irving, who was pretty much the frontrunner, one of those kind of guys who was just a killer business guy."

According to the 1990 book *Hit Men: Power Brokers and Fast Money Inside the Music Business*, about the seamy side of the record industry, Irving Azoff once delivered a snake to a business associate as a way of underscoring a stern message. The book's author, Frederic Dannen, alleged that friends of the five-foot-three, curly-haired Azoff "called him the 'Poison Dwarf.' [E]asily one of the most loathed men in the music business. . . . once . . . when service was too slow at a chic Beverly Hills restaurant . . . he set his menu on fire." And then-CBS Records chairman Walter Yetnikoff asserted, "Irving lies even when it's to his advantage to tell the truth. He just can't help it."

"Sure I lie," Azoff once told a *Rolling Stone* reporter. "But it's more like . . . tinting. I've inherited a lot of dummies' deals. What then happens, you gotta make it right. It's all just negotiating theatrics."

The diminutive, scary Azoff was described as the "*enfant terrible*" of the music business. "To get his clients top dollar, he'll rip up a contract, yell, scream, terrorize."

Azoff's much younger, glamorous wife, Shelli, became one of Kris Kardashian's close friends, a confidant, and a member of her Beverly Hills posse. The two pals had children around the same time—Kim Kardashian and Allison Azoff grew up together and were friends—and sometimes the two moms sported the same outfits by chance for social occasions, and were said to party together at times.

"They were always on the same page," noted a friend of both.

When O. J. Simpson's wife Nicole and her friend Ron Goldman were discovered brutally butchered with a knife, it was Shelli Azoff who first informed Robert Kardashian, telling him on the phone that his best friend's wife had been "shot and killed," based on erroneous gossip from her hairstylist, Alex Roldan.

Like Kris Kardashian Jenner, and like tough-talking husband Irving, Shelli Azoff had a reputation for being one tough cookie. She reportedly once sent a live snake to the singer George Michael's manager, Michael Lippman, after Lippman invited her husband to a party but asked that he not bring Shelli, pissing her off. When executives at Sony Pictures denied the Azoffs access to screen the film *Sex Tape* on their yacht, Shelli reportedly threatened then-studio boss Amy Pascal with a refusal to license music from Azoff's talent pool or permit them to appear in Sony films.

The talk around town was, "Don't fuck with Shelli."

And when Kris first met boy-toy soccer player Todd Waterman, who became her lover in the late eighties and the main reason for her divorce, Kris was accompanied by Shelli Azoff, the two of them vacationing together in Europe, according to an account Kris's furious husband told his friend Joni Migdal.

Billboard was considered the leader of music industry tip sheets, but *Billboard* listed retail sales of records, while *R&R*, sold on newsstands and subscribed to by people in the broadcasting and record businesses, had its own niche. It listed presales, which, according to Tom Kardashian, was "more relevant to a radio station or a record store because those were the most important songs that listeners sixteen to thirty were requesting."

The year 1978, when Kris Houghton became Mrs. Robert Kardashian, among the top tunes being pitched to industry readers in Wilson and the Kardashian brothers' tabloid-size publication were the Bee Gees' "Stayin' Alive," "With a Little Luck" by Wings, and Chic's "Le Freak."

While founder and creator Bob Wilson declined to be interviewed for this book, his onetime assistant, Donna Kramer, remembers life at the *R&R* offices—where Kardashian was a daily presence—as being sex, drugs, and rock 'n' roll personified, and that was the main reason Kramer eventually left. "It was a more wild scene," she said, looking back. "More hip people, more partying people, and I'm not that way. So I didn't love working there. They definitely were smoking marijuana, that type of thing. It was pretty extreme for me. I just didn't look forward to going to work every day."

When she gave Wilson notice, he told her, "On your last day I want you to come into my office and smoke a joint with me and tell me what you think of me and why you're leaving," she recalled. It was the far-out ambiance and culture of *R&R*, at least to her, that convinced her to resign, despite Wilson's constant promise that " 'If you stay with me, I'm going to make you a rich woman.' But I didn't hang around long enough to see that happen."

As part of his investment deal, Kardashian had a posh, private office in *R&R*'s headquarters, located in a small office building in the Century City West complex of Beverly Hills, between Santa Monica and Olympic Boulevards. Initially, it had been located in offices on Sunset Boulevard. Also headquartered in the *R&R* building was RKO General, one of the major radio station chains.

While Tom Kardashian kept his money in, but stayed away from the business, remaining a silent partner, Robert was there virtually every day, but the born-again Christian looked the other way when certain staffers took breaks up on the roof to "do drugs, smoke pot," and possibly have a sexual interlude, according to what Donna Kramer gleaned around the office.

The place was an eclectic mix of young people, hipsters, and music buffs, and there were as many as a hundred employees who covered and researched the weekly trends in rock, pop, and country and western.

Like Kardashian, his personal secretary, Lynn Wright, a portly woman with a pretty face, was born-again and had been one of the original members of the Bible studies that became Pastor Kenn Gulliksen's Vineyard church. She was very active in the life of the church, like Kardashian, and Gulliksen thought of Wright as "one of the most genuine, kind, loving persons" he'd ever met. Kramer got the position as Wilson's assistant through Wright, who was friends with Kramer's cousin, Lani Riches, also a born-again Christian.

Kardashian looked the part of a hip late-seventies and early-eighties Hollywood music executive, even though he wasn't involved in any way in the day-to-day operations of *R&R*. While he sometimes wore an elegant suit at the office, Kramer remembered him as being "pretty casual—he sort of had a 'Tommy Bahama' look in a floral pattern short-sleeve shirts, beautiful slacks and shoes—the *best* of everything, and he had beautiful hair with that white streak."

The office and the secretary were part of the benefits for Kardashian's investment, but it was somewhat of a mystery what he actually was doing there every day. "He certainly wasn't practicing law, unless he was helping friends," recalled Kramer.

Robert and Kris were still living in the Deep Canyon Road house in Beverly Hills that the Kardashian brothers had once jointly owned and often shared with O.J. The house was just minutes from the *R&R* offices, which allowed Kris to pop in when she was out splurging in the chic shops on nearby Rodeo Drive. They took long, leisurely lunches at eateries like Kardashian's old hangout the Luau, where he once played the role of an Armenian Mafioso to impress a girl, and where he was first introduced to O.J.

To Kramer, the boss's young, "sexy" wife appeared "sweet and nice," and when Kris gave birth to Kim, Kramer was invited to Deep Canyon to see the infant, bringing a baby gift for the future porn video and reality TV star. However, years later, when Kris and Kim and the Kardashian-Jenner gang became infamous, Kramer's positive view, especially of Kris, radically changed.

"I don't know that Bob Kardashian would be happy about the paths that Kris and the children have taken," she asserted. "Bob was a very Christian, good man, and I just don't think Kris and the children's lives are something he would approve of. And in retrospect I would think that Kris would be sorry that she lost Bob. He was a good catch and a wonderful person. And with the girls, I just don't get it. I would think their father's rolling over in his grave."

While Kramer worked for Wilson, the president and CEO, and had a good working relationship with him, she adored Kardashian, who she believed was sort of the chief financial officer. "Robert was the angel, not Bob Wilson—an angel in terms of being a kind, wonderful person. *Everybody* loved Bob Kardashian, the sweetest, kindest man." She found Bob Wilson to be a bit gruff. "I'd hear him talk to people and he liked to make them squirm almost. He just wasn't a gentle, nice soul like Bob. I couldn't imagine that they were really personal friends; they were *so* different."

Virtually overnight, *R&R* grew successful, became known as the "radio industry bible," coined format terms such as "Contemporary Hit Radio" and "Adult Contemporary," and began holding annual conventions for industry people—disc jockeys, radio station executives, and record company honchos, at hotels like the posh Century Plaza in Beverly Hills. Donna Kramer was involved in helping to organize them. Every year there was a featured entertainer. When Kramer worked there, it was Donna Summer one year and the Blues Brothers—John Belushi and Dan Aykroyd, who made their act famous on *Saturday Night Live*—another year.

"They were putting a lot of money into the business," Kramer said, "and *R&R* was a very respected company."

And the company was making a lot of money.

And that's when Bob Wilson thought it was time to cash in.

"It was time for us to move on," said Tom Kardashian. "And that only happens when things are going good."

In the eighties, the partners sold *Radio & Records* to Harte-Hanks Communications, a public company that operated newspapers in Texas—twenty-nine dailies and sixty-eight weeklies—and had gotten into the radio and television business.

"Bob Wilson was the one who came up with the idea for *Radio & Records*, and my brother and I came up with more the business side of what to do, and the company really started growing and took off to where Bob Wilson said, 'I don't need you guys now,' so it was time to break it up and sell the company," asserted Tom Kardashian. "It was all Bob's idea."

And Kardashian "absolutely" maintained that the *Radio & Records* partnership ended amicably.

Still, in 2015, Wilson said he didn't want to talk about the whole affair.

The brothers Kardashian and Wilson happily divided what was said to be at least a twelve-million-dollar-and-change windfall profit from the sale—25 percent for each of the Kardashians and 50 percent for Wilson. Robert pocketed some $3 million, equal to more than $6 million in 2016 greenbacks, which to him was big money, but relatively small change in the Hollywood entertainment nexus, where deals in the tens and hundreds of millions of dollars were prevalent.

"The sale *really* was lucrative for us," boasted Tom Kardashian. "It gave us money to do whatever we wanted. The return on capital was good. After we got our separations from *Radio & Records*, my brother and I had our separate deals for a while. I invested in other things than he did."

For a time, Robert and Bob Wilson stayed on with the new owners under contract, and Tom Kardashian signed a noncompete agreement.

"Bob was like a pig in shit," recalled a colleague. "He was suddenly a millionaire and saw himself parlaying all that bread into new projects and making more millions. Maybe we were at one of Joe Stellini's restaurants, and I remember O.J. high-fiving it with Bob and telling him with true admiration, 'Man, you are now one nigger-rich motherfucker,' and they embraced. I saw Bob wipe away tears."

After Kardashian's contract expired with the new owners of *R&R* he began working for his close friend Irving Azoff at the MCA Radio Network, headquartered at Universal Studios.

As Kris saw it, "Life was great and getting greater all the time."

ONE OF THE FIRST THINGS Kardashian did after the sale of *R&R* was begin searching for his dream house, one that would befit a man of his newly found means. Rather than an all-glass Southern California contemporary, or a mansion with pillars, he bought a handsome two-story, six-bedroom, eight-bath, almost seven-thousand-square-foot circa 1977 Cape Cod–style home, at 9920 Tower Lane, in one of Beverly Hills' most prestigious areas—a secluded enclave off Benedict Canyon, in an area that was home to the rich and famous.

As a favor to his pal O.J. and his girlfriend, Kardashian rented Deep Canyon to Nicole Brown and the Juice, who was still not totally committed to marrying her but moved in. They would finally tie the knot a dozen days before Valentine's Day 1985.

"After Robert sold *Radio & Records*, that house on Tower Lane was a prize for him," said Larry Kraines.

On a private cul-de-sac, the Kardashian grand estate sat on a big piece of land and was gated with a swimming pool shaped like a duck with its own well-stocked bar and a pool house, a tennis court, and a Jacuzzi shaped like an egg.

"That house was huge and beautiful and private and they decorated it beautifully and spent a *lot* of money in decorating it," recalled Joni Migdal.

Two of his next-door neighbors were the Cantors—Iris and Bernie, he the founder of the financial firm Cantor Fitzgerald, which lost many employees in the 9/11 terrorist attack on the World Trade Center in New York City. In back was the Bruce Springsteen estate, on a big piece of property at the end of the cul-de-sac. Another neighbor had llamas and peacocks, and very young Kourtney and Kim had two cats, Coco and Chanel, named pretentiously by their striving-to-be-a-Beverly-Hills-fashionista young mother, Kris. Their father and the master of the house now had two Dobermans, the new one with the Armenian name Anoush, along with Sarkis.

The Tonight Show host Jay Leno lived close by. And across the road was the home of the actor Robert Vaughn, who appeared in the popular sixties TV series *The Man from U.N.C.L.E.* as the suave spy Napoleon Solo.

"It was quite a famous area," noted Kraines. "When Kris and Robert had parties, they would invite Vaughn and he would come over."

Living large, the Kardashians entertained often—Kris's idea—and the estate was considered "party central." One New Year's Eve, she hired cancan dancers to entertain. The invitations she sent out were chocolate female legs.

Later, the gorgeous home that Robert Kardashian loved with all his heart—a platinum symbol of his success as a businessman, and a property that gave him the respect and street credibility he always craved—would become part of a vicious tug-of-war between him, his ex-wife, Kris, and her soon-to-be new husband, Bruce Jenner.

OF THE MANY VENTURES entrepreneur Robert Kardashian got into, *Radio & Records* was the most successful, according to his brother.

After Kardashian cashed out of *R&R*, asserted Larry Kraines, "Robert was trying to find a handle on something. He was very creative, very visionary. He'd always come talk to me about business. He would share his ideas with me. In his wallet he had twenty different business cards of different ventures that he had his fingers into. That was his whole M.O., always looking for a home run. He had all these ideas for business—probably fourteen or fifteen or sixteen different kind of companies, or concepts, over a period of a handful of years, and had other stuff going on, but they weren't successful, to be honest."

One of Kardashian's big ideas that seemed to have grand-slam, bases-loaded potential written all over it was called Movie Tunes. He had close ties with the AMC movie theater management chain and with record company executives from his *R&R* experience, and his idea was to have the theaters play music that promoted artists before the start of films and during the intermissions. The record company paid the bill and the theaters gave Kardashian's operation exclusive play rights.

"It was just music, like you would have in a doctor's waiting room, which was transmitted in," said Tom Kardashian, who got involved with his brother on this venture. "But in movie theaters we were able to play music on a CD, and it would play playlists of songs that we sold for the month to a record company, say, Capitol Records, or whoever had an artist that they wanted to expose.

"The beauty of it was we had a *captive* audience," he continued. "Our concept was to tell the customer—the record company—that the song was going to be heard so many times, by so many people—*millions* of people throughout the theaters around the country—and the audience *can't* change the channel. We'd have an announcement, 'You just heard Barbra Streisand, with her new album, soon to be released on Capitol Records.'"

On paper, it seemed a brilliant, very lucrative idea and concept. As Neal Raymond Hersh, Robert's lawyer and close friend who would handle his divorce from Kris, observed, "He created a whole genre of advertising that had never been done before. It was just a remarkable endeavor. It was incredible."

In reality and in actual practice, not so much.

Complaints started to pour in from moviegoers, for the most part parents with young children who heard an obscene lyric and were angry and appalled. Some walked out and demanded their money back. Theater managers were not happy.

"That," said Kardashian, "was a major problem."

As a result, the theater chain required that songs with questionable lyrics be edited, which was a major undertaking with all sorts of pitfalls.

Worse, there was a sudden consolidation of movie theater chains, which meant less competition and less business for Movie Tunes, and movie theater technology advanced, all of which required the Kardashians to pour more money into the business, which wasn't the way they operated.

"We just didn't want to make a big capital investment," said Tom Kardashian. "We were more traditional and old school."

WHILE MOVIE TUNES HIT a roadblock, Robert Kardashian still believed he could arrange a moneymaking marriage between movie theaters and music, and, even better, with concert video of the performers this time. It was called Concert Cinema. And he was joined in the venture by his buddy O. J. Simpson and Bob Wilson, whom he had partnered with in *Radio & Records*. This time, though, Kardashian was the president and spokesman. They called their company, formed in 1984, the Movie Theater Network.

The idea was that the nation's movie theaters would get five-minute film clips of music stars in concert free of charge, and the Kardashian group would make their money from selling a fifteen-second commercial that was inserted in the film, with such promised stars as born-again Christian Bob Dylan, the Police, and Van Halen. Their acts were taken directly from a recent concert, and the clip was shown before the feature film. The first sponsor, claimed Kardashian, was the Pierre Cardin company, and he boasted that some seven hundred theaters in twenty-eight states had reportedly signed up.

In what probably was the first time Robert Kardashian was quoted in the press—a decade before his name became internationally known in the O.J. murder case—he confidently told United Press International, with a Hollywood dateline, "There are eighteen thousand screens in this country and we expect to put Concert Cinema in five thousand of them with about forty-five sponsors a year. The concert preconditions the audience for what it is going to see. Our tests show they help increase attendance and are a popular addition to the program."

While he told the press that everyone profits from the venture—exhibitors, audiences, and the performers "who are getting exposure in a new medium with enormous audiences," he appeared to be blowing a lot of smoke, and the project quickly disappeared from America's silver screens. As the *Los Angeles Times* reported, "The yearlong enterprise became expensive and neither Simpson nor Kardashian made money on it."

By the time of the O.J. case in the mid-nineties, Kardashian was involved in pitching movie theaters on the idea of having lobby vending machines dispensing compact music discs. That concept, called Hit Tunes, also disappeared without any great financial reward.

Fortunately, Robert Kardashian had hit the jackpot with *Radio & Records*, since nothing afterward had profitably panned out for him, despite his myriad of ideas.

As Joni Migdal noted, "When he sold *R&R* he did very well with that. He got a lot of money and he lived off of that for a while."

And when things weren't going well, he applied in July 1988 for a real estate license in the hot Southern California home sales market. His license expired in July 1992. There is not evidence that he had ever sold a home.

FIFTEEN

Who's Your Daddy?

Having walked away with a bundle of money from the sale of *Radio & Records*, a another bundle of joy entered Robert Kardashian's life.

Kris claimed she got pregnant with Khloé Alexandra Kardashian while on a European vacation with her husband in September 1983. After Kourtney and Kim, "Robert and I decided it was time to have another baby. We conceived again in Italy," she asserted in her memoir some years after her ex-husband was no longer around.

And Kris said much less about the conception and birth of Khloé on June 27, 1984, compared to how she elaborated about Kourtney's, Kim's, and Rob's entrances into the world.

However, Kris did note one important fact: Khloé "looked different."

With her blond hair and green eyes, she resembled no one else in her family—from her dark-haired, olive-skinned, brown-eyed, Armenian-featured siblings to her swarthy Armenian-American father. And even Khloé's mother had very dark brown Natalie Wood eyes and hair.

When Khloé got old enough, people in the Kardashians' circle began to notice just how different she really did look and raised questions. Kris would explain away the suspicions by saying that Khloé looked like her maternal great-grandmother, Lou Ethel Fairbanks. And Robert's friend Joni Migdal recalled how Robert would shrug off their suspicions and claim that Khloé looked just like his mother, Helen, who was Armenian but didn't have Armenian features.

However, when the Kardashians became famous, questions arose in the tabloid and gossip media about whether the late Robert Kardashian, who had divorced Khloé's mother because of her philandering, was really the girl's biological father.

Even Khloé's half sister Kylie Jenner, fourteen years old and already with a fashion line, jumped on the "Who's Khloé's Real Father?" bandwagon when she caustically posted a seemingly dummied-up but possibly authentic photo online of then twenty-seven-year-old Khloé with Alex Roldan, who reportedly cut and styled Kris's hair and that of a number of women in her Beverly Hills circle. Kylie wrote: "First official photo of my sister and her dad! Like father like daughter!"

Rumors about Kris and Roldan—he and Khloé actually did look alike—had been making the gossip rounds seemingly forever. Another whisper was that Khloé was the illegitimate daughter of O. J. Simpson after stories circulated that Kris and the Juice had had an affair, which Kris laughed off. Khloé termed false all the salacious chatter about Roldan, and Kylie subsequently tweeted, "It was a joke everyone! Lol!" Kris simply scoffed at the crescendo of titillating innuendo.

Long before Kylie's snarky comment, however, the two women who Kardashian married after he divorced Kris—the first Jan Ashley; the second Ellen Pearson—went public in the celebrity press, stating that Kardashian had told them that Khloé was not his.

On May 19, 1999, four years before his death from cancer, Kardashian signed a sworn declaration in the office of his prominent attorney-to-the-stars and close friend, Neal Hersh, who partly handled his 1991 divorce from Kris. The legal paper was part of Kardashian's successful case to nullify his November 25, 1998, marriage to Ashley after just a few months. In the statement, Kardashian claimed that he had married her, a glamorous, childless widow, "with the expectation of having a child together. I am the one who changed my mind."

But it was learned that Kardashian had actually deceived Jan Ashley from the beginning about having a child with her because, as he had long before revealed to confidants, he had secretly had a vasectomy after the birth of Rob, the last of his children with Kris. At least that's what he claimed to two close friends. "Robert said he had a vasectomy. He didn't want any more kids," asserted Larry Kraines. "He told me, 'I'm done having kids. I've had enough kids.' So that whole deal [with Jan Ashley] was a joke. And I never knew about Jan Ashley saying, 'Let's have kids.'"

Kraines wasn't the only friend to whom Kardashian confessed about his claimed vasectomy. "He told me he had it done after his son was born," said Joni Migdal. "He did *not* want other children. And that whole series of weddings, with Jan and Ellen—I don't think his heart was in either of them. He just did it because he probably was lonely. Those last two wives were spur-of-the-moment wives. I don't think he cared very deeply about either of them."

Unless Kardashian had had his claimed vasectomy reversed, which sometimes works, he could never have been able to father a child with Ashley.

Meanwhile, the key point that Kardashian made in his sworn declaration—the one that Kris Jenner and Khloé Kardashian have pointed to in the media to prove, they claim, that Robert Kardasahian is, in fact, Khloé's father, stated:

"Approximately two months after our marriage, I changed my mind [about fathering a child with Jan Ashley]. I decided that since I already had four biological children, I did not wish to have any more. . . . I declare under penalty of perjury under the laws of the State of California that the foregoing is true and correct."

By claiming "four biological children"—meaning Kourtney, Kim, *Khloé*, and Rob, and sworn to under oath by Kardashian—Kris steadfastly maintained that no other proof was needed as to the identity of Khloé's biological father. Therefore, allegations by two ex-wives and a supposedly practical joke social media posting by a half sibling were to Kris nothing more than salacious gossip and crazy fun.

The news media, with nothing more to go on, went along—after all, a sworn statement is a sworn statement.

But just like how Kardashian reportedly pulled the wool over Jan Ashley's eyes, he conceivably could have pulled a fast one in his lawyer's office by swearing he had fathered four biological children. In 2016, his lawyer Hersh said he had "no memory" of Kardashian ever making such a declaration, despite the paperwork.

However, there is further evidence that Robert Kardashian believed that Khloé was not his biological child, that someone else was the father.

As Kardashian's longtime friend and minister, Kenn Gulliksen, put it, "Kris and Robert had four children. Well, they had three kids and somebody else's kid. Bob never asked my counsel, but I simply heard from him that Khloé wasn't his biological daughter. He gave me no names of who he thought the father was. But I certainly know it wasn't O.J.

"Bob just was very straightforward. We were simply having a conversation about everything he'd been through. It was my strong impression from him that he loved Khloé very much but he said it in a way that implied 'she's not my blood daughter,' meaning his biological daughter. That was the implication."

Continued the man of God: "My understanding from him was that he and Kris hadn't had sex during the period of time they would have *had* to have had sex when Khloé was conceived. And there were other things that I know he kept to himself about all of that, things he didn't talk about. He was obviously wanting to protect his family."

Larry Kraines said he was at the hospital when every one of the

Kardashian kids were born, and when the issue of Khloé's conception came up, Kardashian's only response was, " 'It's all bullshit.' And that's the way he wanted to handle it."

In her memoir, Kris makes brief mention of her romantic and sex life with Kardashian, some of it in a negative fashion. At one point she mentions that the two of them would have what she called "date night." With her babies—then just Kourtney and Kim—put to bed and with a nanny on duty, the two would "head out for a night in Beverly Hills. We were living *la vida loca*!"

At another point in her book, however, she claimed that after calling Robert and telling him she wanted to have sex (which they hoped would result in her becoming pregnant with a son), her husband would "race home and it was wham, bam, thank you, ma'am. We didn't have sex frequently, but just enough."

Joni Migdal said that she and Kardashian talked about the Khloé situation often. "But he was unwilling to take a DNA test." Such tests were first available in 1985, when Khloé was a year old.

When Migdal first saw Khloé and noticed how different she looked from the rest of the Kardashian family, she kept her mouth zipped. "I just didn't say a word. What was I supposed to say? I had two children of my own. I didn't think it was appropriate to mention her looks, so I didn't say anything."

As with Gulliksen, Migdal believed that Robert and Kris weren't having sex when Khloé was conceived.

"Robert would joke around and say the father was probably the swimming pool man," recalled Migdal. "But Robert was not angry, because he didn't care. He said, 'Whatever she is [ethnically], whoever her father is, whatever has happened, she is my child.' He made a decision that no matter who Khloé's father was that Robert was going to love her as his own, and it was all done. That was his decision. It was the honorable way of doing it, and the respectful way.

"He didn't want a DNA test done, he didn't want to find out *any-thing*. He told me, 'I love Khloé. She's wonderful. She's mine, period.'

But he knew she wasn't his. His confirmation to me was, 'she's mine and I don't care who the father is.'"

WHILE ROBERT KARDASHIAN ACCEPTED his third daughter, Khloé, as his own, and loved her as his own, he felt tortured thinking that his wife of six years, Kris, had made a baby allegedly with another man.

As Robert and Kris's minister, Kenn Gulliksen, in whom he had confided his innermost feelings about the Khloé situation, later observed, "Robert knew people had affairs, and he'd certainly been a swinger in his time. But he was a man who, once he was married, expected Kris to be faithful to him forever. When he found out she was unfaithful, he was done."

But presumably that didn't happen with the birth of Khloé. It happened when Kris had an affair four years later that Kardashian discovered, and he learned the identity of her lover, tracked him down, and confronted his cheating wife, which would result in an acrimonious divorce.

It's hard to imagine that Kris, from lower-middle-class roots and with no more than a high school education, would give up all that Robert Kardashian had given her—a new life for a decade with all the luxuries that money can buy, and with the "picture-perfect" family that she often boasted about, for a clichéd roll in the hay with another man.

But that's what happened.

In her memoir, published in 2011, Kris, then the wife of Bruce Jenner, spoke glowingly of her late first husband and her Beverly Hills life with him.

"I was so much in love with Robert," she stated at one point. And at another she declared, "There wasn't one thing that I wanted that Robert didn't eventually give me. He was the most thoughtful, generous, amazing guy I had ever met. He was my prince."

Still, she cheated on him. But first came new breasts.

In 1988, when Kris was thirty-eight and nearing the onset of middle age, Kardashian paid for her to have implants, which she desperately wanted—the first pair replaced with a bigger second pair—because that's what many of her friends were getting, and Kris, mother of four, wanted to look hot, desirable, and porn-girlish just like them. And in that eighties go-go era in Kris's circle of trophy wives and high-end-escort-like girlfriends, all of them, she noted, "wanted to have big, enormous boobs. We were all obsessed."

A friend who visited her just after she got her first implants and was recovering raved, "You look like a supermodel!" But they weren't big enough, or perkier enough, or attention-grabbing enough for Kris's taste. Therefore, she had them redone after she saw her pal Nicole Brown Simpson's newly implanted silicone breasts, which she noted O.J. loved. And so did Kris.

"My mouth fell open," when Nicole revealed them to her, she declared. "They were *gorgeous*. I thought, *I want two of those, please!*"

By the time they both had new breasts, Kris was well aware that Robert's best friend, the Juice, had been beating up Kris's close friend Nicole, then the mother of two—Sydney and Justin. In 1989, when Kris would begin the final affair that would end her first marriage, O.J. was charged with the spousal abuse of Nicole. Their fatal attraction would only grow worse.

During those turbulent eighties, Kardashian's pal O.J. and Kardashian's ex-girlfriend Priscilla Presley, who never did remarry, costarred in the three zany *Naked Gun* movies with Leslie Nielsen. O.J., who played a dumb cop, received a producer credit, and was riding high.

Despite Kris's new breasts, her Beverly Hills lifestyle, and a husband who was "absolutely devoted to me," she still didn't feel fulfilled, and therefore life in the House of Kardashian wasn't as copacetic as it had once been, or had ever appeared to be.

By the end of the eighties, Kris had come to the stark realization that she no longer was in love with Robert Kardashian, to whom she had then been married for a decade.

SIXTEEN

Another Affair

When Robert Kardashian twice saw the film *The Stepford Wives* back in the mid-seventies, he was turned on by the dominance the husbands had over their robot-transformed mates. Later, Kris would claim it was an eighties TV miniseries she had watched, *The Thorn Birds*, with Richard Chamberlain and Rachel Ward, about romantic passion, which had turned her on to finding hot sex again with someone else.

With Robert, she felt a "switch" had been turned off and she no longer had a desire to make love with him. What she wanted, she declared in her memoir, was "so much more passion." She was now still relatively young, and bored with her husband, and she had a pair of what she viewed as great, new faux breasts, for which he had paid a whopping twenty thousand dollars for both surgeries.

Thus armed, it was time for Kris Kardashian to find a lover.

While she doesn't deal extensively with it in her book, Robert

Kardashian's friends contend that beyond Kris's loss of passion for him, she was sick and tired of his controlling every aspect of her life.

All she says in her book about his dominance is "He was always the boss of everything."

With his children, Kardashian surprisingly was a "very strong disciplinarian, very firm," asserted Larry Kraines, "and he was that way with Kris, and that was the problem. What started out to be good for Kris, Kris didn't want anymore. She had enough of his controlling ways and strong ideas. Kris had her own ideas about what she wanted to do with the rest of her life."

One example Kraines had never forgotten, was Kardashian's directive to Kris to listen and learn from self-help cassette tapes that he gave her on a variety of subjects in order to make her smarter and more efficient as a wife, after which he would test her on what she had learned.

And later, when Kris went ahead and found her new lover, Larry Kraines and his housekeeper would discover the two of them in the lower level of his Beverly Hills mansion when they thought no one was at home.

"Kris was only eighteen when Robert met her, and she was young and beautiful, and Robert molded her, and Robert helped her to become a strong person, and what happened was he became very possessive of her, and she fought that," maintained Joni Migdal, looking back. "Kris did not want to be possessed, and the harder Robert tried, the more Kris backed off, and I was hearing that from both of them. He wanted her to be the perfect housewife—the perfect *Armenian* housewife—the perfect cook, the perfect party maker. When he met her she was poor with not much education. But Robert taught her *everything*—how to give parties, how to entertain. He taught her how for every holiday to decorate beautifully in their home. Finally, she rebelled against Robert, against his rules and what he really valued. Robert really loved Kris. He thought that that was going to be *the* lasting relationship."

But bored and rebellious Kris had other ideas.

"Kris would tell Robert, 'I need to go out. I need to have fun. I want to have fun,' and she would go out and stay out really late. She would go out drinking with [the wife of a powerful Hollywood executive] who had a boyfriend, and Kris was coming home at two and three in the morning drunk, and she would tell Robert, 'I need my freedom. I need my independence. I have four kids and I have not lived life.'

"She cheated on him because she believed he cheated her out of life—that she married him when she was young and that she never had a chance to go out and be herself," was the way Migdal, who knew them both well, saw it. "Kris may have been trampy, but she was still a good mother to her kids. You can be a good mother and still be a tramp. You put the kids to bed, you have a nanny, and you go out. You just do it late at night."

It was as if Kris had completely erased the fact that she had long ago gone out, acted independently, and had an affair, oddly with her parents' approval, when she was just eighteen, and with a much older man, a golf pro with a child. And back then he, too, had caught her cheating on him. The other man was none other than her current cuckold, her husband of a decade, Robert Kardashian.

KRIS TOLD ROBERT THAT she thought it best that they have a trial separation, but Kardashian was adamant: He told her Armenians don't go through separations. They either stay married or they get divorced. But he did leave for a couple of days, and she felt free. But then to her dismay he returned. He thought a brief break would give her time to think, and get back to normal, and allow their lives to continue as before.

It didn't happen.

As she put it, "I was going crazy inside."

Subsequently, when Robert was away on a "boys' ski vacation," Kris, always the opportunist, took advantage of his absence to go to a party at a close friend's home, she claims, met a guy, had "an instant attraction" to him, and was off and running.

In her book, Kris gave her first known lover, Cesar Sanudo, the phony name "Anthony." The fake name she gave to her latest, Todd Waterman, was "Ryan." Golf pro Sanudo was a dozen years older than Kris when she caught his eye at seventeen. This time around, the unhappily married mother of Kourtney, Kim, Khloé, and Rob was at least eleven years older than her new lover. And Waterman was, at twenty-three, a relatively unknown soccer player with the struggling L.A. Heat, and not a "producer," as Kris identified him. He was definitely no David Beckham.

When Kris Houghton had first encountered Robert Kardashian at the Del Mar racetrack a decade earlier, igniting their romance behind Cesar Sanudo's back, she was initially attracted to him because she thought Kardashian resembled the singer Tony Orlando. Now, ten years later, still apparently attracted to celebrity look-alikes, she thought Waterman looked like and actually was the actor Rob Lowe when she first laid her big, brown Natalie Wood eyes on him.

Moreover, Lowe was famously rumored in Hollywood for being very well endowed, which equally was an attraction for Kris. Around the time Kris fell for Waterman, the real Rob Lowe proved the gossip to be true when he was caught in a scandal—on video having sex with a sixteen-year-old girl of legal age who he met in a nightclub. The tape also showed Lowe and a male friend having intercourse and oral sex with a model in a Paris hotel room, which later became one of the first celebrity sex tapes commercially available to a porn-hungry public with a VCR; a later one, in 2007, would famously feature Kris's very own second-born, Kim, and her then-former studly black boyfriend, William Raymond Norwood Jr., better known as Ray J, a hip-hop record industry figure.

Not long after Kris and Waterman began chatting at that party at Kris's friend's house, she claims, he followed her upstairs, grabbed her, and kissed her. She thought, as she crudely states, "What the fuck?" and passionately kissed him back.

Taking a slap at her late husband and the biological father of at least three of her four Kardashian children, Kris states in her book that she "hadn't been kissed like that in ten years," which meant *all* the years of her now crumbling marriage. As the affair with Waterman quickly progressed to sex everywhere and anywhere, she boasted, "I hadn't had that feeling for Robert for years." And she noted that her loss of sexual attraction to her husband was even before she hooked up with Waterman, who was a decade younger and in his prime. And she'd eventually rationalize her affair as more "running away" from Robert rather than "running to" Waterman.

Other than the honeymoon period before and right after their marriage, and when they made babies together, Kris was admitting that she had long lost all interest in Kardashian and was just playing along to enjoy her Beverly Hills benefits as his wife. And when she declared all that negativity about her ex-husband in her book, he had been dead for eight years.

Despite Kris's account that she met Waterman at a party at a friend's house, he later claimed they got together at a Los Angeles nightclub after he first saw her photo at the Beverly Hills home of a friend and was intrigued.

But Robert Kardashian told his confidante Joni Migdal that Kris and Waterman had actually met in Europe, where Kris was said to be vacationing with Shelli Azoff, wife of Robert's close associate, the music mogul Irving Azoff.

Once back in Los Angeles, according to what Kardashian told Migdal, "Waterman moved to Malibu and rented an apartment at Kris's urging and Kris furnished it." A furious Kardashian had shown Migdal a cache of receipts he had found hidden in his Tower Lane mansion documenting furniture purchases Kris had made—presumably with her husband's money—for Waterman's love nest.

Where and how they met aside, Kris became consumed with Waterman. As she graphically put it in a description straight out of a campy made-for-TV Lifetime movie, or a pulp romance novel, they had "Wild crazy sex all the time, sex everywhere we could think of."

She claimed they had sex in cars, had sex on a tennis court, had sex in a pool house, had sex in a garage, and had sex on stairs, and she compared their "out of control crazy, dangerous" sex games to a movie she

had once seen starring Richard Gere and Diane Lane, appropriately ti-
tled *Unfaithful*.

And in another slap at her late first husband, she suggested that she
was not only unfaithful, but also "unfulfilled."

She made no mention about the sneaky sex she had with Waterman
in the home of Robert's best friend, Larry Kraines, who confronted her
about it and told her to stop cheating.

Reckless, dangerous, devious, and hurtful. That was the kind of game
Kris Kardashian was playing. At first she was said to have lied to Waterman, leading him to believe she was separated from her husband. Then,
even more strangely, after she did acknowledge she was still married and
was cheating on her husband, she would actually take some of her
children along on dates with Waterman, who particularly took a liking
to Kris's then-youngest daughter Khloé, who was just five.

At the same time as Kris's twisted rendition of her adulterous eighteen months with Waterman, she described herself as both a "Christian
girl who loved the Lord"—which Pastor Kenn Gulliksen found sad and
laughable when he read her book—and "a fuckup because I couldn't get
my marriage together."

Todd Waterman was furious when he learned that his affair with Kris
was detailed in her memoir some two decades after the fact. So, a year
after her book was published—and even though she didn't identify him
by name or profession—he broke his silence and talked to various
celebrity-oriented media outlets that through the years had helped make
the Kardashians famous with constant, gossipy coverage, among them
Star magazine, Britain's DailyMail.com, and *Radar*. She would later demand that he sign a confidentiality agreement never to publicly discuss
her or their relationship, according to his mother, Ilza Waterman, who
also talked to one of the celebrity gossip Internet sites. Moreover, she
claimed that Kris set up her son to make an appearance on the Kardashians' reality show in season seven in 2012 by showing up with her camera crew at his country club and surprising him.

When the affair was happening, Waterman's mother stated that she was led to believe that Kris was separated from Kardashian. "She wouldn't talk about her husband with me. If she did I would have said, 'What are you doing here with my son? What are you doing coming after my young son with all of these kids?' "

According to Todd, the first time he had sex with Mrs. Kardashian "was in her friend's closet. We found a little place in the house and consummated the relationship. It was a magical night, surreal," he stated, sounding almost scripted. "I think it was two people who were both open to experiencing something in their life at that time. It was fate; we invited it and we just ran with it and from that point on, we didn't look back."

Brazenly, Kris had even brought Waterman back to her family's Tower Lane estate, where he is "sure" he had sex with her, but probably not in the Kardashian marital bed. Kris would tell her husband that Waterman was just another tennis instructor teaching her how to play, or a friend of a friend. On one occasion Waterman volleyed on the Kardashian court with the cuckolded master of the house watching.

Waterman's tennis partner that day was his British pal the openly gay soccer player Justin Fashanu. "Robert was watching us play. We're in the affair now and I'm sure he suspected at this point," Kris's one-time lover recalled later. "He was trying to throw me off my game actually. He was just calling out 'foot fault' while I served." A decade after that game, thirty-seven-year-old Fashanu hanged himself in 1998, in London. In a suicide note, he denied allegations made by a seventeen-year-old youth that he had sexually assaulted him in Fashanu's apartment in Maryland.

Along with Kris bringing her lover to her home, she brought daughter Khloé along on dates with Waterman. "Khloé would go out with us," Waterman stated. "She'd be in the backseat of the car if we were going to lunch. I had a special relationship with her more than the other children. She just was the cutest. When talking to her sisters, she would say, 'You don't like him, do you?' "

During the affair, Waterman quit soccer because, he claimed, the pay wasn't good enough, and Kris began picking up his bills, treating him like a gigolo.

"She was generous," he stated. "She was paying a lot, or it was Robert I guess. There was no way I could support her or help maintain what she was accustomed to financially." He says she was the one who helped pick out his apartment, and, according to the receipts Kardashian found, Kris also helped to furnish it. Waterman would go to parties with Kris openly "as her boyfriend," running into such celebrities as Magic Johnson, Billy Idol, and George Michael.

Kris was lying to everyone, even her close girlfriends Joyce Kraines and Shelli Azoff, when they began questioning why she wasn't around much anymore to go shopping, or to have long, gossipy girly lunches. She'd give them lame excuses, while she was actually off supposedly having it off with Waterman.

Faye Resnick, a member of Kris's posse and a close pal of Nicole Simpson, remembers overhearing Kris talking on the phone to O.J., and the subject was why Nicole had stopped talking to Kris. The reason was because the abused Nicole had heard about Kris's affair.

"After Kris hung up, she explained to me that Nicole was a free spirit in many ways, but she did not condone people having extramarital affairs," Resnick noted in a tell-all published in the wake of Nicole's murder. "Nicole was adamantly against infidelity because O.J. had bedded women every chance he got. Nicole, Kris told me, had never fooled around on O.J. during their entire marriage."

Resnick called Robert Kardashian's close friend O.J. "one of the fastest cocksmen in town."

A decade older than her lover, Kris wanted to look her sexiest: She dieted and lost "fifteen pounds"; some of that might have been attributable to the stress of cheating on Robert. She also began going to a tanning salon and "every other day" she was getting bikini waxes.

Kris was always running out of the house to meet Waterman with one lame excuse after another for her husband.

"I constantly lied to Robert," she states. "I would tell Robert I was going to lunch . . . I had a baby son at school who needed me. But I would drop Kourtney, Kimberly, and Khloé off at school" and meet Waterman at his apartment.

Kardashian told Migdal, as he had told Larry Kraines, that he knew Kris was having an affair. "Robert told me, 'I need to know where Kris is going,' and he said, 'I'm going to follow her.'"

And he showed Migdal a pile of receipts he had found hidden in their palatial Beverly Hills home, receipts for a refrigerator, a table, and four chairs. "Robert said, 'What is Kris doing buying all this furniture? We have all this furniture.'"

He soon discovered that she was paying to decorate her lover's small Malibu apartment, which Kris described in her book as a "tiny, dumpy" place in the San Fernando Valley. "I was surprised that Kris furnished the guy's place," said Migdal. "And I was not real happy with Robert and the extent that he would follow Kris and spy on her. I just thought the whole thing was wrong."

Robert told Kraines he had followed Waterman in his car, and Kraines warned him to be careful, that he could get into trouble. On one occasion, Kardashian tailed Kris to a Beverly Hills restaurant, where he caught her having breakfast with Waterman and confronted them. Later that day he caught her leaving Waterman's apartment. He also had hired a private detective to tail her and document her activities.

Robert, Kris acknowledged, "caught us three different times."

Physical violence nearly ensued one late afternoon when Kardashian showed up at Waterman's apartment complex and Kris's lover threatened to call the police.

With Kris in his Jeep, Waterman pulled out of his garage, when Kardashian "comes charging out" of his Mercedes-Benz 450 SL convertible, wielding a golf club. "He took a swing and whacked the back of my car," claimed Waterman. "I said, 'Holy shit, Kris, can I pull over and confront him? What do you want to do?' She screamed out, 'No, no, keep driving, he might have a gun in the car. I know he keeps a gun.'"

A short chase in traffic ensued, but Kardashian pulled himself together and gave up the pursuit without further incident.

Oddly, the confrontation echoed what happened many years earlier when Cesar Sanudo had confronted his fiancée, Kris, and Robert in Sanudo's bedroom and chased both of them out of his condo, which ended their relationship. Now, Kardashian catching Kris with Waterman would end the Kardashians' marriage.

Kardashian had told O.J.—a man who knew something about cheating—about Kris's affair. Later, with Kris standing next to the Juice in his Rockingham mansion, he telephoned Waterman and threateningly bellowed, "You just fucked Snow White. Do you know what you've done to this entire universe, you asshole? You motherfucker. Now you're going to have to deal with me."

When he hung up he confronted Kris about why she was cheating on his best friend. Her response was that she didn't have the "same feelings for Robert."

O.J.'s advice?

Get a vibrator.

Kardashian's family—his parents, Arthur and Helen, his sister, Barbara, and his brother, Tom, were heartbroken when the prodigal son revealed that his wife was cheating on him. Tom Kardashian said he actually heard about Kris's fooling around through rumors in Beverly Hills, not anything that his embarrassed brother had told him.

"When Kris was cheating on my brother or whatever, I don't know what went on behind his doors," said Kardashian, looking back. "He wasn't the type who would come to his brother and say Kris is doing this, or this. So I don't have a take on what went on. But I lived in Beverly Hills, so it didn't take much for me to hear the gossip. My ex-sister-in-law's made a success, she's made some major accomplishments. But the cost of what went into that success, I'm not so proud of."

Waterman claimed that the affair ended when he realized private detectives were tailing him. His mother, a onetime regional sales director for a company that did building maintenance, claimed it had ended when Kardashian telephoned her home asking for his wife.

"Robert called in the middle of the night. He was very upset. I picked up and he said, 'She's with your son.' I said to him, 'It's two thirty in the morning, your wife is thirty-six and my son is twenty-four. I suggest you talk with your wife and I'll talk with my son.'"

Ilza Waterman said she did have a mother-son chat with Todd about his relationship with the married mother of four, and at that point Todd moved to London in hopes of getting Kris Kardashian out of his system, and to escape the wrath of her cuckolded husband.

SEVENTEEN

Emotional Wreck

Robert Kardashian, in his mid-forties, filed for divorce in the summer of 1990. He retained one of the top domestic relations attorneys in Los Angeles, if not the country, Neal Hersh, reputed to be *the* "divorce lawyer to the stars." Hersh learned the ropes from five years as protégé to the charismatic attorney he terms the "Godfather of family law in Beverly Hills," Simon Taub, whose one and only brief marriage had ended in divorce. Taub knew to not try marriage for a second time; it was all too risky. Instead, he handled the emotional and angry marital issues of big stars for big bucks.

Following in Taub's footsteps, Hersh made his reputation in the late eighties in the glare of the tabloids, representing the actress Robin Givens in her divorce from the boxer Mike Tyson. Then came the headline-making Brad Pitt–Jennifer Aniston divorce. He handled buxom *Baywatch* star Pamela Anderson's divorce from Kid Rock. And he was in Halle Berry's corner in her divorce bout with Eric Benet. Kim Basinger retained him in her complex divorce case with Alec Baldwin. He was there for a number of the stars in the *Real Housewives of Beverly Hills* reality TV show. And even some of the Kardashian women enlisted his services long after their father had passed on.

But Hersh has never forgotten his relationship with Robert Kardashian, and how hurt he was in the wake of catching Kris cheating on him.

"Robert was emotionally devastated," when they first met to discuss Kris's adultery and what the cuckolded husband should do about it within the bounds of the law, recalled Hersh. "The divorce was not something he was happy about. He was a family guy, and all he was interested in was his wife and his children. But he and Kris had different ideas about what that entailed. So he was very distraught, and he was wishing the divorce didn't have to happen. I think he wanted to salvage the marriage despite anything Kris might have done in terms of having a boyfriend.

"There was an age difference," continued Hersh. "Kris wanted to go out and have a different lifestyle than Robert did. But Robert was a homebody, *the* most dedicated, loving, kind person and father that you could ever imagine. He was Armenian, but he was like the typical nice Jewish guy who wanted to keep his family."

Hersh met the defendant, Kris, for the first time when he arrived at the Kardashians' Tower Lane estate for a settlement meeting and "to divide furniture, which I rarely did. Lawyers don't really go to people's homes to divide up their crap, but Robert asked me. And Kris was very gracious. When I looked at Kris I didn't think to myself, 'Oh, Christ, she's going around with her exercise guy or whoever he was.' Kris was endearing."

The divorce went smoothly and without much anger, he stated.

But that's not the way Kris saw it. The divorce, she asserts, "got ugly."

She, too, had hired a lawyer to the stars, Dennis Wasser, who specialized in representing famous athletes and Hollywood celebrities who wished to end their marriages. A female friend of Kris's, the wife of a professional ballplayer, had recommended Wasser, but Kris had to borrow ten thousand dollars from the friend in order to pay the high-powered Wasser's retainer. His law firm, with his daughter, Laura Wasser, as a partner, would have their own star lineup of clients: Angelina Jolie, Maria Shriver, Mariah Carey, Ashton Kutcher—and the list went on, and one day would include Kim Kardashian.

At one point during the divorce, and as Wasser's client, Kris got a restraining order that banned both her and her husband from "molesting, attacking, striking, threatening, sexually assaulting, battering, or otherwise disturbing the peace of the other party."

Kris claims she was dead broke when he filed for divorce. "I had no money—not one dollar." And now, without him, she claimed she was lost when it came to handling money because he took care of all their finances. Kris had been treated like such a delicate princess by Kardashian that by the end of the marriage she didn't have a clue regarding the cost of her Beverly Hills lifestyle.

The ex–junior flight attendant, who once earned five hundred dollars a month, but had moved on up to the Beverly Hills big-time, didn't even know how much the gardener got paid, let alone what their monthly mortgage payment was. The only credit card she used was for the upscale market where her help shopped for the family's groceries. She had no idea whether there were monthly payments due on the family's fancy cars, which she drove. Her first-world complaint was, "I had never paid a bill."

And she swore she'd never be in the position of having "no power" ever again when all this was in the past.

In her book, Kris maintains that Kardashian had canceled her credit cards and that her grocery shopping privileges at an upscale food market had been revoked, and her lowest moment came when she was faced with the realization that she couldn't afford to "buy pizza" for her then-chubby children—Kourtney, Kim, Khloé, and little Robert Jr., then ranging in age from two to eleven.

Not so, asserted Hersh.

COUNCIL

Student Council is composed of Student Body officers and other elected leaders. Under the guidance of Mr. Joseph Drury, they plan and supervise all student events.

As head of Student Council this past semester, Bob Kardashian has more than proved his leadership as displayed by excellent executive ability tempered with a wonderful sense of humor, good judgement and fairness at all times. Bob leaves Dorsey held in the high esteem of all those who know him.

Robert Kardashian, the patriarch of the reality TV Kardashian brood—Kim, Kourtney, Khloé, and Rob—was a social and academic star in his class at Dorsey High School, in Los Angeles. In his friend, Donna Tom's yearbook, the future lawyer and entrepreneur wrote "best of success." (DORSEY YEARBOOK)

BEST ALL-AROUND	BEST DRESSED
Sylvia Duran	Joan Salatich
Bob Kardashian	Bob Kardashian

Robert Kardashian was one of his Dorsey High School class's most popular, and was considered a jokester by some. Others worshipped him as best looking and most athletic. Later, he would become close pal and confidant of O. J. Simpson, and one of Simpson's lawyers in the "murder trial of the century." (DORSEY YEARBOOK)

Kristen Mary "Kris" Houghton, the future "momager" of the Kardashians' immense success, fame, and infamy, clowns it up at sixteen with Clairemont High School pal Joan Zimmerman, in a 25-cent photo booth, in their cookie-cutter University City development, in Clairemont, California. (COURTESY OF JOAN ZIMMERMAN)

The future Kris Kardashian Jenner's Clairemont High School yearbook graduation photo. She was uninvolved in school activities and couldn't wait to get out in the world and meet and marry a wealthy man, with her mother, Mary Jo, as her enabler. (COLEMAN-RAYNER, LLC)

Indictments returned in meat bribe case

LOS ANGELES (AP)—A federal grand jury has indicted 13 persons and five Los Angeles area meat packing firms on charges of bribing U.S. Department of Agriculture meat graders.

The FBI announced Tuesday 11 of the indicted had been arrested, another has already been arraigned on similar charges arising from a different complaint and the 13th person was expected to surrender today. Five of the indicted were owners of meat packing plants. The charges stem from alleged offers of bribes ranging from $60 to $300 per day to federal meat graders to upgrade beef quality. Agriculture Department graders are responsible for determin-

ing whether meat should be classified USDA Prime, Choice, Good or some lower quality.

Asst. U.S. Atty. Robert C. Bonner said the indictments "only scraped the surface" of the payoffs and a two-year probe of the meat industry by federal investigators would continue.

The FBI said none of the indictments involved any of the meat graders because those involved accepted money only to cooperate with authorities.

Bribery attempts included one instance in which a meat grader was offered money to overlook tapeworm-infested beef, officials said.

The firms indicted were: Highland Meat Packing

Co., O.K. Packing Co., Great Western Packing Co. and Apex Meat Co., all of Vernon, and Globe Packing Co. of San Fernando.

The 13 indicted were: owners, Aaron Magidow, 45, of Apex; Bernard Fineman, 48, of Highland; Peter B. Brun, of O.K. Packing; Rueben Krasn of Globe; and Maier S. Gerson, of Santa Ana Packing Co., Santa Ana, and employes Dale Clark, Martin S. Pollock; and Thomas Kardashian of Great Western; Ellsworth Eichinger of Apex: Donald Morgan of Santa Ana Packing; David Shubin and Ben Diehl of O.K. Packing; and Hugh Towle of Union Packing Co., Vernon.

George Bush

PRESIDENT OF THE UNITED STATES OF AMERICA

To All to Whom These Presents Shall Come, Greeting:
Be It Known, THAT THIS DAY THE PRESIDENT HAS GRANTED UNTO

THOMAS ARTHUR KARDASHIAN

A FULL AND UNCONDITIONAL PARDON

AND HAS DESIGNATED, DIRECTED AND EMPOWERED THE DEPUTY ATTORNEY GENERAL AS HIS REPRESENTATIVE TO SIGN THIS GRANT OF EXECUTIVE CLEMENCY TO THE ABOVE WHO WAS CONVICTED IN THE UNITED STATES DISTRICT COURT FOR THE CENTRAL DISTRICT OF CALIFORNIA ON AN INDICTMENT (DOC. NO. CR 74-962) CHARGING VIOLATION OF SECTION 201(f), TITLE 18, UNITED STATES CODE, AND ON NOVEMBER TWENTY-FIFTH, 1974, WAS PLACED ON THREE YEARS' PROBATION AND FINED TEN THOUSAND DOLLARS ($10,000).

IN ACCORDANCE WITH THESE INSTRUCTIONS AND AUTHORITY I HAVE SIGNED MY NAME AND CAUSED THE SEAL OF THE DEPARTMENT OF JUSTICE TO BE AFFIXED BELOW AND AFFIRM THAT THIS ACTION IS THE ACT OF THE PRESIDENT BEING PERFORMED AT HIS DIRECTION.

DONE AT THE CITY OF WASHINGTON, DISTRICT OF COLUMBIA ON January 18, 1993.

By Direction of the President
Deputy Attorney General

Scandal and shame rocked the Kardashian family in 1974 when Robert Kardashian's older brother, Tom, as this newspaper clip documents, was indicted and soon made a plea deal for bribing federal meat inspectors as an executive of his family's business, Great Western Packing. A long-held family secret, he lived under a dark cloud for two decades before he was granted a pardon by President George H. W. Bush.

After living under a dark cloud for some twenty years, Tom Kardashian, brother of Robert Kardashian and uncle of the current generation of famous and infamous Kardashians, received a pardon from President George H. W. Bush for his bribery conviction. (U.S. DEPARTMENT OF JUSTICE)

Kris Jenner's estranged father, Bob Houghton, with girlfriend, Leslie Johnson Leach, on his lap. She dumped him because of his excessive drinking. (COURTESY OF LESLIE JOHNSON LEACH)

After a rocky courtship, during which Robert Kardashian dated Priscilla Presley, he wed junior flight attendant Kris Houghton, a union officiated by Kardashian's confidant and minister, Pastor Kenn Gulliksen, who later witnessed the decline and fall of their marriage when Kris cheated on Kardashian. (COURTESY OF PASTOR KENN GULLIKSEN, VIA ROBERT KARDASHIAN)

When Kris was seven, and her sister, Karen, was four, their father, an emotional and abusive alcoholic, abandoned the family, which ended their troubled marriage. Mary Jo later remarried another drinker, but had him quit before they tied the knot. (COURTESY OF LESLIE JOHNSON LEACH)

Gorgeous Vicky Kron Thomsen poses for a pal in the blue dress she intended to wear when becoming Bob Houghton's second wife. But tragedy struck when he was killed and she was seriously injured when the Porsche he was driving while inebriated slammed head-on into a truck on their way to be married in Mexico. (COURTESY OF VICKY KRON THOMSEN)

Robert Kardashian became a born-again Christian in the wake of his family's bribery scandal. Here he and his longtime pastor Kenn Gulliksen and other fellow Christians gather at Gulliksen's home—from left to right Gulliksen and wife, Joanie, Pamela Rice, Happy Rue, and Kardashian. At dinner he revealed that a prophetess foretold the Kardashian name would become world famous. (COURTESY OF HAPPY RUE)

Tykes Kourtney and Kim with baby Khloé, who looks nothing like her sisters. Their father would later confide in close friends and his pastor that Khloé was not his biological child, but that he loved her and would raise her as his own. Both Khloé and her mother, Kris, would deny such tabloid gossip. (COURTESY OF PASTOR KENN GULLIKSEN, VIA ROBERT KARDASHIAN)

All grown up and looking hot, the Kardashian girls with their "momager" mother, Kris, at a benefit in the summer of 2010 for the Ovarian Cancer Research Fund, in Water Mill, N.Y. (BARRY TALESNICK-IPOL-GLOBE PHOTOS, INC.)

Fame, fortune, and infamy came to pals Paris Hilton and Kim Kardashian, both of whom made their first millions and launched their popularity by starring in separate sex videos with their boyfriends. (PHIL ROACH-GLOBE PHOTOS, INC.)

Kim's boyfriend, dapper William Ray Norwood Jr., better known as Ray J, was Kim's co-star in her porno film that became public in 2007, and Kim reportedly settled with Vivid Entertainment for $5 million. (LISA ROSE-GLOBE PHOTOS, INC.)

Khloé married 6'10" Lamar Odom in September 2009, but the pair would have a turbulent union. He would have problems with drugs and alcohol, and made headlines in 2015 when he was found unconscious in a Las Vegas brothel. Their marriage ended in divorce after much public and private drama. (NANCY KASZERMAN/ZUMAPRESS.COM)

Kris Jenner's aging mother, Mary Jo, is helped into a car by her daughter Kris Kardashian Jenner's boyfriend of the moment, Corey Gamble. According to sources, Mary Jo was Kris's "enabler" in finding and marrying rich men beginning when Kris was still in high school.

(MICHAEL WRIGHT/WENN.COM)

Robert Arthur "Rob" Kardashian, only son of the late attorney Robert Kardashian and his then wife, the future Kris Jenner. Like his sisters, Rob became a tabloid and reality TV fixture. Here with his one-time fiancée, Blac Chyna, who had his baby daughter, Dream Renée Kardashian, in 2016. (MJT/ADMEDIA)

Kim Kardashian West, showing off her famous derriere for the paparazzi at the 2015 Costume Institute Benefit Gala in New York City, with her third husband Kanye West, the sometimes troubled rapper and designer, and the father of their two children. Together, the tabloids have dubbed them "Kimye." (STARMAXWORLDWIDE)

Not long before a gang of veteran thieves broke into Kim Kardashian West's hotel room in Paris in October 2016 and stole some $10 million worth of jewelry, leaving her tied up, she is shown here being escorted by her muscular bodyguard. (STARMAXWORLDWIDE)

Kris Jenner with her boyfriend, Corey Gamble, described by Britain's Daily Mail as her "toyboy lover" as spotted together during Paris fashion week in 2016 when Kim was robbed of a fortune in diamonds. (STARMAXWORLDWIDE)

Before Gold Medal Olympian Bruce Jenner married into the Kardashian clan, he was wed to Elvis Presley's longtime girlfriend Linda Thompson, who published a 2016 memoir revealing her long-held secret that he was a cross-dresser with sexual identity problems. (GLOBE PHOTOS, INC.)

Kris Kardashian married Bruce Jenner not long after her Kardashian divorce was finalized after she was caught having an affair. She would later claim that she had no knowledge of Jenner's long-rumored sexual dysfunction, which was not an issue in their divorce. (KEVAN BROOKS/ADMEDIA)

Worldwide headlines proclaimed Jenner's transition from Bruce, who famously shed his athletic male image to that of towering reality TV beauty Caitlyn Marie with big feet, strong arms, and supple breasts. Here she rides in a limo to attend a party in London. (STARMAXWORLDWIDE)

Football great, movie star, and rent-a-car spokesman O. J. Simpson in happier times with his mother and his gorgeous, much younger wife, Nicole Brown Simpson, who he met when she was an eighteen-year-old waitress in Beverly Hills. In 1995 she and a friend were murdered and Simpson was charged with the crime. (GLOBE PHOTOS, INC.)

Before the infamous murders in exclusive Brentwood, Simpson was a friend of the rich and famous. Here he is paling around with baseball all-star Keith Hernandez and the future president of the United States. (GLOBE PHOTOS, INC.)

The shock on longtime friend and O. J. attorney Robert Kardashian's face, a reaction felt by many across the country when a jury returned a not guilty verdict in the murder trial of the century. It was Kardashian's last hurrah. He died of throat cancer at fifty-nine in 2003. There are those who say he would be "turning over in his grave" with how his children turned out. (LISA ROSE-GLOBE PHOTOS, INC.)

"Quite frankly, I don't remember cutting her off," he said. "It isn't my style to cut credit cards off. It's my style to put a limit on credit cards, and the reason is not so altruistic. Walking into a courtroom when you cut off a family from all funds is very risky business, because the judge thinks you're a prick, and what do I need that for. My recollection is that the divorce was very amicable, pretty amicable. I don't think we ever walked into a courtroom. I don't remember it being contentious at all."

But according to court papers, Kardashian signed an affidavit on January 11, 1991, swearing that the previous December he had ended any form of employment he had and declared, "I am now unemployed and have no income," which clearly was an excuse for not helping Kris financially.

Kardashian began representing himself near the end of the divorce case, which Hersh termed a "strategic decision" that he was on board with, but he declined in 2016 to state why in order to avoid breaching his long-deceased friend's "client privilege confidentiality." But another well-informed source claimed Kardashian wanted to "play hardball with Kris; he was furious, he didn't want to give her a dime, and he probably felt Neal was being too nice of a guy."

Kris must have taken note of Hersh's compassion, because he later would represent her daughters in marital issues. When Khloé married the six-foot-ten black pro basketball player Lamar Odom in 2009, it was Hersh who handled the prenup at Odom's request, which was "cleared" by Kris. When Kim divorced Damon Thomas, the first of her three African-American husbands, it was Hersh who handled the case.

While remaining friends with Kardashian, Hersh also had developed a bond with Kris through a friendship Hersh's wife had with Kris's "very close friend" Stephanie Schiller, the ex-wife of the writer Lawrence Schiller, who later penned a book about the O.J. case, using Robert as a key source. But that collaboration would not turn out to be in Kardashian's best interest.

And the relationship between Kris and Hersh would end on a sour note, too. A gossip item about the Kardashians had appeared in the press, and Kris freaked out and blamed the leak on Hersh. "I said it wasn't me," said Hersh, "but she got very upset with me. I'm sure she'd say hello to me," he believed, but thereafter he had lost all the Kardashian women's domestic affairs business, which, in their bizarre lives, could make for sizeable billables. "But they didn't use me again. They didn't reach out to me," said Hersh. "Their business manager refers them to Laura Wasser, who is much more age appropriate for Kim and her group. But I don't think there's bad blood."

ODDLY, KRIS KARDASHIAN DIDN'T THINK having an affair would anger her husband to the extent that he would actually file for divorce. What was she thinking? Nor did she believe that her affair combined with the divorce would have a negative impact on her children, but the girls and boy were devastated. "They cried," their mother stated. "It was horrible."

Years later Kourtney, Kim, and Khloé would dedicate their first book, published in 2010, *Kardashian Konfidential*, not to their momager mother, who helped make them wealthy reality TV stars and more, but rather to their late father, who "without you, we know we would not be the women we are today. We know that every blessing in our lives is because you are our angel watching over us. . . . We are sisters because of you. We love you, Daddy."

A publishing source with intimate knowledge of the book project recalled, "The girls specifically wanted to cite their dad and not their mother in the dedication, and I'm sure they saw it as a put-down of her."

And Rob Kardashian, the troubled namesake who was just sixteen when his father died a quick and horrific death from cancer, honored him in a special way, too, recalled his uncle, Tom Kardashian.

"My nephew came up to me and said, 'Uncle Tom, you're not going to like this.' Rob would always preface with those words because he already knew I would not like what he was going to tell me. It was about a tattoo, a tattoo of my brother's image that Rob had put on his [left] forearm in memory of his father. And he says, 'I know you're not going to like this. I know you're not going to like what you're going to see. But I had my reasons.' "

Tom Kardashian said he wasn't happy about what Rob had done "just like I'm not happy about anybody's tattoos." But he said he understood why his nephew had had the ink applied to his body and close to his heart. "It was his way of memorializing the father he lost so early in his life. All of that was after my brother was gone."

AROUND THE TIME KARDASHIAN filed for divorce, and just when Kris thought the self-inflicted cloud over her couldn't get any darker, her mother, Mary Jo—her "mentor" and "support system"—was diagnosed with colon cancer, which she'd survive, after having previously beaten breast cancer.

According to Kris, Robert, after filing for divorce, had moved out of their Tower Lane estate.

But that's not the way Larry Kraines remembered the tense and strange situation. Despite the Kardashians' divorce drama, they remained under the same roof, he said.

"They both stayed in the house together, and I'm thinking Robert stayed longer than *most* guys when they get separated and file for divorce and are pissed with their wives," he said, looking back to that time. "I don't think Kris really had a place to go, and Robert was probably playing a heavy hand. He was a stubborn guy, and didn't want to leave, so they went back and forth, back and forth arguing. She wouldn't leave, and he wouldn't leave, and that went on for some time, and it was more strange than not. I'd been once divorced, and once you made a decision to get out, one or the other got out. But not in their case."

Continued Kraines: "Because Joyce [Kraines's wife] and Kris were close I didn't want to get in the middle of who was doing who. But

Robert would call me, and we'd sit and talk, and he was angry, and I told him, 'It's time to move on.' But he was saying, 'She's the mother of my children. How could she do that to me?'

"I felt sorry for both of them, but more particularly for the kids, and they were good kids. I told Robert, 'You've got to stay close to the kids. Don't get into a pissing contest with Kris.' But Robert was very upset, very depressed, like you'd normally be when you're losing a wife and children and a home, and you're basically starting all over again."

Despite all the problems Kris had ignited with her affair, she still couldn't get Todd Waterman out of her system. Amazingly, she still hoped to be with him.

On a weekend when Robert had left the house and taken the children to Palm Springs, Kris tried to reach Waterman by phone. Unsuccessful, and even though it was the middle of the night, she drove to his apartment, which she had helped furnish. There, she claimed, she discovered the young bachelor in bed with another woman.

Her instant response?

"You fucking son of a bitch!"

In her book, she says she suddenly realized she had ruined her life to be with him.

But after finding him with another woman, she still wasn't over him.

As she stated, "That's how crazy I was."

She had actually invited Waterman to go on a weekend ski trip with her close friends Candace and Steve Garvey—he a businessman and former first baseman for the Los Angeles Dodgers and, at the end of his career in the late eighties, the San Diego Padres. During his time at bat, he was a Most Valuable Player and all-star, who had earned the sobriquet "Mr. Clean" because of his wholesome public image in baseball.

In her book, Kris portrays her pal Candace and her hubby the iconic ballplayer as a golden couple, a virtual Barbie and Ken.

But Steve Garvey had a tarnished personal life unmentioned in Kris's tome.

In the same time frame that Kris was having her affair with Waterman, Garvey's first wife, a local L.A. TV personality, published a tell-all entitled *The Secret Life of Cyndy Garvey*. She was the mother of Garvey's two children, and one of her shocking allegations was that he had bizarrely given her away after seven years of marriage to a friend of hers, the award-winning composer Marvin Hamlisch, after the two men privately met in the Garveys' den. "He was giving me away," she wrote. "This was . . . too cold-blooded, even for Steve," who had a reputation as a womanizer, and had a number of women in his life. Although he did not deny that he spoke with Hamlisch, Garvey remembers the conversation differently, claiming that his concern was with Cyndy's happiness. Hamlisch, who died in 2012, married a woman named Terre Blair, an Ohio TV weather girl, the same year Cyndy Garvey's book was published.

Steve Garvey later met Kris's close friend the former Candace Thomas, a divorcée in her mid-thirties with two adolescent daughters. They got engaged on the night of the 1989 Super Bowl, within weeks after meeting at a Deer Valley, Utah, ski event.

People magazine, in a 1993 profile of Garvey and Candace, under the headline, "A Swinger No More," noted that at the time Garvey married Candace, a popular bumper sticker read, "Honk If You're Carrying Steve Garvey's Love Child." Kris's friend Candace was quoted as saying, "The pain was excruciating. We cried and cried." Back then Garvey, a staunch Republican, supported George H. W. Bush for president, and considered a run for the U.S. Senate from California despite what *People* called the "tacky publicity."

The tabloids were having as much of a field day with the Garveys' private life as they would later with the bizarro world of the Kardashians.

In April 2006, the *Los Angeles Times* detailed how Garvey was "plagued" with debt, even though he and Candace owned a mansion in tony Park City, Utah. "For years, Garvey and his wife, Candace, have neglected bills large and small, leaving dozens of people who either worked for them or sold them merchandise wondering if they were ever going to be paid," the newspaper reported.

A lawyer who reportedly was owed $235,000 by Garvey declared, "Once a Dodger, always a dodger."

Despite the personal problems, and at Kris Kardashian's invitation, Candace Garvey instantly became a close member of Kris's hot, all-girl, hard-partying, big-spending Brentwood–Beverly Hills entourage, along with Nicole Simpson, Faye Resnick, and a few others. Like them, Garvey would be a witness for the prosecution at the O. J. Simpson murder trial.

Blond, blue/green-eyed and with a grand-slam home-run figure, Garvey was everything Kris liked her friends to look, plus back in high school Candace was on the cheerleader squad, which Kris had failed to make.

Asked in 2015 about Kris's close female friends, her former brother-in-law, Tom Kardashian, responded, "Those are all—sorry, I just can't say the word."

At the ski resort with Waterman and the Garveys, Kris hoped her hot times with her decade-younger lover could be rekindled. The setting was perfect: an outdoor Jacuzzi, a crackling fireplace in every room, champagne—until she spotted him flirting with sexy, much-younger Hawaiian Tropic bimbos who also were skimpily flitting around the resort.

She was furious.

When they got home, Kris told Waterman it was over. Seeing him eyeing women who were almost half her age, and with even bigger breast implants, Kris had come to the realization that she had made a "*ginormous* mistake" by giving up Robert and all the luxury that came with him for a sexual fling. Instead of criticizing Kardashian as a lousy lover and kisser, as she had done after getting a taste of Waterman, she was once again schizophrenically lauding him as "The greatest guy in the world . . . who encouraged me to be a good Christian," according to the story she hawked to readers of her book.

Meanwhile, back at Tower Lane, with both parents stubbornly refusing to vacate the luxe premises as their divorce proceeded, Kris Kardashian noted that her children were "living on a battlefield."

Joni Migdal observed what was happening and maintained that Kardashian was "always there" for his children. "He did his best to be a good father. They always had wonderful birthday parties. They went to church. Back then they were all down-to-earth kids, and the divorce devastated all of them. And there was the anger that Robert felt toward Kris, and the anger that Robert felt toward his life and himself.

"It was *horrible*."

DURING THE WHOLE DIVORCE and separation mess, Kris had befriended another young, attractive mother, Anita Friedman, whose unidentical twin daughters, Johanna and Elizabeth, had become chums with little Khloé Kardashian at the public El Rodeo Elementary School, in Beverly Hills, and the children had a number of playdates together.

A Messianic Jew—one who believes that Jesus is the Messiah—Friedman was the wife of a journalist and author, Robert A. Friedman, who, like Robert Kardashian, had become a born-again Christian. One of his books was entitled *What's a Nice Jewish Boy Like You Doing in the First Baptist Church?* He also wrote dialogue, she said, for Mickey Rooney, and boasted that his father had invented the flexible drinking straw, and the Sheaffer refill pen.

While Anita Friedman had no knowledge at the time of Kris's affair with Todd Waterman, she knew her marriage was on the rocks, that there was a separation in progess, and that the turmoil at home was having an emotional impact on six-year-old Khloé, who she recalls was "sweet, but *very* passive." And Friedman viewed Kris as a "bored housewife" who sported Chanel everywhere she went.

Later, when it all came out about Kris's affair and the divorce, Friedman said she looked back to that time and realized that Kris must have been thrilled knowing she could run off to meet her lover and be able to drop off Khloé "for a playdate, and Khloé was my girls' go-to friend."

And Friedman found her to be a wonderful child.

"I remember looking at Khloé at Christmas break, and she's standing there with a cage with a guinea pig in it and she was by herself and everybody was getting picked up, and I go, 'Hi, sweetheart, are you getting picked up?' And she says, 'Yes, my daddy's picking me up.' And when I looked at her, I thought, this girl has no guile whatsoever. She's just the sweetest, and the nicest—very unpretentious, not pushy, and I think my daughters kind of pretty much ruled her—'let's play this, let's play that.'

"She had those beautiful greenish-blue eyes and that golden hair and she did absolutely look different from the rest of them," continued Friedman. "Lately, when they [the tabloid and celebrity media] are showing possible fathers for Khloé, she looks just like that hairdresser, and he looks like Khloé—they have the same facial structure, and those eyes."

Later, when Khloé was a teenager, she was working with her older sisters in a boutique they had in the L.A. suburb of Calabasas, and Friedman and her daughters spotted her there. She looked completely different and had lost her childhood cuteness.

"She looked like the dregs," recalled Friedman. "Black hair and black bangs, and very goth."

In the midst of the Kardashians' divorce battle, Kris had invited Friedman to a birthday party for little Khloé, and because it was a swim party at the Kardashian pool she decided to stay to keep a watch over her daughters because Kris didn't have a lifeguard present, and it was "just a free-for-all type party."

The only man present was Khloé's father, who Friedman had never before met, and Kardashian was seated "away from everybody," cleaning a separate spa pool with a net on his property. Since Kris was visibly ignoring him and not making any introductions, the gregarious Mrs. Friedman, seeing how glum and lonely he appeared, decided to introduce herself.

"So I went and sat with him," she said, "and he was *very* downcast, *very* sad, *very* disturbed, and *very* angry because they were breaking up, even though they were still living in the same house. He was very cordial, very sweet, but *very* down, but not just depressed—it was more of an anger, and he had a right to be angry. He was looking at the kids in the pool in the distance and he seemed sad.

"I was talking to him and the talk turned to England because my family had lived there for a year, and he says out of the blue, 'I have a castle in Ireland.' Castles in Ireland weren't that pricey in those days, and since this was Beverly Hills, it didn't strike me as an outrageous idea that he had one in Ireland." (However, no one in Kardashian's circle recalls that he had ever owned such a property.)

Friedman noted that there was absolutely no communication between Kris and Kardashian during the party. Kris was in a bikini, and carrying Rob, then about three, and "she's got her sister with her and they were whispering and giggling about Mr. Kardashian. There was great tension in the air. There was a great disconnect, and there was animosity."

What surprised Friedman, too, was how Kris looked stripped down to a skimpy swimsuit.

"It's not like she had lard, it didn't look like she had cellulite, but she didn't look that great," recalled Friedman. "But I'm looking at her and I remember thinking, this gal is divorcing her husband and she's got four children, but she's looking like she's getting ready to be over the hill—not run-down or anything, but not looking her best, even though she was a pretty woman."

At one point, Friedman walked into the Kardashian home and the first thing that struck her was an immense oil painting of the Kardashian family "when they were all younger, and wow, did Kris look beautiful in that picture, which was the focal point of the living room."

Wandering to the kitchen, she stopped suddenly in the entrance to avoid interrupting the tender scene she had come upon.

"Kourtney and Kim were hugging Robert, saying, 'We love you, Daddy.' They kept telling him how much they loved him, and that they were going to miss him because he was going to San Francisco for the weekend, and he had his bags with him."

SOME MONTHS LATER, EL RODEO Elementary was holding an open house for parents and, Friedman had never forgotten, "Kris rolls in and she now looks *really* good. She's reinvented herself, and she looks really skinny, and she's wearing this short little pencil skirt and a beautiful, gorgeous Irish green Chanel jacket and carrying a Chanel purse, of course, and who does she have in tow but Bruce Jenner, who was her new beau, but they weren't married yet, and he's kind of hanging out, and he was *not* in a pencil skirt at the time.

"Today I can just imagine Robert Kardashian *watching* this whole Kardashian-Jenner insanity from heaven. Who would have thought that chick in the bathing suit carrying baby Rob around at that party for little Khloé was going to do what she was going to do. I thought her glory days were almost over back then. Little did I know."

EIGHTEEN

Enter Jenner

Bruce Jenner, the gold medal Olympian with a mind-boggling secret, entered Kris Kardashian's dysfunctional world courtesy of Candace Garvey. It was late in 1990 and Jenner—having just turned forty-one a few days before Halloween, his favorite holiday; he loved to dress up—had been divorced for four years from his second wife, Elvis's former live-in, Linda Thompson. When Garvey, playing cupid, arranged to set up Kris with Jenner, he was then the prolific father of three sons and a daughter from two failed marriages. But he was open for a new and better relationship; a three-time loser *back then* he wasn't.

Jenner was intrigued when his friend Candace told him about her friend Kris, especially when he learned that she was a stylish dresser, and Bruce always liked the way certain women outfitted themselves. Garvey, for instance, favored a preppy look and, according to Kris, "dressed like a Ralph Lauren model." For Jenner, that was a turn-on, kind of butch but still sexy. But back then, long before he became Caitlyn Marie Jenner, he didn't care much about how he himself dressed, at least in public, and usually was attired in sweats like the jock that he was reputed to be.

As Kris put it after meeting him, "He had been living alone too long and didn't care about his appearance."

It would be almost a quarter century later that Bruce Jenner, having transitioned in 2015 to her new identity—with nails and toes and lips painted red—could openly be all dolled up like she had always wanted to be, and with famous designers vying to dress her.

Candace Garvey thought Bruce and Kris, then with eight kids between them, would make for a perfect match. Kris wasn't so sure, but agreed with Garvey that she'd go out on a blind date with Jenner, mainly just to get Garvey off her back.

Her divorce still wasn't finalized, but she went on her pal's word that Bruce Jenner was one "great guy."

Based on Kris's checkered history, golf courses and racetracks were her usual venues for meeting future lovers—for instance, Cesar Sanudo she had met at the Hawaiian Open, Kardashian she had spotted at the Del Mar Thoroughbred Club—so it was no surprise that her first get-together and date with Bruce Jenner was at the Riviera Country Club in Pacific Palisades, where he and Steve Garvey were playing in a tournament. Jenner was a minor sports celebrity earning a meager living off his name, appearing in obscure athletic events, or giving paid speeches to organizations such as the Boy Scouts of America, who still revered him as a long-ago Olympic headliner.

But the moment Kris laid eyes on him she thought he was "adorable," and he spontaneously gave her a big "bear hug."

The next day he called and invited her to come to Florida with him, where he was going to be in some sporting events for a few days, and she jumped at the opportunity. During that trip she discovered that her still-far-in-the-future reality TV husband turned transgender diva was "such an exciting guy. . . . We just loved each other from the start."

By early 1991, Kris, still entangled in divorce proceedings with Kardashian, was sleeping with Jenner and rated him her "best lover."

But it wasn't all a bed of roses.

Todd Waterman, Kris's other "best lover," later claimed that they were still seeing each other even after she had gotten involved with Jenner.

"I wouldn't say we were dating, we were still communicating," he asserted in 2013. "She was still coming over to the apartment, and we were still sleeping together when she had started dating Bruce. I would say that she was getting serious with him and we were still occasionally seeing each other, and it was messing with my head. I think we just had a hard time keeping away from each other."

In her book, Kris made it seem that Waterman had just suddenly appeared out of the blue again, and she made no mention of continuing a physical relationship with him.

When gossip items began appearing about the relatively long-forgotten, twice previously married Bruce Jenner suddenly being romantically involved with the then publicly unknown Kris Kardashian—items that attention-hungry Kris herself might have leaked—Waterman showed up "on a wild and drunken binge" late one night at Tower Lane, Kris claims, yelling, "Fucking Bruce Jenner!? That is horrible. I want you back!" She says she convinced him to leave.

He next reached her on her car phone a few days later, and Jenner picked up and told him to take a hike, or else.

"Finally, I was able to close the door forever" on Waterman, who Kris still identified as "Ryan" in her book.

Jenner then had a Hamburger Hamlet mano a mano with Kardashian and told him, Kris claims, that she wanted nothing out of the divorce—not the Tower Lane estate, worth millions, none of the luxury cars, nothing—except for child support, if he would just end this "nightmare of a divorce."

Kardashian, who would have fought tooth and nail to avoid giving Kris one red cent because of her blatant promiscuity and mistreatment of him, was thrilled with the offer, and agreed without hesitation.

In early 1991, Kris called her lawyer and told him it was a done deal. The Kardashian marriage was over.

DURING THE DIVORCE PROCEEDINGS a six-page psychological profile was done, which showed Kris to have "histrionic and narcissistic traits," and stated that both she and Kardashian were prone to "impulsivity" and had "a strong need for attention." The report, first quoted in a celebrity weekly, also disclosed that Kardashian had a "more intense need for closeness and the approval of others," while Kris appeared to have "less need for others' approval, but a greater need that her sense of specialness be mirrored." The profile went on to state that Kris had a "Cinderella attitude where situations resulted in everyone living 'happily ever after.' " And Kardashian was viewed as "impulsive when overwhelmed."

Along with child support, the deal Jenner and Kardashian hashed out at that Sunset Boulevard burger joint was that Kris and the children could remain in Kardashian's Tower Lane estate—his prize bought with the several million dollars he had made from the sale of *Radio & Records*—for a period of six months, until she could find other housing. But Jenner, who had little money of his own, who was living in a dumpy little house and "was no Rockefeller," according to Kris, also moved into Robert's beloved domicile. To steam Kardashian even more, Jenner brought with him as temporary tenants his own parents, Esther and Bill Jenner, to enjoy all the Kardashian luxury.

Simply put, Kardashian was "very pissed off," according to friends.

While Kris didn't mention in her book where Robert settled after she, Jenner, his folks, and Kardashian's children became the sole temporary occupants of Tower Lane, it was his childhood friend, close confidante Joni Migdal who gave her emotionally wounded one-time lover shelter from the marital storm.

"When she asked him to move out of Tower Lane and he moved into my house, and Bruce Jenner moved into his house with his parents,

Robert was devastated," said Migdal. "And he turned from being the sweet, wonderful friend I had for a lot of my life to being an angry, unsettled, depressed human being. I have always adored Robert. He and I have always been best friends, but he just changed with that whole thing with Bruce moving into his house."

When the move happened, Kris had also asked Robert for a "lot of money," and, as Migdal recalled the situation, Kardashian told her he'd give her not a penny. "She needed lots of money to support the kids. I said, 'Robert, you've got four kids, and now she has the kids and you've got to support them,' and he finally gave it to her, but he gave it to her unwillingly and with anger."

Migdal believed the stress, anger, and anxiety Kardashian felt was a factor in his cancer and his death a decade later. "And that's when he first started getting sick with his esophageal stuff, with serious acid reflux. . . . He had *never* been an angry man, but with the divorce with Kris he became an angry man."

For about three months, Kardashian stayed in the guest room of Migdal's Marina del Rey home with a view of the Pacific, but the beauty of the setting did nothing to alleviate his depression and anger. Migdal tried as best she could to help him through. After breakfast, she would run with him on the beach, and they would have long talks "for many, many hours," she'd never forgotten. "We'd talk about his anger, how Kris could do this to him, how she could have Bruce move into his home. Robert was *not* happy. He was very angry. He was devastated. He *lost* it."

Kardashian couldn't take it anymore and decided he wanted his house back and vacated—with Kris, with her lover Jenner, with her lover Jenner's parents, and even with his own beloved kids, out of there. He just wanted to be back in the home he loved—his Beverly Hills version of Manderley, and with all his possessions, but without all the gothic drama.

But he was in for still another depressing shocker.

Kris and the gang had trashed the place.

"When they eventually left that beautiful, beautiful house, it was a mess," asserted Migdal. "I was there when Robert was walking through after they all left. The kitchen was trashed. There was food everywhere. They had this quilted wallpaper and there was paint on it and crayon markings. They had just done everything they could to trash the place.

"Robert had spent so much money fixing it up when he bought it, so he was amazed—because it now looked like a squatter had come into the house and just written on the walls, damaged the place. It was *horrible*. There was writing all over the walls. The kitchen was burned. When Robert moved back in, the house was a mess, and that made him *really* angry."

Looking back to that time and the heated atmosphere between Robert and Kris, Migdal believed that the vandalism "was purposeful" and done because Kardashian had told them all "they needed to move out. They had been there for a few months."

Kardashian's other close friend, Larry Kraines, part of the same clique going back as many years as Migdal, was shocked when he heard about the damage, mainly because he had known Jenner far longer than Kris had and couldn't comprehend him participating in any form of vandalism. "Bruce was an outgoing guy, an interesting, nice guy. I can't imagine him doing anything like that."

The two had become acquainted in the late seventies, early eighties when Kraines's company, Kraco, founded by his father, was sponsoring Indy 500 cars and Jenner was then covering the Indy car races as an announcer for NBC Sports. "I know Bruce knew that Robert and I were closest friends, and Kris made no mistake about that. When Kris met Bruce and they later got married, we didn't communicate a lot. If I stayed close to someone it was my friend from high school, Robert."

In her book, Kris makes no mention of the mess she and Jenner left behind when they moved out of Tower Lane, as witnessed by Migdal and Kardashian. Instead, she simply states that she and Jenner leased a house in Malibu. She called the move a "nice transition . . . It got me out of Beverly Hills."

But once again she skipped over what had really happened.

Kardashian, in fact, had put up all, or most of the required rental money for Kris's new place after being convinced to help by his confidante Migdal. "I said, 'You have to do it. Your kids are going to live there, and you want them to live in a nice place.' His heart was so good. He was always generous in spirit."

On February 10, 1991, five months after they met, Jenner asked Kris to marry him. The big event happened at dinner over champagne (and Jenner was a beer drinker) with their friends Candace Garvey, who had first introduced them, her husband, Steve, and a mutual friend, the actress Mary Frann, a divorcée best known for playing Bob Newhart's wife in an eighties sitcom. Kris claimed that Jenner got down on one knee, the same fairy-tale claim she had made about Robert Kardashian on the day when he asked her to marry him.

Their wedding, his third, her second, took place on April 21, 1991, in the Bel-Air home of friends of his. Jenner was so obscure as a celebrity at that point, and Kris was an unknown in the public eye, so their union passed with little or no publicity.

"It was," she gloats, "the perfect day."

They would have one hell of a ride together before their next divorce, his third, her second, just before Christmas, 2014.

NINETEEN

Kissin' Cousins

In the late eighties, Robert Kardashian's close friend and pastor, Kenn Gulliksen, had gone east for a time to start a Vineyard church in Boston, and the two had lost touch during that horrific period when Kris had her affair, resulting in the tumultuous Kardashian marriage ending in divorce, and with Kris soon marrying Bruce Jenner.

All that was now in the past. Gulliksen and his wife, Joanie, had returned to California, with Kenn as North American Director of the Association of Vineyard Churches. The Gulliksens were spending some time in a condo loaned to them by a friend in Palm Desert, near Palm Springs. And it was there that the Gulliksens ran into Robert and the new woman in his life, Denice Ann Shakarian Halicki, and the two couples decided to catch up and have a long, relaxed lunch together.

As far as Gulliksen can recall, it was the first time he had met Denice, even though he knew much about her family history, and how her grandfather, Demos Shakarian, a wealthy and successful Armenian dairyman, had founded the influential Pentecostal-rooted Full Gospel Business-men's Fellowship International. Gulliksen had even met the charis-matic Demos in the past, and had attended some of the group's meetings featuring testimonies regarding miracle healings, and with adherents exuberantly speaking in tongues while praying.

And long before Gulliksen was introduced to Denice at that desert lunch, Kardashian had told him about how the Kardashians and the family of the famous Demos were related. But what now came as a surprise to Gulliksen was that his friend and fellow born-again Christian, Robert, was now seriously involved romantically with his third cousin, Denice. It was the relationship issue, that they were kissin' cousins, that gave the minister pause. But the open-minded man of the cloth under-stood how his friend could fall for such a stunning, sexy younger woman.

"I always knew Bob was attracted to glamorous women," noted the pastor. But Denice fit into a very special category of glamorous women, as pointed out by Gulliksen's middle son, then about twenty, who also was there at that lunch, and later "made a joke about what parts of Denice were real," recalled Gulliksen with a chuckle. "I'm not into plastic sur-gery and breast implants—I'm not into that look, but I was happy for Bob."

The pastor's view was that the woman snuggled up to Kardashian across the table in the restaurant, who was thirteen years his junior—even younger by two years than Kris was when Kardashian met her—resembled a real-life, silicone-enhanced, cosmetically redone love doll.

Denice had the look that Robert clearly savored, as evidenced by how he had served up thousands of dollars for Kris just before she cheated on him.

"Denice was very nice and very sweet, and she sat very close to Bob at lunch," recalled Gulliksen. "After all, he'd been through a lot and he had a need to kind of return to his roots, and Denice was both beauti-ful *and* Armenian."

• • •

WHEN DENICE BECAME ROMANTICALLY involved with her Kardashian cousin, she had recently been widowed by the sudden and freak death of her husband of little more than three months, the cult car-crash film-maker, Henry Blight "Toby" Halicki, who had made a bundle with his first big low-budget movie in 1974, called *Gone in 60 Seconds*.

During his relationship with Denice, the eccentric and creative film-maker had transformed her from a plain Jane Armenian-American girl who had attended the TV evangelist–founded, staunchly conservative Oral Roberts University in Tulsa, Oklahoma, which banned students from drinking, smoking, and having premarital sex, into a Barbie-esque bombshell.

"She had mousy brown hair, a flat chest, and a big, long Shakarian nose, and that's what she looked like when she first started out, and then came the remodeling," claimed the filmmaker's brother Bud Halicki. He said Toby spent thousands of dollars on plastic surgery to transform Denice. "She went from that mousy look and she got her second or third breast augmentation from a size 30 or 32 cup to a 40-something God-awful thing. They started with her eyes and then her proboscis [nose], and then her buttocks, and God knows what else."

At one point, Toby Halicki complained to his brother-in-law, Robert Glaser, about his "big-time" expenditures for Denice's beautification makeover. "He said that he had ten thousand dollars alone in the tits. I don't know if that was for each one. Toby made her all up. Her boobs were *way* oversized, and he put a lot of money in cosmetic changes. I saw her before all the work was done, and she was skinny and not a glamorous person at all. Toby did it with his money."

Forty-eight-year-old lifelong bachelor Halicki married thirty-two-year-old Shakarian on May 11, 1989. But on August 20, a little over three months after their Miami honeymoon, Halicki himself was gone in sixty seconds, killed instantly when a cable attached to a water tower snapped and severed a telephone pole that fell on him while filming his latest car-crash epic in the Buffalo area near Dunkirk, New York, where he grew up in a family of thirteen children with a father in the towing and wrecking business.

At the time of his death, Halicki had an estate with an estimated value of $14.7 million (but actually worth a lot more in the long run), and his widow, Denice, would fight tooth and nail for years with the Halicki family for every penny (and gold watch and Dick Tracy collectible toy) that she deemed was her property. And Robert Kardashian, who hadn't been licensed with the California Bar Association for many years, would aid her in that probate battle, acting as her legal advisor, but also hoping to make a bundle in fees and commissions.

"Eventually, love blossomed between them, and they were truly a wonderful couple," recalled a cousin, Michelle Willett Orist, who roomed with Denice for about a year after Halicki's sudden death. "To me, it appeared Robert always was quite amused by Denice. He got a kick out of her, and they had a very strong bond between the two of them, very connected. She trusted him and they worked really well together through those trying times. Robert was a very down-to-earth human being. He had a lot of flair and confidence, but his base was truly simple and down-to-earth."

Denice Shakarian Halicki declined to be interviewed for this book, claiming she was writing her own—a claim she has made for a number of years—and noting in an email that she had never spoken publicly about her relationship with Kardashian and the "depth, heights, and length of my life with Robert . . . I pray that you are guided by the truth, sincerity, joy, laughter, and love that precious Robert lived his life by, especially our life together. . . . My father and mother loved Robert and Toby as I did. May God guide you in love."

Denice's mother, blond, blue-eyed Evangeline "Vangie" Shakarian, of Norwegian descent, did break her family's silence, and noted that Kardashian "came in to help Denice with the [Halicki] estate and it got to be a little more than that. They were engaged for six years. Denice got Robert involved because he was part of the family. The Shakarians are related to the Kardashians, and Denice is a third cousin.

"Robert was very religious—very much so," continued Vangie. "He used to say to people, 'If you want to know who I am, here's who I am,' and he'd give them the book *The Happiest People on Earth*, about Demos Shakarian's life, who was Denice's grandfather." The book, which was first published in 1975 and had many reprints, was written by a husband-and-wife team who specialized in penning Christian-themed stories. Denice's father, Richard, who would take over the Full Gospel organization from his father, wrote a sequel, *Still the Happiest People*.

According to Vangie, "Denice was already involved with Kardashian regarding the Halicki estate when he was still going through his divorce with Kris in 1990–91, and the [Kardashian] kids still adore her. Robert kept asking her to get married. He was *begging* Denice to get married, but she wanted to finish out her husband Toby's estate, which was very complicated, and it was a big deal, and worth a lot of money."

Robert and Denice's close live-in relationship and engagement was underscored by a family-style Christmas card they mailed that had the panache of a page out of the chic Neiman Marcus Christmas catalog. It showed the master of the richly appointed house dapperly outfitted, with the well-coiffed mistress of the house, Denice, glamorously attired in an off-the-shoulder velvet gown and high heels. Robert's four brightly smiling children of divorce and of a philandering, now remarried mother—Kourtney, Kim, Khloé, and Rob Jr.—were seated on the festive garland-wrapped staircase.

"The Kardashian Family wishes you a Merry Christmas," reads the undated card. "May the Joy of the Lord be your strength. Nehemiah 8:10."

It was signed in gold letters, "Robert and Denice," with the names of the Kardashian children inscribed below.

In her memoir, Kris Kardashian Jenner made a single, brief mention of Denice. Kris and Jenner had moved from the rental that Kardashian had helped finance in Malibu to a rental in Beverly Hills in 1992 to be closer to the Kardashian girls' private school, Marymount, and to Tower Lane and their father, who would care for them when the new Mrs. Jenner and her husband were traveling.

If Kris was jealous of the new woman in her ex-husband's life, she gave no indication, but, instead, was rather complimentary. Robert, she stated, "was dating an amazing woman . . . whom I'm sure he was in love with. She was really, really cool, but especially amazing to my kids." She made no mention that her ex-husband and Denice were actually related, or anything about Denice's past marital history.

BUD HALICKI, WHO WAS co-executor of Toby's estate with Denice and did battle with her and her many lawyers, including Kardashian, was of the opinion that she was a gold digger, out to get every penny from the valuable estate of her husband of some ninety days.

Toby Halicki had always feared that when he died his multimillion-dollar estate would be fought over and consumed by legal costs and fees. In order to avoid such a terrible ending, his one-page will, which looked like it had been written in chicken scratches while the author was on an LSD trip, offered a simple solution: "Split the money, guys, and have a good time. No probate."

It didn't turn out that way.

Toby had specifically left Denice a 1987 Rolls-Royce and a dream home he was forever constructing on eight acres of land—then valued at as much as $8 million—in the tony Rolling Hills section of the Palos Verdes peninsula overlooking the Pacific south of L.A. Plus he willed her another $1.5 million in either "cash, cars, or property."

She claimed that she never received the latter but did convince a court that as Halicki's widow she should receive a "widow's allowance" that averaged about ten thousand dollars a month for almost two years and totaled $250,000. The administrator of the estate ordered the payments stopped, fearing they might make the estate insolvent.

By the time of his death, Toby's headquarters on Vermont Avenue in Gardena was piled high with an acre of model trains, cap pistols, Little Big Books, piggy banks, pedal cars, model cars, planes, boats, and more. On his desk was a Mickey Mouse telephone. In all, there were some 100,000 different toys that Halicki had collected over some fifteen years.

As the battle for his estate raged, a Los Angeles Superior Court judge ordered the liquidation of the collection, then owned fifty-fifty by the warring co-executors Bud Halicki and Denice—in hopes of ending the probate battle between the widow and the deceased's family, and finally settling the case.

At that point, Denice got her unlicensed legal counsel, cousin, and lover, Robert Kardashian, to oversee the sale of her late husband Toby's beloved toys, and hopefully get a healthy piece of the action out of the deal for himself.

A month after Kris became Mrs. Bruce Jenner, her ex-husband was already heavily involved in aiding and abetting his cousin and new love, Denice.

On May 22, 1991, Kardashian sent a letter—typed on official-looking stationery, with his name engraved in fancy script, and with his profession falsely listed as "Attorney-at-Law"—to Patrick McCarroll, the court-appointed executor handling the entire hellish Halicki estate matter.

Kardashian wrote that he was confirming conversations McCarroll had had with Jeffrey B. Wheeler of Rosenfeld, Meyer and Susman, one of the law firms retained by Denice, regarding "my authorization to obtain a sale" of the Halicki toy collection. "It was agreed," Kardashian continued, "that I am to receive Twenty Per Cent (20%) of the gross proceeds of any sale of said toy collection if the sale is consummated through my efforts. Said monies are to be paid immediately upon monies received by the estate. I shall have total negotiating power with the purchaser to negotiate a deal acceptable to the court. It is my understanding that One Million, One Hundred Fifty Thousand Dollars ($1,150,000.00) is the minimum for which I am authorized to sell said toy collection."

If the sale had gone off as Kardashian, and especially Denice, were hoping, the unlicensed lawyer would have walked away at the end of the day with a commission of a cool $230,000, and the widow of three months would have gotten the balance, $920,000, minus any fees. But the sale of the collectible playthings, just one fascinating piece of the wider Halicki estate, didn't happen the way they had hoped and planned, and it wound up in an auction, realizing little of its worth. As for Kardashian's role in the matter, Bud Halicki said, "He was like a shark, for sure." But he got not a penny out of the deal.

Kardashian also got caught for acting as Denice's lawyer, but without a law license to practice.

The matter involved a yearlong trial continuance requested by Kardashian of Denice's probate cases. In an August 1994 letter to the Halicki estate trial judge, Robert Feinerman, an attorney for the law firm of Kindel & Anderson pointed out: "The State Bar advises that Mr. Kardashian was not an active member of the State Bar. . . . Therefore, it is not clear how he could have been Ms. Halicki's 'principal legal advisor' during a time when he was not permitted to practice law."

Kardashian quickly got his law license restored.

Bud Halicki had spent many days in court with Denice during the probate fight, and Robert Kardashian always was a part of the scene even though Bud asserted that Denice had "at least six major law firms representing her" at different times. "But every time she'd come to court Robert Kardashian would make a grand entrance and she'd say, 'There's *my* Robert. Here comes *my* Robert,' and it was disgusting. Robert was advising her on *everything*. No matter her law firm, Robert would be telling her what he *thought* was necessary. He *never* once spoke to me. There was no conversation in any way, shape, or form. He wouldn't even look in my general direction. He sat with her and it was obvious to me that he was her next new catch."

Among those in the Halicki family sued by Denice was Toby's sister, Tara, and her husband, Robert Glaser. The widow claimed they had a very expensive gold watch that had belonged to Toby and some other items, and she wanted them returned to her. "She didn't get anything from me, but we had to hire a lawyer," Glaser said.

When the Glasers flew to Los Angeles to appear in court with Denice, they met Kardashian in the courthouse and saw that Denice had permitted Kardashian "to drive Toby's white Rolls-Royce [that Denice inherited]. I saw Kardashian in it," recalled Glaser. "He was a little, short squirt, and I don't know how he could see over the steering wheel."

TWENTY

Fatal Friendship

Robert Kardashian's close friendship and business partnership of more than two decades with O. J. Simpson—a tight bond that would end horrifically—didn't begin on the campus of their alma mater, USC, or on a football field as most believe. Their brother-like relationship was actually first forged in a swinging Polynesian-style celebrity and singles hangout called the Luau, at 421 North Rodeo Drive, in the heart of trendy Beverly Hills.

Decorated with enormous wooden tiki gods, and with a moat around the exterior with a bridge leading to the entrance, the hip and hopping Luau was owned by the actor-restaurateur Steve Crane, the second of the seven husbands of screen goddess Lana Turner's eight turbulent marriages.

In the early seventies, the Luau became a hangout for the affluent, semi-playboy brothers Robert and Tommy Kardashian when they were both considered—in their minds at least, and by some women like Kris Houghton—to be two of the town's "most eligible bachelors."

Those were the days before Tommy was arrested and before Robert began toting a Bible.

If you drove a fancy car (and the valet parked it in front) like the Kardashians' wheels—Tommy had a Rolls-Royce Corniche, along with a Jaguar XKE and a Lamborghini, and Robert went from a lowly Pontiac Grand Prix with a black leather interior to a Corvette and then a Rolls—and you wore your expensive clothes from the ivy-covered walls of Fred Segal's boutique on Melrose, like the Kardashians did, the leggy, man-hungry young women who hung at the Luau's frenzied bar figured you were cool and *very* eligible.

The big Polynesian drinks, the hungry babes, and the great ribs with the secret sauce, later revealed to be nothing more than catsup, were the draws.

When Robert began introducing Kris Houghton to the glamour of Beverly Hills in the mid-seventies, before they were married, the Luau was the first place he took her to dinner. The waiter brought what Robert told Kris was an exotic appetizer, coconut rolls, a Polynesian dish. The unsophisticated Clairemont High graduate turned junior stewardess was more accustomed to Pink's Hot Dogs on La Brea than a hip eatery on Rodeo Drive. Long after, Kardashian would tell the story often, embarrassing Kris by revealing that the coconut rolls were actually warm hand towels.

Many years later, after two heart bypass operations and dealing with diabetes, seventy-five-year-old Tom Kardashian reminisced in 2015 about those seventies glory days on the prowl in Beverly Hills. "On most evenings, unless it was one where I had to get up and go to the office early, as a single guy you would just go by the Luau and see who was there, and you'd run into girls who knew all these guys who were hanging out there, and you'd run into your guy friends, and then you didn't even care about the girls. The girls came and followed the guys."

The Kardashians, both slick charmers—Robert in his mid-twenties,

Tom in his late twenties—had become regulars and had befriended the Luau's smooth maître d', Joe Stellini, a native of the tough New York City borough of the Bronx, who happened to be married to Joni Migdal's manicurist but who later reportedly dated the actress Jill St. John. It was Stellini, once described as "somewhat thin-skinned" and "macho," who first introduced Robert and Tom to O.J. and his pal Al Cowlings.

"O.J. would come in the Luau," said Kardashian, "and Stellini told him you got to meet these other USC guys, the Kardashians. They are guys you should know."

Robert hero-worshipped O.J., once the god of the USC football team, and instantly bonded with him. The term "bromance" wasn't invented back then, but that's what existed between the Armenian-American and the African-American.

"O.J. had charisma and he was just a very energetic guy that people enjoyed being around," said Tom Kardashian. "And O.J.'s closest friend at that time was Al Cowlings [who had grown up with Simpson in the San Francisco–area projects], and Al was the same kind of charismatic guy. My brother was charismatic as well and he had things. He had girls around him that were attractive—and O.J. needed to associate with that."

Stellini also told O.J. that the Kardashians had a couple of wealthy friends, also brothers and Luau regulars, whose father was a multimillionaire oilman. Like the Kardashians and O.J., Harry and Peter Rothschild (both of whom died in 2015, in their seventies) had been USC alumni.

"Harry and I were friends," said Kardashian, "and we would go to the USC football games together, and I used to take tennis lessons at Harry's house, and then O.J.—who had a Black Power ghetto-style Afro back in those days—started taking lessons at Harry's house, and so it was another place for all of us to hang out and have parties and stuff like that."

Soon, Robert and O.J. and Tom and others were volleying together regularly on the Rothschild court. And the close bond between the pro football player, who favored being around affluent white guys over his black brethren, and the Armenian-American brothers, who idolized football players, black or white, took hold.

Speaking of the parties at Harry Rothschild's Beverly Hills mansion on Summit Drive—an estate later purchased by Priscilla Presley—Kardashian noted, "If there was anything there was alcohol and drinking, but *never* drugs. I was not a drug person. If you go by the statistics, the firstborn son [Tom himself] is always conservative, but the second-born son [Robert] gets away with whatever he wants to, and takes more chances." He didn't elaborate. But Joni Migdal swore she never saw Robert use drugs, and noted that he rarely ever even drank alcohol. He favored tea, she said. O.J., however, was rumored to have used co-caine when it was *the* go-to recreational drug in the swinging seventies, when he became a charter member of team Kardashian.

Soon after bonding with the Kardashian boys, O.J.—then playing for the Buffalo Bills, and in an emotionally abusive and cheating marriage with his first wife, Marguerite—became like a third Kardashian brother, practically living with them at their house on Deep Canyon Drive in Beverly Hills when he was regularly on the outs with his wife, usually because of his womanizing, and usually with younger white women.

When future momager Kris Houghton first became romantically involved with Robert and was spending more and more time at the Kardashian brothers' bachelor pad, she saw that O.J. was constantly there, was practically one of the brothers, and she likened them to the Three Musketeers.

"O.J. admired and looked up to Robert. O.J. enjoyed the fine things in life. He wanted to be successful. He saw how Robert and Tom lived, in that beautiful home, and he wanted it," Kris later observed to a writer. And her perception of O.J. and Robert was a startling projection of her own desire to have Robert, be successful, and live the high life. "O.J. . . . really respected Robert's opinion in his personal life," Kris continued. "When O.J. needed somebody, Robert was there. O.J. would always stop by Robert's law office. Robert acted as his attorney."

When O.J. decided to buy his English Tudor mansion at 360 Rock-ingham, in the very affluent, fast-lane West Los Angeles neighborhood of Brentwood, made famous during his later murder trial, it was Robert Kardashian who inspected the house with O.J. and gave him the high sign to buy it. And it was Robert who introduced O.J. to the man who would become O.J.'s business manager and financial guru, Leroy "Skip" Taft.

Hanging out with Robert at his house, Kris was once approached by O.J., who walked her to the phone and prodded her to dial a certain number and ask to "speak to Jennifer." Kris made the call, and when Jennifer got on the line, O.J. grabbed the phone. Kris later understood that O.J. had asked her to make the call because the white girl was very young, possibly still in high school, and O.J. didn't want her parents, who might answer the call, to hear his older, masculine, black voice.

"I never asked too many questions in those days," Kris, then mar-ried to Bruce Jenner, said later. "I was so young, I just watched. But I did think it was strange that O.J. was always over at the house with Robert and Tommy, and always calling these girls. I mean, wasn't he *married*? I remember thinking, 'Boy, if *I* ever get married to someone who travels, I'm never going to let him travel without me. Look what happens!"

That from the woman who cheated on her first lover, Cesar Sanudo, with the man she then married, Kardashian, and then would also cheat on him before he divorced her.

IN THE EARLY MORNING hours of June 13, 1994, the brutally butchered bodies of Kris Jenner's close friend Nicole Brown Simpson, thirty-five-year-old mother of two, and her occasional friend, twenty-five-year-old Ronald Goldman, who happened to be in the wrong place at the wrong time, were found outside Nicole's town house, where she had moved after separating from O.J., then forty-seven.

With Simpson as the prime suspect, the case riveted the nation, and then fractured it racially. The murder, trial, and aftermath would make the Kardashian name, for the first time, both famous and infamous, and a part of history. It would also lead to Robert Kardashian's emotional, physical, and financial fall, which would escape the media and the public.

Kardashian would play a key role as O.J.'s loyal friend and defender in the almost nine-month nationally televised trial, and he would—like many across the country, and in particular the prosecutors, Marcia Clark and Christopher Darden—express shock and horror when, on October 3, 1995, the predominately black jury, after just four hours of deliberations, returned a verdict of not guilty.

Whites were seen crying, and blacks cheering.

Just before the verdict was returned, early that morning, Kardashian, the born-again Christian, spent time in the visitor's cell with O.J. and led him in prayer. "I prayed to God, not that this man be set free, but that 'thy will be done.' Only you know, God, what has happened here.'"

In fact, by the time of that brief prayer meeting, Kardashian had lost all faith in his friend's innocence, felt betrayed, and was devastated. That whole loving Kardashian-Simpson brotherhood would end.

Unknown to the public and to those in the media and to the principals who wrote millions of words, or made or appeared in films and television programs about the case through the years, Kardashian's life would become a living hell over the next seven years and eleven months, culminating in his death from esophageal cancer just three days before the eighth anniversary of Simpson's acquittal.

Kardashian thought he would exit the case as a national hero, as the ultimate loyal friend. Instead, he would be demonized as much as the acquitted defendant whom he had stood by. There would be anonymous midnight calls, threatening his life and the lives of his children, and he would be virtually blacklisted in the Beverly Hills society in which he ran.

"No one ever turned their back on someone like they did on Robert over the O.J. thing," recalled his longtime confidant Joni Migdal. "We would be driving in his convertible and people would spit on him—oh, it was *terrible*. Many of his friends wouldn't even talk to him. No one wanted to do business with him. When he would walk outside he would wear a baseball cap so no one would recognize him with that streak in his hair.

"He really believed that by doing what he was doing with O.J. that he would have opportunities to become a paid public speaker and talk to audiences about friendship, about faith, but that opportunity never arose. It was *very* sad for him, and he was *very* depressed that none of his good intentions were ever honored or recognized. And they *were* good intentions. Robert was never an opportunist—*never*. What truly devastated him, what I think truly was a factor in killing him, was the fact that everybody, instead of appreciating the fact that he was a good friend and that he supported O.J.—everybody turned their back on him. *Everyone.*"

And indirectly, Migdal became involved in the O.J. case herself when Kardashian hired her daughter, law school graduate Nicole Pulvers, from Migdal's first of two marriages to a lawyer, to babysit O.J. after his arrest and during the lengthy trial. None of the media covering the trial had ever connected the dots—that the young woman with the last name of Pulvers, who spent eight hours a day with O.J. as his babysitter and, as the lawyers joked, "O.J.'s Jewish mother," was the daughter of Kardashian's close friend Joni.

Pulvers had come to like O.J., and when the trial was nearly over and the verdict was to be announced, she decided to wait for the outcome at O.J.'s home with Al Cowlings and others in the Simpson inner circle.

When he arrived at his Tudor estate on Rockingham in ritzy, leafy Brentwood, free at last, after passing angry crowds of whites shouting "murderer, murderer . . . go home, murderer," he was greeted outside his home by hundreds of blacks who were thrilled with his acquittal, brought about by his shrewd black lawyer, Johnnie Cochran, who had played the race card to the hilt.

Getting out of the van, finally home, O.J. looked around, puzzled at seeing all the black faces there to greet him. His reaction? "What are all these niggers doing in Brentwood?" a white friend said he asked.

In the house, Nicole Pulvers, with tears streaming down her face, gave O.J. a big hug. Robert Kardashian, with a drink in his hand, appeared in a daze, a bland smile painted on his face, as he stiffly stood and watched the homecoming celebration, as a documentary film team shot the scene.

"In the beginning," said Migdal years later, "the O.J. case was my daughter's first job, and she thought it was the best job in the world. But it ended up to be the worst job in the world. The whole case was just very disappointing to her because we all believed O.J. was innocent, but that changed. People were asking her for a comment and for books and she just shied away from the whole thing, as did I." Pulvers left the law and became a stockbroker.

Kris, then married to Bruce Jenner for three years, was furious with Kardashian for defending O.J. because Kris knew how physically abusive O.J. had been to her pal Nicole. Kris and Nicole had had their last chat on the day of the murder, and the discussion centered on making lasagna. The next thing Kris heard about Nicole was a call from O.J.'s mother-in-law, Juditha Brown, saying that her daughter had been murdered.

In her memoir Kris wrote about her relationship with Nicole, but after the book was published, Nicole Brown Simpson's family claimed that what she wrote was strictly with profit and publicity in mind and that her account was not accurate. "Kris Jenner is pathetic," Nicole's sister, Denise Brown, declared in an interview with the *National Enquirer*. In her book, Kris detailed a phone call she received from Denise a day after the murder involving a stash of photographs. But Denise told the tabloid she had never made such a call, and knew nothing about such photos. "I think most people will question her intentions of writing about my sister's murder," said Brown. "Nicole has been dead for seventeen years. Please, Kris, don't profit off of my sister's horrible death."

After learning of the murders, Kris immediately suspected that O.J. was somehow involved, and she quickly learned that her ex was, as she later put it, "on O.J.'s side."

Kardashian knew—and feared—that his involvement in the O.J. defense would create an even bigger chasm between himself and his ex-wife and especially their two eldest children.

In hopes of staving off the animosity he was certain would be directed at him, Kardashian penned a mea culpa to Kris and all four of his children, explaining why he had gotten involved. It was dated January 22, 1995.

The born-again Christian stated that "God allowed this horrible tragedy to occur for whatever reason," and he claimed, "I just happened to be in the 'wrong place at the wrong time.' I am not a public figure and really do not enjoy the horrible invasion of privacy of you, me and my family." He further told them that he didn't want "our family torn apart" by the very public trial and the headlines, and he asserted that he felt "trapped in the position I am in and can't get out."

Still, he showed his loyalty to his longtime friend. "I truly believe in O.J.'s innocence and unless they find him guilty, I will continue to support him."

He concluded by writing, "I love you all and just want the best for our family. Please be understanding."

He ended, "Love, Robert."

But the case would have an immense impact on his children, despite his plea for forgiveness.

When his firstborn, Kourtney, applied to the University of Arizona, the ultimate party and stoner school, from where she earned a degree in theater arts and hung out with another L.A. celebrity brat, Nicole Richie, her application essay was entitled "My Parents Were on the Opposite Sides of the O.J. Simpson Case," their depressed father had told Joni Migdal. "So not only did the O.J. case tear Robert apart, but it tore his family apart, too," asserted Migdal. "That whole backlash was not what he had planned, and it was devastating."

Moreover, when his second-born, Kim, got married in 2000 to music producer Damon Thomas—the first of her three African-American husbands—she was still so angry at her father over his defense of O.J. that she kept the marriage a secret from him until Kourtney revealed all to their father. "That was devastating to Robert, too," maintained Migdal. "Robert was a traditionalist and really believed that his children had his confidence, and he had theirs. But he didn't."

When Kardashian learned about Kim's marriage, he confided in a friend that he was upset and concerned about their interracial relationship. "I know these black guys and I've known them all my life, and I know they love white pussy," the source recalled Kardashian angrily saying. "O.J. always brags about how much he and those guys get. The problem is my kids are liberal, maybe too liberal, and I have no one to blame but myself because I introduced them to Uncle O.J. and others, and they always felt comfortable with them." And the friend noted, "It was my sense, my perception that Robert would have preferred Kimmy to be with a white guy." By the close of 2016, first-born Kourtney was the only one of Kardashian's three daughters who hadn't married an African-American. But she did have three children—Mason, Penelope, and Reign—outside of marriage with the Jewish Scott Disick, a nine-year relationship that ended in 2015.

One of the few friends who, along with Joni Migdal, stuck by Robert Kardashian through the O.J. trial and up until his death eight years later was Larry Kraines. Like Kardashian, Kraines, who had closely socialized with O.J. when Kris was still with Robert and O.J. was with Nicole, believed in the Juice's innocence, always considered him a fun-loving, good-hearted guy who would "sign a football for a nephew, who'd remember to do it and have it done."

Just four months before the murders, in February 1994, around Valentine's Day, Kraines, his wife, Joyce, O.J., Nicole, and Kris Kardashian had dinner together at a restaurant in San Pedro owned by a former USC football player, and throughout the meal and drinks O.J. was "the same old friendly guy, and you'd never know anything was wrong between them. It was just good ol' O.J. and Nicole being Nicole."

Kraines believed that when O.J.'s physical abuse of Nicole was later revealed, "I'm not sure Robert was all that aware of that stuff because there was always O.J.'s side of stuff."

But after the acquittal, Kraines, like Migdal, witnessed the living hell Kardashian was experiencing.

"People would key his car frequently, and throw shit and break his windows," Kraines recalled sadly. "There was a lot of resentment. It did really boomerang the wrong way for Robert. He had problems trying to make a lot of money again. He wasn't doing great financially. He didn't get millions and millions of dollars [in legal fees to defend O.J] like [lead defense attorneys] Robert Shapiro and Johnnie Cochran got."

Practically every night during the trial, Kardashian and Kraines had dinner together. It was during those meals that Kraines got an earful and Kardashian revealed O.J.'s and his own displeasure with some of his "Dream Team" attorney colleagues.

"O.J.'s view was that Robert would be his eyes and ears and keep him up to speed, and come over and spend time with him at his beck and call, and that was very, very difficult for Robert to do," Kraines learned over dinner. "One of O.J.'s biggest fights with the 'Dream Team' was that they were pissing away his money." "That whole deal was a lot of pressure and tension for Robert," continued Kraines. "After the O.J. thing a lot of people didn't want to have anything to do with him—more than anyone can believe. More than *he* believed. He was hoping that him sticking up for his friend and being there at the time of need would bring him fame and fortune, and it may have brought him fame, but for not very long, and did *not* bring him fortune. It brought him misfortune."

None of what Robert Kardashian went through in the wake of the O.J. case has ever been reported before, including in the critically acclaimed, Emmy-winning 2016 TV miniseries, *The People v. O.J. Simpson: American Crime Story*, which starred David Schwimmer as Robert

Kardashian, Selma Blair as Kris Kardashian Jenner, and Cuba Gooding Jr. as Simpson and was based on journalist and attorney Jeffrey Toobin's bestselling 1996 book, *The Run of His Life: The People v. O.J. Simpson.*

In that miniseries there is a scene in which Kardashian, using the alias Richard Kordovian in order to hide his suddenly famous identity and name, takes his children to a restaurant, where he is treated like a VIP because of his new celebrity status. At the table, he tells his children, "We are Kardashians, and in this family being a good person and a loyal friend is more important than being famous."

But in reality, Kardashian wanted both—the fame and being perceived as the loyal friend, according to his close inner circle.

TWENTY-ONE

Dire Warnings

When the murders occurred, O.J. was on his way to Chicago, or already in the Windy City, he claimed. When he returned to L.A.—a few days before his arrest—he was met by a throng of reporters, lawyers, and his loyal friend Robert, who helped in handling his luggage, mainly a Louis Vuitton bag, which would become part of the mystery because there were suspicions that it might have contained the murder weapon, a knife, or the bloody clothes that Simpson had hidden there, and that Kardashian aided in disposing of it. There were also suspicions that the weapon was hidden in Simpson's golf bag, which he and Kardashian picked up at LAX a day after O.J.'s return from Chicago.

So suspicious were the police of Kardashian's role that detectives showed up at relative Sam Kardashian's Southern California Disposal and Recycling Company, in search of the Louis Vuitton bag and possibly other evidence. "We have our own little transfer station, which is like a little dump," said Sam's wife, Paulette in 2015, "and they thought we helped get rid of it. My husband's sister was working here at the time and told the police, 'No, we haven't seen Robert. We don't know anything about it.'"

Larry Kraines, who was seeing Kardashian "no less than four or five nights out of seven" during the O.J. case, had gone to Kardashian's newly rented house in Encino on the day Kardashian brought the bag there, and what he witnessed he believes underscored Kardashian's innocence. "A friend of Robert's and I went up to the bedroom and we saw the Louis Vuitton bag lying there and I said to Robert, 'Is there anything in there?' He said, 'No, just a *Playboy* magazine and some clothes from when he was in Chicago,' and that was it."

O.J. was still free and at his home on Rockingham—family members were standing guard there, fearing he'd kill himself—when Kardashian left Encino to spend time with him. Rather than drive there in his sporty Mercedes, he decided to take Denice's Rolls-Royce, the big British luxury car that had once belonged to her late husband, Toby Halicki. The reason for Kardashian's car change was because he suspected he'd be bringing O.J. back home with him so he could avoid the media and the escalating press coverage, and the larger Rolls could handle any luggage or personal effects he might bring with him.

As he was pulling out of the gated, hilly driveway, Denice came running out to tell him to take the Louis Vuitton bag out of the trunk of the Mercedes and put it in the Rolls so the bag could be returned to O.J., which was done. Kardashian brought Simpson back to the house with him without being spotted by the press. As it turned out, the Rolls made for perfect cover to hide a suspected murderer and his mouthpiece, a scene even a creative filmmaker of mysteries would never have imagined.

Before O.J. fled in the Bronco, Denice was the one who cooked the meals, who accompanied O.J. and Kardashian to Nicole's funeral, who was an eyewitness to the various ways they disguised themselves to avoid the media.

And on the day the arrest warrant was issued, charging O.J. with a double homicide, it was Denice who advised her fiancé to quickly summon Al Cowlings to act as O.J.'s protector in case he tried to injure or kill himself, a decision she'd come to regret.

Kardashian, the man of peace, the born-again Christian, also had a love for guns, and there were at least five in the house—a .38-caliber Smith & Wesson, several rifles, and a pellet gun. Kardashian called a friend who lived nearby to pick up the weaponry to keep them out of suicidal O.J.'s hands. But he had no idea that O.J. had actually smuggled his own gun into Kardashian's home. Kardashian spotted it and, frightened, asked O.J. to pray with him. This was all happening in the room where Kardashian's daughter, Kim, then thirteen, slept when she visited, a bedroom with a feminine canopied bed.

Not long after the prayers, and with the house bustling with lawyers, O.J. disappeared.

Knowing he was about to be arrested, he had penned his mea culpa and fled in the Bronco with a loaded gun and with pal Al Cowlings at the wheel of the getaway SUV, leaving the police, the prosecutors, and his best friend, Kardashian, in a virtual state of shock. An all-points bulletin was issued by the LAPD, setting in motion the famously bizarre televised freeway chase that mesmerized millions of viewers across the country and ended with O.J. in handcuffs at his Brentwood home.

It was one of American television's first authentic, unscripted nonfiction reality shows, and it had the Kardashian patriarch as one of the leading players.

Denice's suggestion to Robert to call in Cowlings to help had gone terribly awry.

FROM THE BEGINNING, JUST AFTER the white Ford Bronco chase, just after Kardashian read the rambling, incoherent O.J. letter to the media, Kardashian was warned to stay out of the case by those who most cared for him, such as his brother, Tom, and his pal Larry Kraines.

"I told Robert *not* to get involved, and Tommy told Robert not to get involved," recalled Kraines. "I didn't feel that to be in the limelight the way he would be, would be good for him, particularly if it would be proven that O.J. did do it. I was trying to be more objective, but Robert was being the loyal friend, *and* I think he wanted to be in the limelight a little bit. He did love the attention, and at that time he needed a little attention. I don't think he had a clue that O.J. could do such a thing—it wasn't even imaginable."

Kardashian refused to believe that his friend of many years and one-time business partner had turned into a killer. And unlike the schmaltzy O.J. miniseries dialogue, Robert Kardashian actually adored being the center of attention, being a celebrity of sorts. It took a horrific murder to give him the fame he had long craved since the days when he was on the edge of the entertainment business in his involvement with *Radio & Records* and Movie Tunes and those other businesses he had hoped would make him rich and famous.

On Friday, June 17, 1994, five days after the butchering of Nicole and Ron, the day of the nationally televised Bronco chase, and shortly after Kardashian read to the assembled press the letter O.J. had left behind—the moment the Kardashian name became known worldwide for the first time—his brother, Tom, paid him a visit at his new home to try to convince him not to get further involved.

Robert was then living with Denice in a gorgeous, gated contemporary rental over the Santa Monica Mountains from Beverly Hills in the affluent community of Encino, in the smoggy San Fernando Valley. He had leased the recently remodeled five-bedroom, five-bath, 7,104-square-foot home on the secluded 16000 block of Mandalay Drive in May 1994, about a month before the murders, at a favorable rate because the builders reportedly had had a tough time selling it. Kardashian had recently sold his beloved Tower Lane estate, where he had raised his children and where his marriage had fallen apart because of his wife Kris's affair.

With his twenty-eight-year-old white girlfriend, one-time model and low-budget movie actress Paula Barbieri, O.J. had been hiding out with Kardashian and Denice—sleeping in the bedroom Kardashian had reserved for his daughter Kim in his new place, where he thought he would be able to start a new, happier chapter in his life at fifty.

It would not come to pass.

WHEN TOM KARDASHIAN TURNED on the TV and saw the Bronco chase, he couldn't believe his eyes. The fugitive had been one of his close friends, as close to him as he was to Robert. Watching the cops chase the Bronco was Tom's second shocker in a week; the first was the actual news of the murders. "That," he stated, looking back years later, "was a terrible shock. That wasn't anything my wife or I would have expected. The only reason I would have thought that O.J. was capable was because he played a violent sport."

Tom's wife, Joanie, had become close to Nicole Simpson, but not as close as Kris, who was younger and had more in common with her. And Tom said Nicole had never given Joanie a hint about the physical abuse she was suffering at the hands of O.J.

Tom never discussed O.J.'s guilt or innocence with his brother. "We never went into that because my brother believed in O.J., so he supported O.J. He went to the trial every day. He visited him in jail while O.J. was incarcerated, so my brother just stood behind him, so that was it. We didn't discuss at dinnertime with my parents, 'Hey, did O.J. really do this?' I have no idea if he did it, and I supported O.J. because I had known him to only do good things for people that were friends that I knew, so the murder was a real shock because *if* he was this kind of [psychopathic] person, I didn't know it."

While there was no talk between the Kardashian brothers about who killed Nicole and Goldman, Tom did step in to advise his brother to distance himself from the case, just as Larry Kraines and a few others had.

"When I heard what was going on in the Bronco, my wife and I went over to my brother's house, and he was already on the phone with different people, with the news media, and they wanted to interview him, and all I can remember is telling my brother, 'You know, you've done your bit, now get out of the deal,'" Tom said in 2015.

"This was just after he read O.J.'s letter to the press, and I told him, 'That was great, you were wonderful. Now I think it's time you lay low, because this will never stop.' I was a different kind of person than Robert, so my advice to him was, 'Now it's time for you to back away and let the professionals take care of it.' It's just what I've seen in this town all these years—usually nothing good comes out of what my brother was doing, which was wanting that kind of notoriety. It usually doesn't work to your favor. I gave him the kind of advice my father would have given him. It wasn't a fair thing for me to tell him what to do, but I just told him how I felt."

Robert basically brushed him off.

"His reaction was like nothing—'Okay, thanks, I hear you.' He wouldn't have taken my advice, because that was him. He was who he was—he *liked* the notoriety. He liked the fame, and that's probably why the girls [Robert's daughters, Tom's nieces] got it the way they got it"— a reference to their fame and notoriety as reality TV stars and more.

Continued Kardashian: "While he was going through the trial he really liked the pictures being taken of him; the press knew who he was. When we went to a restaurant, they would always get him the best table. That's how Beverly Hills was, and he loved that. Before the O.J. case he was an unknown, but if he could have been a movie star, I guess he probably would have done that. He liked the fame and the glory."

And he got both in spades during the lengthy trial, before it all turned against him.

Kardashian was given the full-monty celebrity treatment.

In restaurants, actors like Roger Moore of James Bond fame sought him out to chat. Rod Steiger sent wine to his table. He and his arm candy/ fiancée—leggy, buxom Denice, who fit right into the Hollywood scene with her cosmetically implemented looks, got invitations to A-list par- ties and screenings such as one at the sprawling estate of producer Robert Evans, where the other guests included the Beattys—Warren and Annette Bening—and Victoria Principal, among others.

The powerful Hollywood talent agent Sue Mengers cooed over him, recounting how she and David Geffen got together every morning to watch the case on TV, and she whispered that he could expect a huge advance for any book he wrote when it was time. And Kardashian was secretly hoping that Pacino or De Niro would play him when the movie was made.

Denice's father, Richard Shakarian, who had taken over for his father, Demos, as head of the Full Gospel Businessmen's Fellowship, convinced Robert to speak to the Pentecostal gathering at the big Anaheim Convention Center. The born-again Christian was in heaven, literally and figuratively, telling the praise-the-Lord gathering that he had given O.J. a Bible and prayed with him. "God has a plan for everyone," he told the audience. "I hope you will keep O.J. Simpson in your prayers."

Being in the media spotlight, however, wasn't all that Kardashian had hoped for. The dark side of fame was becoming the focus of tabloid print and TV reportage. The O.J. case and the cast of characters had all the elements. And next to Kato Kaelin, O.J.'s roommate at the time of the murders, Kardashian was considered central casting's version of the slimy hanger-on, the mouthpiece with the edgy music-industry background. His Armenian dark looks, his expensive suits, that streak in his hair, the Rolls-Royce or Mercedes-Benz that were his daily drivers fit the tabloid narrative perfectly. He was the epitome of O.J.'s advisor and pal.

CURIOUSLY, OTHERS PERCEIVED KARDASHIAN DIFFERENTLY, viewing him as one who cared little for the spotlight, as one who was shy.

A few days before the Bronco chase, Kardashian had lunch with his close friend and divorce attorney, Neal Hersh, at Harper's, a trendy restaurant located in what was then the ABC Entertainment Center, in Century City, and later the headquarters for CAA, the powerful Creative Artists Agency.

Kardashian told Hersh that he had been invited to be the keynote speaker at the graduation at his alma mater, San Diego School of Law, which was quickly coming up, and he was asked to talk on the topic of lawyers who succeeded as businessmen. "And Robert was saying to me, 'Neal, I'm too shy. I don't want to stand in front of all those people and speak.' And I said, 'Robert, your story is fantastic. I'll help you write this thing. Don't be silly. Say yes.'

"And something like twenty-four hours later he was on national television, being seen by a billion people worldwide, and at that moment he was probably one of the most recognizable faces in America, if not the world. So if someone says he wasn't shy or unassuming, they are wrong. He *was* shy and unassuming. He just was thrust into the O.J. case."

Joni Migdal agreed with Hersh's assessment.

The woman who had known him since junior high, who had become his confidant, and his lover for a time, who was at his side when he met his future first wife, Kris, and who took him in when they separated over her affair, said the "beauty of Robert was that while he was very, very popular, he did not want to be famous at all."

She said his parents, Arthur and Helen, were furious when he came to O.J.'s defense and put the Kardashian name out into the public domain for the first time.

"When he offered to help O.J., they were mortified because the important values they had instilled in Robert were to stay *under* the radar, and live his life quietly, and with dignity and with respect. They liked O.J., but they hated the notoriety. They hated the publicity."

Robert's family, the Kardashians, were a secretive lot, making money in tough, highly competitive, sometimes dirty businesses—from waste management to historically corrupt meat packing and much in between—so keeping it on the down-low was of the utmost importance. By going public in the most publicized murder trial in contemporary American history, Robert had broken the Kardashian family's vow of silence, its *omertà*.

Thus, members of the sprawling Kardashian family—Robert's generation of relatives whose forebears had fled Armenia and a genocide of its people that was prophesied—weren't at all happy with the attention he had brought to the Kardashian name. And were even more upset later by the even brighter spotlight shone on it by Robert's ex-wife Kris Jenner and the three daughters she had with him, in particular Kim Kardashian, of sex tape fame.

The good Kardashian name, they felt strongly, was being dragged through the mud.

As one outspoken family member, Paulette Kardashian, wife of Kardashian relation Sam Kardashian, proprietor of Southern California Disposal and Recycling Company—famous for the massive thirty-by-fifty-foot American flag flown above his business near the busy 10 freeway in Santa Monica—declared in 2016:

"Nobody would have known who the Kardashians are. We were really put on the map because of a murder and a sex tape, and that's sad. My husband—he's really quite upset that the Kardashian name has been taken down. When you have a clean name, and then your name is known all over the world for different things, it's very difficult. The Kardashian name got recognized because of the murder and when Kim did that sex tape.

"My granddaughter, who goes to university and kind of looks like Kim, told me when her classes start she will text her professors and tell them, 'Please don't use my last name in class.' She doesn't want to be hassled.

"When all this started," continued Paulette Kardashian, "my husband kept thinking it's going to go away, but I said, 'It's *not* going to go away. It's only going to get bigger.' But what is it those Kardashians are selling? They really aren't noted for anything. But people give Kris credit because she's very smart, she's very shrewd . . . a murder and a sex tape."

TWENTY-TWO

Tragic Times

*V*anity Fair writer Dominick Dunne, who covered the O.J. trial, called Denice Shakarian Halicki "A beautiful, rich, blonde widow." He once wrote, "She has very long legs and wears very short skirts and is a knockout." But she once confronted the writer, claiming he had made an error in reporting that she had been out shopping on the day of the Bronco chase, and she demanded to know the identity of the source of his information.

" 'Don't you see what they're trying to do?' " Dunne quoted her as asking. " 'They're trying to minimize me in the case. They're trying to make me look like a bimbo, out shopping at the time. Do you really think, knowing me, that I'm the kind of person who would be out shopping at Neiman Marcus in Beverly Hills when all that was going on in my house? Of course I was there. Remember, that was half my house at the time. Robert and I had just moved in there a few weeks before the murders.' "

Dunne characterized her as "a lady who likes to be in the center of the action."

When Dunne's piece ran in the magazine in June 1996, the long relationship between Kardashian and Denice had ended, and she had moved out.

"The story went at the time that she took all the furniture and the television sets with her," he wrote, which angered Denice when she read it. She claimed she only took the stuff because it belonged to her.

When she told Kardashian she was leaving, a Kardashian friend recalled him saying, "I told her to take her shit and get the fuck out."

AFTER THE TRIAL ENDED, every major TV news personality was chasing Kardashian for an interview. Next to O.J., Kardashian was the big "get," the broadcast journalism term for securing a highly sought-after, exclusive interview. Barbara Walters won the prize with a Kardashian sit-down on ABC's *20/20* program.

The interview was held at Kardashian's Encino home. But Kardashian was far from pleased with how his chat with network television's vaunted celebrity interrogator went. "She had promised him she wouldn't ask him certain questions, and then she went ahead and asked him the questions," revealed Joni Migdal, whom Kardashian wanted present as a witness to the proceedings. "She promised him, 'I'm not going to go here, and I'm not going to go there,' but she didn't honor what she promised. Robert did *not* like it, and he did *not* like her. There were several times when he said *cut*, and Barbara Walters got really pissed off."

But he told her the truth when he admitted, with much Walters prodding, that he now had "doubts" about O.J.'s innocence. He revealed that the blood evidence was the "most devastating part of the whole trial" for him, and that he became "so conflicted" about O.J. that he'd wake up in the middle of the night. "The blood evidence is the biggest thorn in my side that causes me the greatest problems, so I struggle with the blood evidence."

He also revealed to her that if he had to do it all over again, he would not have participated in O.J.'s defense, and he doubted that the Juice would have done the same for him if the tables had been turned.

THE MUCH-BALLYHOOED WALTERS interview was tied to the promotion of a new book about the O.J. case entitled *American Tragedy: The Uncensored Story of the Simpson Defense*, by journalists Lawrence Schiller, a longtime friend of Kardashian, who was a major source for the book, and James Willwerth, a *Time* magazine correspondent. Kardashian had given his friend the pastor Kenn Gulliksen the impression it was his book and that he expected to share the byline with Schiller. However, after reading it, Gulliksen said he came away "wondering how Bob could ever have thought of this as 'his' book, since he appeared to just be another character in the tragic story—his voice wasn't uniquely heard."

The New York Times agreed in its review, noting that Kardashian "comes off merely as a good-hearted bumbler."

In fact, the book's publication underscored Kardashian's own personal tragedy in getting involved in the O.J. drama and in cooperating with Schiller. He complained to confidants that his participation in the book had scarred his reputation and financially injured him. He railed that he had gotten taken in, and bemoaned that he never received the money he was promised or the acclaim he expected. As Gulliksen, who had received an inscribed copy from Kardashian, noted, "It was obvious Bob felt a bit betrayed by the author [Schiller], and Bob decided he wouldn't refer to it as 'his' book anymore."

Kardashian had told Joni Migdal that Schiller approached him with a hard-to-believe offer he couldn't refuse—a payment of "four million dollars" to cooperate in the research and writing of the book. "Robert needed the money then because no one would do business with him because of the O.J. case. But I don't know if he received all of it, or any of it. I know from Robert that that was the agreement—four million dollars."

Larry Kraines, who knew Schiller for years, said his view of Kardashi-an's deal with Schiller was that "Robert was more or less used." While he didn't know the details of Kardashian's arrangement with Schiller, "I know that Robert felt he was going to get *some* money. He had trusted Schiller, and at the end of the day I think that he got the short end of the financial side."

Schiller, who acknowledged in his book that Kardashian "assisted me in the preparation of the book" and that he had told O.J. that the book "would include Bob's story," declined to be interviewed for this book.

Migdal remembered that Kardashian initially saw the book deal as a "wonderful opening for him, that it would result in his making speeches around the country and getting paid for his appearances. He thought the book was his opportunity to regain a little bit about who he was be-fore [the O.J. case] and heal his persona, heal his reputation. But to his total and utter dismay, it didn't happen that way. When the book came out, he was *not* the hero and the compassionate friend. His role in the story kind of petered out as far as he was concerned, and as far as his future was concerned. It depressed him."

About a week after *American Tragedy* hit bookstores, a depressed Kardashian needed to get away, and he rented a house in Ventura, where he sulked. Migdal, along with another friend, visited him, and vividly recalled, "He was a wreck. He was nervous about the book, nervous about *everything*. Physically, he didn't feel well. He looked *horrible*. Emo-tionally, he wasn't in good shape. That book was a major disappoint-ment in his life because he really believed that everyone would read it and he would come out a winner—more respected, more revered, more understood. But with the book, no one in Robert's life wanted to be with him. He never in his whole life had anyone treat him with such disdain and such ill intentions. He was heartbroken."

ROBERT KARDASHIAN'S INTERVIEW WITH Barbara Walters made head-lines the next day. But it can now be told that he had also lied to

America's premier broadcast newswoman and celebrity interviewer. When she asked him what the impact of the trial had been on him personally he responded that its toll included the loss of his fiancée, Denice Shakarian Halicki, suggesting that the stresses and strains had been too much for him and her to bear.

In fact, Kardashian had fallen for another woman.

Unknown to the media, including journalistic big guns like Walters and Dominick Dunne, who had been closely following the O.J. case and the cast of players, Kardashian had ended it with Denice because he had quietly fallen in love with Shawn Chapman Holley, the African-American attorney who was assisting Johnnie Cochran in O.J.'s race-card defense and was a member of his prestigious L.A. firm, the Law Offices of Johnnie L. Cochran.

In the 2016 miniseries *The People v. O. J. Simpson*, Holley was played by the actress Angel Parker, but there was no indication in the program (nor in Jeffrey Toobin's book) of any intimate relationship between Holley and Kardashian, played by David Schwimmer.

Known as Shawn Chapman back then—her later married name was Holley—she was a major player on the defense team. A UCLA graduate and a former L.A. public defender, she had had much criminal defense trial experience when Cochran asked her to be a part of his office's all-black team of lawyers when he joined O.J.'s defense.

Virtually every day of the months-long trial, Chapman and Kardashian were together in the courtroom, in conference rooms, at evening and weekend meetings with the other lawyers, all with the goal of getting O.J. acquitted. And as time passed, Kardashian's feelings grew stronger for her. He was more than smitten, as she was with him. Only a very few in his close circle knew what was going on.

"I am absolutely positive that Shawn would want that part of her life with Robert kept secret," asserted a well-placed source. "It was a big secret. They were very careful."

Denice, who wore his engagement ring and thought she would be the next Mrs. Robert Kardashian, may not have realized what was going on until it was too late. And at that critical point when she did, he asked her to leave and she soon stormed out of his life.

"Robert and Shawn were on the case together, so they spent a great deal of time together, and they began dating, and I got to know her well," said Larry Kraines. "We had several dinners with Shawn, and she was very bright, very liberal, very smart, and so that bothered Denice, and that sort of broke up Robert with Denice. She wasn't going anywhere with Robert, nor was Robert going to go anywhere with Denice. The problem Robert had was getting involved with Denice in the first place. She had the looks. She was sweet to him, she was good with the kids, and if someone was good with his kids, that was good enough for Robert. But Denice didn't mentally stimulate him.

"When Denice saw the relationship was falling apart she came to me several times and wanted advice, and I told her, 'Denice, I think that there's probably some issue here that maybe you can help yourself.' She knew that Robert was cheating on her with Shawn. I told her that one of the problems was 'You're so pretty and you're so attractive, but you don't have anything to say, you don't add to any conversation. I told you ten times to get *The Wall Street Journal*. Go read the *Los Angeles Times*, so when you're sitting with people at dinner and they are all talking, you can say, "Well, how about those Dodgers? Good game last night." Say something of substance.'

"But she did start to read and talk up and I told Robert, 'I talked to Denice. I told her to get a newspaper,' but he said, 'It's probably too late for that.' He said, 'I have to do everything for her. Other than the physical attraction, and being sweet and Armenian, I just don't see myself spending the rest of my life with her.'"

Shawn, on the other hand, was "intellectual," and, noted Kraines, "the complete opposite of what Robert had with Denice. [Denice] was ditzy—totally."

When Kardashian got involved in the O. J. Simpson case, his "thoughts about Denice strayed," a friend said, and he began seeing Shawn and "he needed to get Denice out of his life. I don't know that she knew what was really going on." Kardashian told this person that Denice refused to leave, even presumably after learning about his affair.

"She did love Robert. She loved the lifestyle. She loved living in that house on Mandalay Drive. She loved what Robert had to offer her. She loved the ring he gave her. She loved the engagement—and then he wandered," the friend said. "Denice didn't want to break up with Robert, so he had trouble getting her out of his house and out of his life. Finally, there were her heel marks going out the door."

The accounts given by Kraines and the second close source are in stark contrast to the one claimed by Denice's mother, Vangie Shakarian, who asserted that it was her daughter's decision to end the engagement and the relationship, blaming the decline and fall on the strain of the O.J. trial.

"They'd have probably been married if it hadn't been for that murder and trial because it just got over the top. It was such a drama," Vangie asserted. "My daughter went through that whole O.J. thing with Robert. My daughter went with him every day to court. She picked out Robert's ties. Her and Robert really raised those [Kardashian] kids when they were little. The kids still adore her. And we love the kids, regardless of what they are doing. Robert and Denice were engaged for six years. He *wanted* to marry her. But they broke up after the trial. She's even got an amazing letter from him just *begging* her to come back."

Shawn Chapman was hoping that her relationship with Kardashian would move forward. But Kardashian, whose close friend for decades had been a black man, who had a liberal household in which his children called Simpson "Uncle O.J.," and two of three of whose daughters and even his ex-wife would later date and/or marry African-American men, couldn't fully commit to Chapman because of her race.

"Robert realized that because Shawn wasn't white that he couldn't get really serious with her, and that was the part where he had to give her up," said the friend, looking back years later. "Shawn was devastated because she really loved Robert, and I think he really loved her much more so than he had loved Denice. Shawn was smart and lovely and a wonderful person. He told me he loved her but had to come to grips with his own biases—his racial biases. It didn't matter that his best friend was O.J. He just knew that he could never give Shawn a commitment the way that she wanted it because of her race."

Shawn Chapman Holley did not respond to voice-mail messages and e-mails left by the author asking for comment about her relationship with Kardashian. Over the years, she became one of L.A.'s power lawyers to the stars, and her connection to the Kardashian name continued: When Kim Kardashian's third husband, Kanye West, got into a civil suit with a paparazzo, he retained Holley to defend him. Kim's one-time boyfriend Reggie Bush, of the NFL, also hired her. Other star clients included Michael Jackson, Axl Rose, Snoop Dogg, and Lindsay Lohan.

Denice never remarried. As for Kardashian, she said in an e-mail in 2015, "The view the public received of Robert during the O.J. case and more recently is not representative of the Robert that was building a life with me, even though in the [O.J.] case we were caught in the eye of the storm . . . Robert will always be loved."

In 2007, Simpson was charged in a bizarre robbery in Las Vegas in which he tried to take back sports memorabilia that he claimed belonged to him. He was arrested in a sting operation, tried, convicted, and sentenced to thirty-three years in prison. Simpson haters called it karma. Others believed it was the judicial system and prosecutors taking revenge for his acquittal. O.J. could be released from prison as early as 2017, when he turns seventy.

TWENTY-THREE

Lonely Farewell

With fiancée Denice Shakarian Halicki long out of his life, and with his furtive interracial relationship with Shawn Chapman having failed, a lonely, depressed and financially strapped Robert Kardashian got married for a second time, eight years after he divorced Kris. This time he chose a one-time beauty queen whom he thought had plenty of money and moxie.

Janice Lynn "Jan" Ashley, fifty-one, a Miss Tulsa back in the late sixties, and a recent widow—her husband had been the B-movie television actor-producer John Ashley—became Mrs. Robert Kardashian. He was then fifty-five.

They were wed in a Las Vegas–style rental chapel in Vail, Colorado, during a Thanksgiving 1998 ski trip, with friends and with Kardashian's four children in attendance—four very unhappy children, because they didn't like the new woman in his life and the fact that Daddy was getting remarried.

One of the wedding guests was Kardashian's Jewish pal Larry Kraines, who had been present at Kardashian's first, big, fancy church wedding with Kris back in 1978. This one was different. The latest ceremony was a "regular gentile wedding, probably a little more so than if Robert got married in a chapel in Vegas," said Kraines. "In the Vail chapel, if you were Jewish they'd put a menorah up there by the pulpit. If you were Catholic, a cross would go up. It was like Vegas, but nicer."

Kardashian's longtime pastor, Kenn Gulliksen, who counseled him as a born-again Christian and officiated at his marriage to Kris, was not on the guest list. The two had lost touch for a time when Gulliksen had moved from L.A. to "plant" a new Vineyard church.

After the ceremony, the bride and groom had a celebratory dinner with their guests, and then spent their honeymoon in Vail—with his kids present.

Known as "Uncle Larry" to Kourtney, Kim, Khloé, and Rob, Kraines was looking for signs about how Kardashian's children felt about his decision to remarry. They certainly had liked Denice when he was living with her; she was sexy and dramatic looking, and the Kardashian girls loved that about her. When their mother quickly married Bruce Jenner after the divorce, it was only Kourtney, the eldest, who had qualms. But regarding their father's new marriage, "I couldn't get the girls to give me a read on Jan," Kraines recalled vividly. "They weren't talking. In other words, they didn't like it that he was getting married again. They felt that it was too soon, and why marriage anyway, and so on and so forth."

From the beginning of his relationship with Jan, Kardashian raved about her to Kraines, telling him how gorgeous she was, how much fun she was.

"We all went out together, but I didn't think much of her—I thought she was a phony," said Kraines, looking back. "She had a little bit of the Hollywood thing—'aren't I great, aren't I this, aren't I that.' And I wouldn't call her beautiful, but she was pleasant looking, for sure."

Having moved out of Mandalay Drive, Kardashian was house-hunting in the upscale Encino Hills–Lake Encino area of Encino—known as

Beverly Hills North—with his friend Joni Migdal, who had become a real estate agent.

"He was very specific in what he wanted," recalled Migdal. "He wanted a bedroom for each of his children, and he would use the dining room as his office because he planned to work at home," having lost most of his friends and not bringing in any real money. He finally settled on a one-story five-bedroom with a pool, and decorated it in a conservative Ralph Lauren style, just like the first house he had had years earlier with his brother, Tom (and frequently O.J.), in Beverly Hills. He wanted the big, modern home because he saw it as a way to bond again with his children after the hate he felt during and after the O.J. trial.

"He really felt that the house would be a good support system and a good foundation for his kids so that they would have a place that wasn't Mandalay, that wasn't Denice, that wasn't O.J., that wasn't anyone except him and them in that house," observed Migdal. "It was very cute once he moved in. He would get up in the morning and he would *pretend* like he was going to work—he'd shower, dress, and then head into his dining-room office. He *loved* that house."

And it would be the last house he would ever buy. He didn't know it at the time, but he had less than five years to live.

At the same time that Kardashian was buying, Jan Ashley was selling her home in the same neighborhood. Kardashian was shown it, and during a walk-through he saw Jan's photograph in a frame and decided on the spot that he had to meet that woman. He soon contacted her. They hit it off and dated for seven months. And on a romantic getaway in Hawaii, Kardashian proposed and recent widow Jan accepted on the spot.

Just like lonely Kardashian, "Jan didn't want to be by herself," said Kraines, who got to know her as a couple with Kardashian. "She was very charming, and she wanted to win over all Robert's friends and family, and she *really* wanted to marry the guy. She wanted to be with a guy who was fun, personable and that's what Robert was.

"All of a sudden she's inviting Robert's friends over to a barbecue, and she's saying, 'Bring the kids, too!' Everything's going great, and somehow Robert feels he should marry this gal, but keep in mind he was lonely."

And he also was in bad shape financially and he "assumed through her that she was very wealthy—because she told him so," said Kraines. "She was wealthy to a degree, but I don't think she was as wealthy as she told him, and her money came from the death of her husband."

About a year before Jan Ashley tied the knot with Robert Kardashian, she had been widowed. A tall, slender beauty in her day, she had been voted Miss Tulsa, Oklahoma, in 1966. Born in Texas, she grew up in a modest Tulsa family, the daughter of James and Monnie Glass, and had been the actor-producer John Ashley's third wife. Before she married Ashley in 1978—the same year Kardashian married junior flight attendant Kris Houghton—Jan had been the attractive executive secretary to the nation's then-youngest corporate leader, "Boots" Adams, president of Phillips Petroleum Company.

Jan's husband, John Ashley, was sixty-two when he died suddenly of a heart attack in New York City in 1997, while working on a new film. Discovered by John Wayne because of his boyish good looks, Ashley played in low-budget American International Pictures horror films and fifties drive-in movies such as *Dragstrip Girl*. He starred in a TV series called *Men of Annapolis*, but didn't make the cut when he auditioned for a mid-fifties classic, *I Was a Teenage Werewolf*. He later coproduced such popular eighties TV series as *The A-Team*, starring the tough guy Mr. T.

As Kraines recalled, Jan had gotten the impression that Kardashian had big money, which was another incentive for marriage, and Kardashian had the impression that she was loaded, too. She was constantly pitching her supposed wealth to Kardashian, who needed money, and he was eating up her stories about how they could live the high life.

" 'We can go to Palm Springs. We can get a house. I'll get you a membership in the country club,' " she cooed to Kardashian. "And he bought into that hook, fucking line, and sinker," maintained Kraines. "Robert told me, 'I think I can marry this girl.' I said, 'Do you love her?' And he said, 'I don't know what love is anymore. But I know I don't want to be by myself anymore. I know she's great with the kids, and she loves the whole family, and she loves you guys.'

"But when I got to know her," noted Kraines, "I didn't feel the love."

Still, as an observer, Kraines felt that before Kardashian tied the knot, his new love had put herself out to make friends with Robert's friends, and was always pleasant and nice.

"But just about as fast as they got married and got back and settled in, the party stopped," he said ominously.

"She didn't like the kids, the kids didn't like her. And the house for both of them, there was not going to be any house. Robert wanted to have a house big enough for all of his kids and for him and Jan, but her whole tune changed."

And even worse, she hated Kardashian's dog, his beloved, closest, and most loyal companion, a Doberman pinscher.

"Jan said, 'You gotta get rid of the dog,' and she had all kinds of complaints—'it's this, it's that, and it doesn't like me, and it's shedding,'" recalled Kraines. "The dog was a sweet dog, and Robert had it for five or six years, and it was a real companion, but because of Jan, I think he gave the dog to one of his cousins.

"When they were dating," continued Kraines, "Jan had barbecues at her house and the dog came, the kids came over—no problem. Then all of a sudden after they married it was different, and Robert quickly realized that he made a bad decision marrying her. So within a short period of months he wanted to have the thing annulled on whatever grounds he could get it annulled on."

He chose the oddest reason.

According to a sworn declaration he filed with his lawyer, Neal Hersh, he claimed that childless Jan wanted to have a baby with him, and that he initially agreed, but then changed his mind and as a result he wanted the marriage nullified.

While it worked and the marriage was ended, none of it made any sense for a couple of reasons: For one, Jan was already in her early fifties and had never before had a child, and the odds of her having one at her age was a long shot. But moreover, her getting pregnant with Kardashian was impossible because he had had a vasectomy, or at least that's what he claimed to Kraines and Migdal.

In any case, the former Miss Tulsa and the patriarch of the Kardashian clan went their separate ways.

On October 1, 2015, sixty-seven-year-old Jan Ashley, who had returned home to Oklahoma, died.

"She left us too early and went to be with the Lord," her obituary read. There was no mention of her tumultuous, brief, annulled marriage to Kardashian.

She was buried next to her husband, John Ashley, in the final resting place for a multitude of Hollywood stars, Forest Lawn Memorial Park, in the L.A. suburb of Glendale.

THROUGH HIS CONTACTS IN THE music business, Robert Kardashian had become chums with Ken Roberts, who in the seventies and eighties owned one of L.A.'s most popular and influential rock stations, KROQ-FM, a once debt-ridden, little-listened-to operation headquartered in Pasadena, home of the "Little Old Lady (from Pasadena)," made famous in a mid-sixties tune by surfer rockers Jan & Dean. Turning KROQ into a powerhouse, with deejays like Freddy Snakeskin and Jed the Fish spinning alternative tunes, Roberts, also a concert promoter, gave new entertainers and unknowns like Prince and Culture Club, Billy Idol and the Go-Go's, big play, lots of publicity, and national attention.

In the late 1990s and early 2000s, Roberts, then in his mid-to-late-sixties and divorced, was throwing elegant parties at his sprawling 112-acre ranch in Mandeville Canyon, part of Brentwood, for his well-to-do, older male friends, and he was inviting lots of attractive, younger women, most of them professionals—bleach-blond Bel-Air real estate agents, Redondo Beach redhead mortgage bankers, surgically enhanced

Barbie-like Beverly Hills divorcées, that sort—who were there for one reason and one reason only—to meet, greet, and marry rich older men.

As Larry Kraines observed, "Ken Roberts wasn't an attractive guy, but if you have a lot of dough and put on a good show you get surrounded by younger gals. He wasn't my kind of guy at all. None of the women were sleazy, nor was he. The women were all basically divorced looking for some guy through some guy through some parties. Ken Roberts was flamboyant, throwing all those parties, but it looked to me like too much show and not enough go."

Roberts would later lose it all, including his party house, when he defaulted on a multimillion-dollar loan from a hedge fund in Connecticut. He died, reportedly broke, at seventy-three, in July 2014.

Kardashian had become a regular at Roberts's parties, usually held on Monday nights, when a dinner was served and the dapper older men mixed with the invited glamorous younger women. In early 2002, through one of those women, Kardashian was fixed up with the latest woman of his dreams. She would become his third wife—and his controversial widow some eighteen months later.

Her name was Ellen Pearson, a blue-eyed, tall, and leggy blond divorcée with a knockout smile, who was at least a decade his junior.

"She wasn't my favorite," stated Larry Kraines.

But she was Kardashian's favorite, and virtually overnight they fell in love, or seemed to.

IN THE EARLY SUMMER of 2003, the happy couple decided to take a luxury vacation. Their destination was Italy, and Kardashian was feeling like a young man again, joyous and in love. They took lots of photos of their trip, and when they returned Robert and Ellen had dinner with Robert's divorce lawyer and friend, Neal Hersh, and his wife, at Mistral, a French restaurant on Ventura Boulevard in Sherman Oaks. Robert couldn't stop talking about how much he loved Italy, and he showed the Hershes the photos he and Ellen had taken.

Neal and his wife so enjoyed Kardashian's show-and-tell that they decided to go to Italy, too. "We had almost mirror-image trips," he said.

Shortly after Hersh got back, he was having coffee with his daughter at a Starbucks in Brentwood.

"I got a call from Robert and he told me that he was feeling sick, and he also told me that he hadn't been feeling well when he was in Italy. Then he went to the doctor and got the news—cancer. It was devastating. It was horrible. I went to see him at his house in Lake Encino, where he was living with Ellen, and he looked bad. He was tired. He had trouble keeping food down, or even swallowing food. He was struggling."

In mid July 2003, Robert heard that Larry Kraines was ill, too, and bedridden, that he had had an emergency appendectomy, that there had been postoperative problems, and that he was recuperating at his lush get-away home in the arid California desert. While feeling lousy himself, Kardashian decided to pay his close friend a visit.

"And I'm sitting all messed up with complications, and I looked at him and said, 'You don't look so good. You've lost a lot of weight.' He was always trying to keep thin, but always eating too much of that Armenian good food. He says, 'We just got back from Italy and I ate like a pig over there, but I don't know what happened because I've lost twelve to fifteen pounds, and I'm still losing weight.'

"I said, 'Forget about me, go check out what's going on with you. This doesn't sound right. You've never lost weight like that in your whole life, let alone in two weeks.'

"And then two or three days later he called and said, 'You won't believe this.' I said, 'What?' He said, 'Are you sitting down?' And then he said, 'I have esophageal cancer.' And I said, *'What the fuck!'*

"And that was the beginning of the end."

There was nothing new about Kardashian's throat problems, according to his brother, Tom, who claimed throat issues related to acid reflux had even kept Robert out of the military draft many years earlier. "He always had problems swallowing, and he did not enjoy going to doctors," asserted Kardashian. "He probably should have done some research earlier on about what was going on with his health, but he just didn't want to go in and get a checkup. He might be alive today if he had."

He said that what quickly became cancer had started "more like an ulcer, and then he didn't go in to see the doctor until it was too mature." He noted that his brother's type of cancer, esophageal, "is worse than others."

Like Hersh, Tom Kardashian said it was during his brother's trip to Italy with Ellen Pearson that Robert began feeling very ill.

"That's where he came up with more issues and he felt he needed to get checked. When he saw the doctor, they found out there was a blockage, a tumor, and I think it was fifty-seven days from when they did diagnose it to the moment he passed."

In part, Tom Kardashian blamed his brother's participation in the O.J. trial and all that went with it as the reason for why he "died prematurely. I'm not a doctor. I can only say that my brother was one who carried stress, and it [the O.J. case and the aftermath] could not have been a positive thing for him."

Larry Kraines said that Kardashian always kept "things to himself, bottled up, and when people keep things to themselves so much, well, we used to say in yiddish, 'you eat your *kishkes* out.' Robert *always* had acid reflux—always, always, always. He would eat a pound of Tums a week. He had boxes of it, and when he did go to the doctor, the doctor would go, 'Oh, it's just the way your system is.' But that later developed into something more than just his system. Robert was never a proactive guy with his health. We always thought, 'We're healthy guys,' so we didn't take care of ourselves."

Kardashian's ex-wife Kris, however, would have a far different story to tell about the end of the life of the father of her first four children. Kardashian, she asserted, showed up at a basketball game in which their son, Rob, was playing in the gym at the Buckley School, approached Kris, and began literally "crying" as he told her he had cancer.

" 'I'm sure it's going to be okay, but I am really scared,' " she quoted him as saying. A week later, according to her account, he telephoned her again. This time he was joyous. " 'Guess what? I don't have cancer. It's a miracle. I am okay. It turned out to be a bad test.' " But then, she maintained, a few months later he called her again—with the bad news. " 'I do have cancer.' "

He informed her, she stated, that he planned to fly in a "healer" from China who would help him beat his terminal illness. As a born-again Christian with close ties to the Pentecostal Shakarian family—Demos Shakarian preached about miracle healing—Kardashian was hoping there was some authenticity to the stories he had heard over the years about cancer victims being miraculously made well through the power of prayer and a healer's touch. Decades earlier, his grandfather and an associate had even announced plans to build a temple in Los Angeles for an Armenian faith healer who had arrived in the United States to heal the sick son of a wealthy Armenian wine merchant.

But none of what Kris Jenner wrote in her 2011 memoir about the tragic last months, weeks, and days leading up to Kardashian's death fits with the chronology recounted by those who were much closer to him at the end than Kris, who was busy building her own life and future career with Bruce Jenner. If Kris is to be believed, Kardashian had gotten sick and gone for tests much earlier in 2003 than any of his closest friends and confidants knew about, and that is very doubtful.

Oddly, in her memoir, Kris made no mention of Ellen Pearson by name, stating only that, "Four weeks before Robert died, a woman he had only been dating a short time married him." But there would be more about her after Kardashian died and Kris and her brood became famous.

ON JULY 27, 2003, in the living room of his home in Encino, a terminally ill Robert Kardashian, looking like a concentration camp victim because of all the weight he had lost, and dressed in just a pair of shorts, a T-shirt, and slippers, wed Ellen Pearson in a very private ceremony attended by his daughters. No one present recalled Kris being there.

What is remembered is that the dying groom was so weak he was barely able to say the words "I do."

"Ellen convinced him in practically his last weeks alive to marry him," said Kraines, who heard about the wedding in a telephone call from the doomed groom and later saw photos of the depressing affair.

Kraines subsequently telephoned the new Mrs. Kardashian and she told him that Robert was too sick to take his call. He finally got him on the phone, "but it was terrible," he'd never forgotten. Kardashian sounded incoherent, mumbling his words. In a later conversation, Kardashian, his voice weak, complained to Kraines, "If I don't die from cancer, I'm going to die from starvation."

At that point he was "going down very quickly," said Kraines.

Still recuperating from his surgery, Kraines returned to L.A. to see his terminally ill friend of four decades, and that visit, he says, occurred only with "complete force" by him because the third Mrs. Robert Kardashian tried to block his way.

Looking back in 2016 to that horrific time, he and Joni Migdal both asserted that Ellen Pearson Kardashian had "sequestered" her dying husband from his closest friends who wanted to spend time with him.

"I talked to Kim several times then and she told me that as soon as Robert found out he was going to die that Ellen kept him apart from any of his friends," said Migdal. While Robert's friends and family were upset regarding Ellen's very protective stance, it is possible that Ellen thought that Kardashian needed his privacy and was only trying to help rather than hinder his life in his final days.

According to Migdal, Larry and Joyce Kraines were the only people from Kardashian's social group who "really stuck with him [in the wake of the O.J. case] and stayed friends with him."

Kraines was determined to see his dying pal. When he drove up to his Encino home one afternoon uninvited, he could see that Robert's parents, Arthur and Helen Kardashian, and his brother, Tom, were in the backyard.

"I rang the doorbell and Ellen comes out and she's acting like a guard," recalled Kraines. "She asks me, 'What do you want?'

" 'What do you mean, what do I want? He's been sick for three months. I haven't been able to talk to him. I want to say hello.' I said, 'I see Helen and Arthur are here, and I'm not in any mood to argue with you.'

"But she says, 'He's got to rest. He doesn't need to see anybody right now.'

"And I said, 'I'm not asking you, Ellen, I'm telling you I'm coming in. Whether you stop me or not, that will be your decision. And I'm walking through you if you don't move aside.' And that's exactly what I did. She may not have been a very nice gal, but Robert was weak and sick and Ellen was a companion, and her daughter was helping to care for him."

When Kraines finally got in to see Kardashian, he said, "It was horrible, just horrible."

Joni Migdal also managed to get in the house one day when Ellen was out, and had a chat with Robert on the patio of the swimming pool. "He knew he was very sick. He knew he was going to die, and I said, 'Robert, what are you going to say to your children?' And he said he was going to tell them that he was dying, and 'to look for signs' that he's around after he was gone, because 'I will always be with them.' I thought that was one of the nicest things that he could say. That's who Robert Kardashian was."

While Kardashians friends complained of being blocked from seeing Robert, his children were there at his side. According to Kris Jenner in her book, as "Robert was going downhill fast. . . . Kimberly and Kourtney spent practically every waking moment" with their father, "taking care of him and feeding him. . . . Kourtney read to Robert, and Kim would make him Cream of Wheat, oatmeal, or a cup of tea."

When Kardashian was dying, Priscilla Presley, whom he had wanted to marry and have children with years earlier, telephoned him and gently told him she loved him.

It brought tears to his eyes.

KRIS JENNER CLAIMED THAT in her ex-husband's last hours, she went into his bedroom and saw that he wasn't conscious but that his heart was still beating. She said some last words to him, but "felt like he just wasn't there anymore," and that when he passed part of her "died with him. . . . I was, by then, Kris Jenner, but in some way I would also always be a Kardashian."

Weighing about eighty pounds, Robert Kardashian, whose only real fame ever came as being a famous football player's sidekick and defender, died on a hospital gurney in the bedroom of his home on September 30, 2003, almost five months before his sixtieth birthday.

His funeral service was held at Inglewood Park Cemetery, also the final resting place of Johnnie Cochran, the attorney who played the race card and won O. J. Simpson's acquittal in the trial of the century. Cochran died at sixty-seven, two years after Kardashian's passing.

Ronald Reagan's minister, Reverend Donn Moomaw, who had gotten embroiled in the Bel-Air Presbyterian Church sex scandal in the early 1990s, and who had been Tom Kardashian's friend and pastor, officiated at the funeral. Besides Moomaw on the stage, eulogies were offered by Kim Kardashian, representing the family, and Larry Kraines, who was asked to represent Kardashian's friends "because we went back a long, long way."

The eulogies dealt with Kardashian's sense of humor, and his loyalty. "And all his old girlfriends, going all the way back, were there," Kraines recalled. "Even though he had lots of dates when he was younger, he kept good relationships and friendships with every single one of those gals, which said he was a good guy, and he thought they were good people, and he never wanted bad feelings with anyone."

At the funeral, Kim approached Joni Migdal and told her about an odd experience she had had on her way to the cemetery. " 'You'll never guess what happened,' " she said. " 'I was driving down the Ventura Freeway to get to the funeral and there was like a rainbow of seagulls that flew over.' The strange thing about that," noted Migdal, "is that the Ventura Freeway is in the Valley, and seagulls do not go to the Valley. I asked Kim what she thought it meant, and she told me, 'It's a sign my father was there with me.' "

After the funeral there was a country club reception. Friends of Kardashian who had abandoned him because of his role in the O.J. trial and his participation in Lawrence Schiller's book suddenly did an about-face and showed up to honor his memory.

But Migdal recalled that "no one—*no one*—talked to the widow," Ellen Pearson Kardashian. "She was like sitting all by herself." She was blacklisted by everyone, just as her late husband had once been.

There was so much to Robert George Kardashian's complicated and turbulent life, but the world would mostly only remember him and his name as connected to his daughter Kim's sex tape and to a reality TV show starring his family with the Kardashian name in the title, but mostly to the O.J. murder case and trial.

As the headline over *The New York Times* obituary quietly summed up his life: "Robert Kardashian, a Lawyer for O. J. Simpson, Dies at 59."

PART III

The "Miscreants"

"Kim Kardashian, Superstar"

Robert Kardashian's death was hardest on his children.
Kim, always closest to him and the favorite of his three daughters, was just three weeks away from turning twenty-three when her father passed, and she was the most affected emotionally. Her behavior that horrific year underscored her anger and pain that she would soon lose him. Around the time Kardashian became terminally ill and had little time left, Kim joined with her boyfriend, a Mississippi-born young black man by the name of William Raymond "Ray J" Norwood Jr., in an act that forever would change her life.

He came from a musically talented family; Norwood's older sister was the popular singer and actress known as Brandy. Using the name Ray J professionally, he had talent, too, and would become an actor, singer, and record producer. Before he was ten, and after the family had moved to Los Angeles, the cute, cuddly kid was being cast in commercials, and soon he had roles in two sitcoms popular with young blacks—*The*

Sinbad Show, in which he played the orphaned son of the African-American comedian. The other was his sister's series, *Moesha*, about a high school girl who, by coincidence, lived in the Leimert Park neighborhood of L.A., where Robert Kardashian's pal Phil Pennino had lived when they were in high school together, and which was then still predominately white.

But Ray J's biggest claim to fame—or rather infamy—in the early 2000s was his costarring role in an interracial sex romp with Kim Kardashian, the real scene-stealer and a genuine exhibitionist, the year her father fell ill and died. It was supposed to be a private video, but it would later gain Kim international fame (and millions of dollars) when it suspiciously became public and was boffo at the registers of adult shops everywhere and downloaded on PCs around the world.

Kim followed in the stiletto-heel footsteps of her close friend Paris Hilton, whose heavily publicized triple-X-rated romp—*1 Night in Paris*—had launched her outrageous career. Kim's, too, would lead to her very questionable stardom.

Robert Kardashian's name and fame and the Kardashian family became known as a result of his ill-fated, ill-advised on-camera defense of an accused black killer. Kim's became known for her ill-advised but successful on-camera sex with her black lover.

The first decade of the 2000s was the era of the spoiled, wild girls of L.A.—the Hilton "celebutantes" Paris and Nicky; the emotionally troubled and diabetic Johnson & Johnson Band-Aid heiress, Casey; the difficult *Mean Girls* actress Lindsay Lohan; singer Lionel Richie's rail-thin daughter, Nicole, who denied having an eating disorder; pop sensation and rehab veteran Britney Spears, and the then known for little or nothing Kim Kardashian—until her video surfaced. They were the "It" girls, whose raunchy behavior, documented in the tabloids, gossip columns, and celebrity magazines earned them TV shows, lucrative movie and recording deals and sponsors, and, in some instances, jail time.

But Kim was far less visible, and more behaved. Her daddy had always taught her to be a little lady.

As a veteran female senior tabloid editor who specialized in celebrity news and gossip observed in 2015: "Paris Hilton was a bad girl and the public was interested in her when she behaved badly. She had the society thing and people looked at her style and her money, but she just wasn't as fascinating as Kim Kardashian. Until Kim's sex tape, she wasn't considered a bad girl. She didn't do drugs. She didn't stay out all night boozing. And she didn't have blond hair and blue eyes. She was more relatable."

From 2003 onward, Kim's sex tape remained hidden and undiscovered, and it did not surface until 2007—curiously in the same year that her mother, Kris Kardashian Jenner, cut a lucrative deal for a reality show with E! to air all of their bizarre behavior as a family. Around the same time, either by coincidence or by shrewd planning, Kim and Ray J's lusty on-camera romp was purchased by a major producer and purveyor of adult films. Vivid Entertainment, which paid a mysterious someone a reported one million dollars, released it publicly in stores and on the Internet shortly after Valentine's Day 2007, with much fanfare, controversy, and, for Kim Kardashian and her family, free publicity worth untold millions of dollars.

It was called *Kim Kardashian, Superstar.*

But how did it get from the confines of Kim's very private possessions to Vivid?

Blame—or credit—the momager.

"Kris knew people who knew people," said a close Kardashian business insider who was aware of the clandestine sex tape transaction. "She'd learned much from Robert and much from Bruce through the years. She knew her way around town, and had the connections. Kris saw the value in that tape, knew how a sex tape had made Paris Hilton a sensation, and figured it could do the same for Kim. Either directly or indirectly, that tape got to the folks at Vivid. Kris knew what she was doing, and Kim went along for the ride. It was all about money and fame."

Generating even more publicity and visibility, Kim made headlines by suing Vivid for distributing *Kim Kardashian, Superstar*, seeking all profits from its sale and asking for unspecified damages along with attorney fees.

She issued a statement to *People* in February 2007, claiming: "This tape, which was made three years ago, and was meant to be something private between myself and my then-boyfriend is extremely hurtful not only to me, but to my family as well. . . . It is being sold completely without my permission or consent."

Steven Hirsch, Vivid's co-chairman at the time, said his company had "the legal right to distribute" the tape, was "comfortable" in releasing it, and noted, "We would like Kim and Ray J to be a part of it and hopefully we can work that out." Ray J, not named in the suit, had nothing to add.

But his mother, Sonja Norwood, later suggested that Kim was the likely source for leaking the tape. "As a mother, I was very upset," she declared on Wendy Williams's TV talk show (while promoting her family's own reality show on VH1). She claimed that Kim and her son had dated for five years and "were in love," and she noted, referring to the tape, "What you don't want people to see, you don't do. . . . Somehow it [the tape] surfaced." And she was furious that Ray J was being gossiped about and blamed for leaking it to Vivid.

It all ended amicably, however, when Kim, after generating headlines, dropped her lawsuit.

"We met with her several times and finally reached a financial arrangement that we both feel is fair," stated the Vivid Entertainment Group's co-chairman, Hirsch, who noted, "The DVD has become a best seller in adult video stores and online. . . . It is also a popular download."

Other than her role in a sex tape, Kim had no other fame at that point, as underscored by Hirsch's press release, which described her only as the "daughter of O. J. Simpson lawyer Robert Kardashian and a close friend of Paris Hilton." It further noted, "As part of her commitment to drop the suit, Ms. Kardashian agreed to a lump sum financial settlement for the sale of the DVDs."

It was later reported that she got nearly $5 million for her sex play with Ray J, with whom she had broken up in 2005.

Six years after the release of the tape and her daughter's big financial settlement, Kris Jenner spoke publicly about *Kim Kardashian, Superstar* for the first time in a chummy chat with Joan Rivers on her gossipy and very strange show, appropriately called *In Bed with Joan*, which was taped weekly from Joan's bed in her Malibu home and aired on iTunes and YouTube.

Kris, air-kissing Rivers, boasted that her daughters had "star quality on some levels . . . they had a passion about something," like fashion. When asked by Rivers what her reaction had been to her daughter's sex tape, Kris stated that she "literally fell apart" knowing that the public was seeing her second-born doing the nasty. Calling herself "somewhat religious," she claimed, "I had to go into a room and cry for a couple days and say, 'okay, pull yourself to-fucking-gether because you have to be here for all these kids and your family, and you have to show them as an example how to get through this.'"

LARRY KRAINES, BETTER KNOWN as "Uncle Larry" to Kim and her Kardashian siblings, firmly believed that his late close friend Robert, the patriarch, would be "proud as punch that his girls had initiative and that they got success and riches on their own. Would Robert have liked Kim's sex tape, and all that horseshit? Probably not. But would he have liked the fact that they have made a tremendous amount of money? Definitely! Robert wasn't here to do it for them, but he had a lot to do with their work ethic. And I'm proud of what they all did."

Kardashian's brother, Tom, agrees with Kraines's assessment.

"The girls got their business acumen and entrepreneurial spirit from Robert. Kris, to her credit, just kind of kept a firm hand on all of it. How did all their success come about? It was my brother's influence at home, and how he thought."

He noted, surprisingly, that his mother, the late Helen Kardashian—the Kardashian girls' paternal grandmother—"would encourage everything the girls are into, and what they do. My brother could do no wrong, and the girls could do no wrong. But my dad might not have been pleased with their choices. Yes, Kim did a sex tape, but who in the family is going to talk to her about it, and how would you talk to her about it? Would you say, 'Oh, Nana, what do you think of my sex tape?' It would be my mother's lady friends who would want to throw in shit like that. 'Helen, did you see that tape with Kim and her boyfriend? Did you just see what Kim did?'"

IN HER 2011 MEMOIR, Kris Jenner made absolutely no mention of her daughter Kim's very lucrative venture into the porn world—shot in 2003, released in 2007—and how it made her so famous—and a millionaire at least five times over.

For Kris's readers, it was as if *Kim Kardashian, Superstar* had never happened.

Instead, Kris noted that her daughter was "getting some attention" for another completely unrelated reason by going out and being seen by the paparazzi and gossip writers with her friend, the scandalous Paris Hilton. Making no mention of Hilton's own sex tape, which made her a household name, Kris stated that somehow the Hilton girl "took off in the public eye and became very, very famous."

Kim had become Paris's sidekick—both with sex tapes on their résumés—and the two of them, according to Kris, began "traveling to places like Vegas or the Hamptons together. . . . Paris started asking Kim to go everywhere with her" and "the media started noticing Kim because she was always with Paris."

They were being noticed, in fact, mainly because they were two young, exhibitionistic, narcissistic, fame-hungry hotties who had become celebrities by doing it on camera and being generally outrageous.

IN HER BOOK, KRIS curiously described her second-born as the "hopeless romantic among my girls."

By then Kim was long divorced from her first husband, the African-American music producer Damon Thomas, with whom she had eloped in 2000 when she was nineteen and he twenty-nine. They divorced in 2003 after a very stormy three years together.

In divorce papers that were later leaked to a tabloid, Kim alleged she had been both emotionally and physically abused by Thomas, that he had slammed her against walls, thrown her across a room, and battered and bruised her, or so she had alleged. The divorce papers quoted her as claiming that on one occasion "He became enraged and punched me in the face. My face was bruised and swollen as a result. I thought about calling the police but was afraid and decided not to do so."

Thomas opened up to another celebrity weekly, denying all Kim's allegations, and charged that she had made them up in order to get "a lot of money" in their divorce.

He reportedly was ordered to pay her $56,000.

He said he was the one who filed for divorce—shades of Robert and Kris—when he discovered she was allegedly cheating on him. He claimed that her alleged philandering had occurred with "multiple guys." One of them was identified as actor/dancer Cris Judd, ex-husband of Jennifer Lopez. Kim denied the accusations of adultery.

Moreover, Thomas claimed he paid for Kim's extravagant shopping sprees, along with her breast implants and liposuction. He had complaints about the same kinds of expenditures that Robert Kardashian had had about Kris when he dumped her.

Kim was clearly following in her mother's footsteps, marriage-wise.

The cliché "Like mother, like daughter" fits well when comparing the two. From their history, Kim was clearly a chip off the old block. Kris even acknowledged in her memoir, "Kim and I are like twin souls."

And as Thomas asserted, "Kim is obsessed with fame. She can't write or sing or dance, so she does harmful things in order to validate herself in the media. That's a fame-whore to me."

JUST AS WITH KIM'S sex tape and the scandalous divorce, there was more tabloid drama when, a decade after Robert Kardashian's death, his angry and emotional words about his marriage to Kris and her roles as wife, mother, and adulterer became candidly and publicly known. They ignited an explosive legal war between the Kardashians, led by Kris, against Robert's widow, Ellen Pearson, who sold excerpts from his 1989–90 private diaries and some family photos to the publisher of several celebrity weeklies.

It was as if Kardashian were speaking from the grave.

On one page of his diary, he had written, "Imagine, if you can, a couple happily married for over 10 years, with 4 gorgeous children, and then to the husbands horror, he discovers that his wife is having an affair . . . Imagine his hurt, frustration, and anger, not only for himself but for their children. Imagine what effect this behavior ultimately will have on the children's future morals . . . a real nightmare, isn't it?"

At another point, Kardashian wrote that Kris's lover, Todd Waterman, "slept in my bed" while cuckolded Kardashian's daughter Khloé and son, Rob, were in the house. "She doesn't care! She left [the] kids & screwed all nite." Regarding the Christmas holiday of 1989, he claimed he "was home alone with 4 kids. I put them to bed & played w/them." In still another entry, Kardashian claimed that Kris pulled Kourtney's hair and twisted her arms, and that both Kourtney and Kim were "scared and nervous, have been beat up several times before and are very, very intimidated."

His "dear diary" references about what a horrific life he had with Kris went on and on.

Not surprisingly, the publication of Kardashian's angry words did not go over well with the momager, who, on April 4, 2013, had her Hollywood attorney, Marty Singer, sue Pearson.

He claimed that the diaries and photos belonged to Kris and her brood, that by selling them for "tens of thousands of dollars" the widow had infringed on the copyrights owned by the Kardashians. Moreover, he alleged that the Kardashians weren't even aware of the materials, that Pearson had held the "private writings" and photos "in secret," until all was published. Singer claimed that all Kardashian's tangible personal property was meant to go to his children, and that Pearson had kept the writings and photos "with the express intent to one-day capitalize on and exploit the valuable property and celebrity of the famous Robert Kardashian, and/or deprive the Kardashian Siblings of the benefit of private information, and memories about their father."

The lawsuit went into Pearson's own financial situation, claiming that after "years of unchecked spending living off of her inheritance and amassing significant debt, including to her country club" she had filed for chapter 7 bankruptcy in March 2011, but never listed that her assets included "the Diary and Photograph and Family Albums as valuable assets" in her possession, as required by law.

Singer charged that with all Pearson's "financial woes," she tried to "sell (often false) tabloid stories and Kardashian family photos to exploit and cash-in" on the Kardashians' celebrity. His suit cited *In Touch Weekly* and *Life & Style* magazines as the publisher of the stories.

Pearson fought back.

Legal papers filed by her lawyers in federal court in Los Angeles on August 12, 2013, alleged defamation, intentional infliction of emotional distress, and civil conspiracy to defame. As part of its request to file a countersuit, the Beverly Hills–headquartered Peter Law Group took note of the Kardashians' reality TV program, describing it as the "often sordid, decadent and scandalous lives of the Kardashians," and said its success was based on a "basic premise embraced [by] . . . Kris Jenner in particular—to expose their outlandish and controversial activities to world-wide television viewers for commercial profit."

And Pearson's lawyers claimed that the series was "predicated entirely on the revelation of private information of the most salacious variety." Pearson claimed the Kardashians had filed their lawsuit against her because it would be part of a "carefully orchestrated aspect" of episode two from season eight of *Keeping Up with the Kardashians*.

In that episode, according to Pearson's lawyers, "the Kardashians repeatedly attribute highly incendiary and provocative statements about Kris Jenner's fitness as a mother to Ellen when they were in fact made by Robert Kardashian about his ex-wife and their mother."

Pearson's lawyers further claimed that Robert Kardashian's revelations in his diaries "are inconsistent with Kris's portrayal as a loving and caring mother who puts her children first. Robert's diaries and notes exposed Kris as a manipulative and devious mother and ex-wife who simply used and exploited her children and family."

The copyright claim was settled in 2014. Pearson returned the diaries and photos to the Kardashians, and the Kardashians were awarded about $84,000. Tabloid hell also broke loose for Kris and her children in the fall of 2014 when Kardashian's short-time second wife, Jan Ashley, claimed publicly that the Kardashian siblings had caused the marital problems between her and Kardashian. She told a celebrity magazine, "Did the kids have anything to do with it? Of course, they did! All I know is he was upset all the time. Not with me, [but] with his kids and his ex-wife. . . . They were after him for money, money, money. I don't think he could handle them." She also claimed that Kardashian "pretended" he was wealthy, and that his children "acted like a bunch of spoiled brats. . . . He didn't have any money," she asserted. "He always pretended he had money."

Even in death, Robert Kardashian, who always tried to be a good Christian, couldn't catch a break.

TWENTY-FIVE

It's Reality

According to Kris Jenner, everyone who knew her and Bruce and their five daughters and one son thought they were all "so crazy" that they deserved their own reality TV show.

The man of the house, the secretly cross-dressing former Olympian who considered himself a woman trapped in a man's body, had already experienced reality TV as part of the first-season cast of the nightly U.S. version of the British-made game show *I'm a Celebrity . . . Get Me Out of Here!* in which he lived for weeks with ten other B-listers (Robin Leach, Alana Stewart, Melissa Rivers, and Cris Judd, among others) in a difficult (but scripted) jungle environment in the Australian outback. Tessa Jowell, Britain's minister of state for culture at the time, described the cast of Jenner's show to the *Financial Times* as "has-been celebrities."

Jenner's reality appearances aired in that same strange year, 2003, that Robert Kardashian died and his beloved daughter performed sex acts on camera with her lover.

Jenner didn't like the reality TV gig at all, but needed the money and adored being in the public eye. Like his stepdaughter Kim Kardashian, Superstar, he was an exhibitionist.

In any case, reality television, as the free world now knows, was the Kardashians' platinum future. As Kris observed, "I always thought our family was certainly entertaining enough—or maybe just crazy enough—to make a good reality show." Ryan Seacrest thought so, too.

If anyone should take the blame, or the praise, for bringing the Kardashians to the world's stage, it should be the handsome, boyish bachelor wunderkind of television land, who had been discovered years earlier by the closeted homosexual talk show host Merv Griffin. Once described in a profile as "an asexual icon for traditional cultural conservatism," Seacrest became a power as the host of one of television's most popular shows, *American Idol*, which premiered in 2002.

Before that, he had a history of hosting other reality and game shows, and even did radio. When Dick Clark—long billed as "America's oldest teenager," of *American Bandstand* fame—had a stroke in 2004, Seacrest stepped in in 2005 to host the popular New Year's Eve Times Square ball-dropping show, and when Clark died Seacrest signed a deal to host and be the executive producer. He also had his own fashion line and had his hand in numerous other lucrative media endeavors.

In 2007, Seacrest and his two-year-old company, Ryan Seacrest Productions, were on the lookout for a family that a reality show could be built around. His model, one that he regularly watched, was *The Osbournes*, starring the heavy metal star Ozzie Osbourne and his family—his wife, Sharon, their son, Jack, and daughter, Kelly. It began airing on MTV in March 2002—it was one of the network's most popular programs—and ended its successful run in March 2005. Jack and Kelly would later reveal that some of the family's off-the-wall antics were staged, which was no great secret in the world of reality TV. Much of what would be filmed when the Kardashians hit the airwaves was set up by the producers, according to news accounts.

Seacrest approached casting directors in Los Angeles and said,

" 'We're interested in meeting families who want to be on a series or are interested in being in the world of television.' "

The Kardashians, led by Kris, were first in line. She would call her family a "modern-day Brady Bunch," probably not realizing that some cast members of that iconic early-seventies family sitcom had serious issues. Mike Brady, the father, was played by Robert Reed, who died after contracting HIV. Maureen McCormick, who played daughter Marcia Brady, had serious drug issues. And Mike Lookinland, who played Bobby Brady, had a drunk driving record.

The real-life Kardashian bunch were far from the TV model Brady Bunch, but Kris saw parallels, and she had even gone so far as to buy a new home, a Cape Cod style that she felt resembled the one the fictional Bradys occupied on television. It was "the perfect house," she called it, "for our crazy Hollywood family." Moreover, she saw her new address as "a stage . . . a house *dying* for an audience. I never could have dreamed of how large that audience would become."

A casting director set up a meeting with Seacrest, Kris, Bruce, and the gang. "I had met the girls before, but I didn't know the family well," said Seacrest in 2015. "So I said to a guy in my office, 'Why don't you buy a video camera and go out to their house on a Sunday when they're having a family barbeque, shoot it, and then we'll watch it and see what we think.' "

After spending a bit of time with the Kardashians, Seacrest got a call from his man on the scene: " 'It's absolutely golden,' " he joyfully reported. " 'You're going to die when you see this tape. They're so funny, they're so fun, there is so much love in this family and they're so chaotic— they throw each other in the pool!' "

Seacrest watched the tape first thing Monday morning, was knocked out, saw a hit on his hands, and rushed the material over to E! As Seacrest told *Haute Living* in January 2015, "That was the beginning."

Of all of them, he admired Kris, the momager, the most. "She has done an amazing job," he believed, "at taking what was just a television show and building it into a massive empire for the family."

Kris had a somewhat different take on how the idea for the show came about. A friend, Deena Katz, had sparked the idea after spending an evening with the Kardashian-Jenners. Katz was in the TV business, was a casting director, saw how crazy the family's lifestyle was, and suggested she talk to the Ryan Seacrest crowd over at E! "Get me a meeting," Kris claimed she told Katz. The next morning Kris was in Seacrest's office. She felt she was in good company because two of her daughters' pals, Paris Hilton and Nicole Richie, had done their time on E! with reality shows. At the meeting she told Seacrest's partner, Eliot Goldberg, that her idea for the show would be a "blow-by-blow look at our crazy, loving, fun, and incredibly close family."

And her big pitch was that her daughters would be the show's stars, especially Kim and all the controversy that was swirling around her—"both positive and negative." But her sex tape was not mentioned by Kris in her book as the reason for all that controversy.

The producers, Seacrest and Goldberg, surely aware of *Kim Kardashian, Superstar* and its XXX rating and all the buzz attached to it, bought the show on the spot.

It was a "magical moment" Kris had never forgot.

When she told the family that night, Bruce was "dumbstruck," but went along. But he had to be wondering how much he might have to reveal about himself.

Meanwhile, Kris was about to merge her roles as mom and manager.

She called herself Momager.

People who knew Kris from way back when—when she really was a Kardashian through marriage to Robert—perceived that she had the kind of ambition and drive and ego that would one day bring her to this point.

Robert's lifelong confidant Joni Migdal, pondering Kris's success in 2016, maintained, "This was her vision of what she always wanted to do. She had a plan. She had a goal. Look what she did with Bruce. When she first met him he was a nothing. Yes, he was an Olympian, but she really turned his whole life around. What she's doing now is creating her own dream. I am *not* surprised. I am *not* shocked at all. She always had the capabilities, and she just went with it."

A 2015 profile of Kris in *The New York Times* had a similar take about her and her family. "[W]e have reached the point at which the Jenners and the Kardashians are not famous for being famous: They are famous for the industry that they've created, the Kardashian/Jenner megacomplex, which has not just invaded the culture but metastasized into it, with the family members emerging as legitimate businesspeople and Kris the mother-leader of them all."

A month after the deal for the Kardashian show was signed, filming started.

One last detail was left to be finalized—what to name it.

The producer and showrunner, a woman by the name of Farnaz Farjam, had been all over the place with her camera crews trying to document the varied real and staged activities of the Kardashian bunch.

Showing up exhausted and late once to a meeting early on in the process, she said, "I'm just having a really hard time *keeping up with the Kardashians.*"

Ka-ching!

Keeping Up with the Kardashians had its premiere on October 14, 2007, a date that will live in television and pop culture infamy.

It became a gold mine. A Hollywood fairy tale come true.

BY 2016, THE KARDASHIAN-JENNER franchise and empire would have a a reported net worth of more than $191 million, a mind-boggling and seemingly impossible success story for a dysfunctional family with little or no discernable talent besides self-promotion.

Along with the show, their empire included clothing lines, skin-care products, fragrances, lines of jewelry, cosmetics, and more.

Kris's bundle came mostly from her company, which involved the Kardashian show, reality TV spin-offs, and the development of products by her daughters—such as Kourtney, Kim, and Khloé's "Kardashian

Beauty" line and Kim's Collection Fragrance. Sears would commission Kris to manage a global lifestyle line, and she would have the "Kris Jenner Kollection for QVC." And much more.

The Kardashian sisters would have their own lucrative brands and businesses, together and separately.

Kim alone would have a net worth of $51 million, and was the richest and most powerful. From the main show, she received a reported $80,000 per episode, and has received as much as a gossiped-about $1 million for a personal appearance. One report stated that people who want to be in her presence were actually charged a fee. At her birthday party in 2014, guests were charged as much as $2,500 each. And she was making huge deals for exclusive rights to events in her life like bridal showers.

Kourtney, the eldest and the least scandalous, and the only sister who didn't marry, although she had three children out of wedlock, would be worth as much as $15 million. From the reality show, she would be paid as much as $50,000 per episode, receive $125,000 for a personal appearance, and for tweeting a product endorsement, she would be paid $15,000. And she had spin-offs from the main show—*Kourtney and Khloé Take Miami*, and then *New York*.

Khloé, whose birth as a biological Kardashian has been seriously questioned—even by her father of record, the late Robert Kardashian, reportedly had a net worth of $11 million. From the family program, her take-home was $40,000 per episode, and when she made a personal appearance she took home another $75,000. Asked to make a product endorsement on Twitter, she would get a check for $13,000. From a fragrance line, she earned an estimated $20 million.

Kris's daughters with Caitlyn Jenner, formerly known as Bruce, would become overnight fashion stars. Kendall and Kylie were far more attractive physically than the Kardashian sisters, and developed a hugely successful clothing line with PacSun. For their participation in the show, they each earned about $5,000 per episode. And Kendall would become a much-publicized fashion model. At fourteen she was signed by the prestigious Wilhelmina agency, and she would begin showing up on the covers of such fashion bibles as *Vogue* and *Harper's Bazaar.*

And in the spring of 2017, the Kardashian's reality television empire and brand expanded to include the youngest of the Kardashian-Jenner clan, Kylie, to the schedule with her own spin-off—eight episodes called *Life of Kylie*, set to begin airing that summer on E! "Kylie's beauty, business savvy, and fashion icon status have made her one of the most famous and successful young women on the planet," boasted an E! v.p. "Kylie has achieved so much at such a young age, and we know the E! audience will be thrilled now that she is ready to share an inside look at her everyday life." The momager, Kris, was billed as executive producer.

The least famous—but a constant tabloid figure—would be Robert Kardashian's namesake and only son. Robert Arthur Kardashian's net worth was almost $3 million, and he would be paid $20,000 per episode at the top of his game. He was cast in a season of *Dancing With the Stars*, and would serve as a judge in the 2012 Miss USA pageant—paid a reported $25,000. There would be other deals, too.

"All those millions and very little talent says something terrible about our culture," observed a member of the Kardashian team. "But, hey, take it while you can."

The many seasons of *Keeping Up with the Kardashians* would be seen in 160 countries. There would be countless reruns and countless critiques by respected cultural critics. The Kardashians were *the* zeitgeist of the early decades of the 2000s, love 'em or hate 'em.

The opening sequence of the first episode was classic. The camera zeroed in on Kim's signature body part, her enormous ass, as she scanned the contents of the Kardashians' fridge.

"Junk in her trunk," commented Kris.

"Mom, she's always had an ass," declared Khloé.

Kourtney called her mother "catty."

And Kim replied, "I hate you all."

_____

TWENTY-SIX

A "Complex" Lie

In early 2007, the freelance writer Nate Denver had never heard of Kim Kardashian, like most everyone else. It was some months before the premiere of *Keeping Up with the Kardashians* and just before the pornographic *Kim Kardashian, Superstar* was released, that Denver, in Los Angeles, received a call from his editor, Noah Callahan-Bever, at *Complex* magazine, in New York, assigning him to interview her.

"I remember asking who she was, and they said she was a friend of Paris Hilton, and I kind of joked, 'So now we're interviewing Paris Hilton's friends?' But they told me who her biological father was, and some of the men she was involved with. That gave me some context. But that's the first interview I'd ever done with someone I truly was unfamiliar with," he said, looking back in 2015.

For Kim, this interview with Denver and the photos that were going to be taken were a big deal because *Complex*, billed as the "men's guide to consumer culture," was the first magazine ever to approach her and put her on the cover and make her a pin-up girl. She appeared in the February-March 2007 issue in a breast-enhancing black bra, black panties, and peep-toe stilettos, with a headline that read: "WHO IS KIM KARDASHIAN? PARIS HILTON'S B.F.F. ON SEX, LIES, AND VIDEOTAPES."

But readers of her mother's memoir would never have known that. To Kris, the only men's magazine that meant anything in Kim's blossoming career was *Playboy*, and during the first season of *KUWTK,* and after Kim did her first TV talk show appearance on *The Tyra Banks Show*, and after Kim became known as a porn star, *Playboy* called and wanted to do a spread, and got the green light with Kris's exuberant approval.

Not nearly as naked—and nowhere nearly as raunchy as she was in her sex video—Kim, in a plunging red negligee, posed sublimely in the December 2007 issue of *Playboy*. Kris raved about Kim's Hugh Hefner adventure in her book. But Kim's dealings with *Complex* were completely ignored.

While Hefner gave Kim and her people the royal treatment for the shoot at the Playboy Mansion, Nate Denver, then thirty-one, met twenty-six-year-old Kim for her interview and the *Complex* photo shoot in a far less glamorous venue. They arranged to meet in a West Hollywood bar in the middle of the day when she was still a virtual unknown.

He was "not surprised" when she arrived and he found her to be one hot number. "If I hadn't been married to my beautiful wife at the time," said Denver, "I would have been interested. Kim was attractive and extremely friendly."

The idea for the cover story, said Denver, "was to kind of introduce her to readers, because this was her very first magazine interview and first cover. She had a really nice kind of optimistic feel to her about the world and where her career was going, and it seemed like she knew this was probably going to be a nice stepping stone for her, and it was a really easy interview. She had a lot of energy and I felt she was going to turn it into something."

Kim openly talked about herself, or so her candor seemed in that bar, revealing at one point that sometimes she referred to herself as "Princess Kim," claimed she was an "outdoorsy sports person," and that she and her then–bosom buddy Paris Hilton referred to themselves as seniors of a fictional "Hollywood High," meaning they knew their way around La-La Land. "I go to parties and hang out," she said when Denver asked her what she did for fun. But there was something very important about her past that was missing from her answers.

After Denver finished the interview, his editor telephoned and queried whether he had, by chance, asked her if there was any truth to a rumor that was circulating in media and gossip circles that she had made a porno with her lover, Ray J, and that it was soon to be released commercially.

"At the time, I had no idea that it existed," acknowledged Denver, "so I called her back, and we set up a second interview for on the phone. She was very friendly, she said it [the tape] existed, 'but I need to talk to my lawyer first.'

"She called me back the same day and completely denied that it existed. She said, 'There's no such tape. It doesn't exist.' She had been completely coached and was ready to deny that it existed, and gave me a completely rehearsed answer. It was silly because we had just talked a couple of minutes before and she had said she wanted to talk about it. I think the next week the tape came out."

In the published interview, a Q and A, Denver asked her about the sex tape rumors, and she was directly quoted as saying, "There is no sex tape! Ray J's not the kind of guy who would do something for revenge. There is no amount of money that could ever convince me to release any tape, even if I had one. I don't need the money!"

Kim had been caught in a major, embarrassing lie.

Soon after, Denver watched Kim and Ray J's porno when it went online. "My curiosity drove me to find it and take a look," he recalled. "It was interesting to see a person I met and interacted with in a production like that. At the same time it was a strange voyeuristic thing to watch."

But *Complex*, blatantly lied to, wasn't through with Kim Kardashian.

Joe La Puma of the magazine's staff did a follow-up interview with her in the spring of 2007 and confronted Kim about her denial, and she gave a rather convoluted answer, to wit:

"Well at that point I really didn't think that one was coming out. I heard rumors of things as degrading and disgusting as a golden shower . . . that never even happened in my lifetime, so I didn't think that what everybody was talking about had any truth to it. So I apologize for not publicly being honest, but no one wants to hope that that's the truth and you hope that will never come out so I felt like at the time that's all that I could have said."

Asked whether she thought the tape would never surface even though she knew "Ray J was filming it," Kim admitted, "I knew that we had one tape, but it was a few different times throughout the few years in our relationship. I obviously knew that that existed, I just never thought that it would happen."

She also denied that she ever had any intention to see it made public, or thought that it was a good idea to see it commercially released as a career enhancer as it had been for her pal Paris.

"Never once have I thought that . . . My dad would've been mortified and I'm not happy about it. You know, I thought I was gonna marry this guy; we were in a three-year relationship. I didn't think that our personal business would be for the world to see."

THE WORLD, HOWEVER, DID SEE Kim Kardashian *again* in the buff— then married for the third time, and soon to be a mother of two—when she "broke the Internet" by posing seven years later on the cover of the winter 2014, ten-dollar edition of *Paper* magazine—her big, bold, inflated, shiny, naked ass front and center for all to see.

The infamous Kim Kardashian derriere had even caught the attention of the respected British actress Helen Mirren, who was quoted in the UK's *Telegraph* as musing, "I'm not into the Kardashians, it's a phenomenon I just don't find interesting, but—and this is the big word: B-U-T-T—it's wonderful that you're allowed to have a butt nowadays! Thanks to Madame Kardashian . . . It's very positive. . . . I love shameless women. Shameless and proud!"

In promoting the *Paper* magazine issue, the magazine's advertising declared, "There is no other person that we can think of who is up to the task [to Break the Internet] than one Kim Kardashian West. A pop culture fascination able to generate headlines just by leaving her house, Kim is what makes the web tick . . . All we can say about the images inside . . . *holy fucking shit.*"

It was not the first time that Kim had been featured in the trendy magazine. A few years earlier, when it did a social media issue, *Paper* featured Kim and Khloé inside—a photo of the sisters with their eyes glued to their mobile phones, "and it was a huge success online," said *Paper* editor Mickey Boardman, looking back in 2015.

The idea to do the Kim cover and use the image of her to break the Internet was the brainchild of the magazine's then-new chief creative officer, Drew Elliott, who had spent a year in Los Angeles working for a social media company—one that had done work for President Obama and many celebrities. "One of Drew's mandates was to do people who have a much greater reach digitally, so that's why Kim was the ultimate in a way because she is really *the* most famous woman in the world, especially if you go on the Internet. . . . The story has to live online, create interest and traffic, and get people talking," said Boardman.

Curiously, when Kardashian West's name was brought up at an editorial meeting, Boardman said they weren't thinking of doing a nude cover with her. Their thinking was that she was among a very tiny list of celebrities who have "a gigantic following, and everything they do creates news." Besides Kardashian, that elite group included Rihanna, Justin Bieber, and Miley Cyrus.

"But Kim is gorgeous. And she's become *very* fashion," said Boardman. "Her metamorphosis is kind of fascinating. And we just thought she was super right—*the* most important celebrity in a way right now."

By using a naked Kim on the cover, maintained Boardman, "We were purposefully trying to get as much attention, as much traffic, as much press, as much everything.

"People always have some kind of reaction to her. Either they *love* Kim or they think she's a symbol of *everything* that's wrong with society. There are very few people who elicit that strong of a reaction."

BY THE TIME KIM was being considered by the *Paper* people as the only celebrity in the world who could break the Internet, she had had a second turbulent marriage, and was then hoping to have a successful third.

Her second husband, after Damon Thomas, was the professional basketball star Kris Humphries, the six-foot-nine, 235-pound son of an interracial couple. But before she tied the knot with him, her baby sister Khloé gave her a dire warning, in her typical classy manner, not to. As she revealed in 2016 to Snoop Dogg on his online show, "I was like, 'He's a fucking loser. Why are you marrying this fucking dog?' "

And Khloé knew from losers as her roller-coaster marriage to her own black basketball star, the six-foot-ten Lamar Odom, would amply and very publicly demonstrate.

Odom had fathered three children with his first wife, and married Khloé in September 2009—they had dated for only one month after meeting at a party. Their wedding was given big play on E! They even had their own E! spin-off, *Khloé & Lamar*, a two-season flop.

Odom would later have a DUI arrest, alleged drug problems, and just before Christmas, in 2013, Khloé filed for divorce, but she later withdrew the papers. In 2015, Odom was found unconscious at the Love Ranch brothel in Nevada, igniting headlines and still another Kardashian scandal and more drama. They eventually did divorce.

Khloé apparently had a real thing about romancing giant-size African

American hoop stars, as underscored in the fall of 2016 when she began seeing the six-foot-nine Cleveland Cavaliers player Tristan Thompson, who is seven years her junior. Khloé's momager, Kris, was introduced to her daughter's new beau and called him a "wonderful guy . . . he's great." She termed her third-born a "delicious girl" and declared, "I just want her to be happy, having a good time." Khloé had begun seeing Thompson after breaking up with the six-foot-five Houston Rockets star James Harden, an Olympic gold medal winner, just like her stepmother, Caitlyn.

BUT BACK TO KIM, who would "break the Internet," courtesy of *Paper* magazine.

She disregarded sister Khloé's sage advice in 2011 and at thirty wed twenty-six-year-old Humphries. It was a lavish affair in Montecito, California, with tons of publicity, and with the ceremony once again aired on the Kardashian family's reality show network, E!, as Kim's momager, Kris, and her handsome husband, Bruce, proudly looked on.

But their ill-fated union lasted just seventy-two days, at which time Kim filed for divorce on the grounds of irreconcilable differences, one of which may have been that at a little over five feet tall, she was at least three heads shorter than the NBA giant. Their split was finalized in 2013.

"For once, Kim should have taken Khloé's advice," was the assessment of commenters—haters and acolytes—on the many Kardashian online forums.

Kim also had a turbulent relationship for three years, this one on and off, with Reginald Alfred "Reggie" Bush Jr., who, like her "Uncle O.J." was an African-American football player who, like O.J., had won a Heisman Trophy at USC, and would even go on to play in the NFL for the Buffalo Bills like O.J.

During their relationship she reportedly tried to initiate an affair with the man who would become her third husband and the father of her two children, the rapper Kanye West.

While Kim was still with Bush, West was believed to have declared his love for her in the lyrics of one of his songs, "Knock You Down," in which he referred to her as the "cheerleader of my dreams." A woman he was involved with at the time, the biracial, bisexual model and actress (and one-time teenage stripper known as "Paris") Amber Rose, would later claim that Kim had sent pornographic photographs of herself to West. Rose, who wrote a book entitled *How to Be a Bad Bitch*, called Kim a "home wrecker," and she was quoted in *Complex* magazine as stating, "They label me a bisexual freak stripper who fucks Kanye on a daily basis."

In May 2014, Kim extravagantly married Kanye with a showy pre-wedding affair in the Paris mansion of the fashion designer Valentino Garavani—better known as Valentino. The couple tied the knot in Italy—Kim wore a gown of custom design by Givenchy and had a much-publicized ride in a carriage in the gardens of Versailles.

Of the many men in his daughters' lives, Robert Kardashian, had he lived, would have most respected and liked West, for his award-winning musical career, his entrepreneurial successes, and for fathering Kim's two children, pretentiously named Saint West and North West. But he sometimes referred to himself as "Mr. Kardashian," which would not have gone off well with the bride's late father, who prided himself on his Armenian heritage.

Along with his music success, West would have his own fashion line like the Kardashian-Jenner women. In a snarky September 2016 *New York Times* story about his show for New York Fashion Week, *Times* fashion editor Vanessa Friedman described West as "musician/impresario/mad tweeter/Adidas collaborator." She declared that his show in blazing Indian summer heat on Roosevelt Island, in the middle of the East River, "cast a pall," and she noted that his clothing line wasn't "original or risky enough" to even be terrible. "They were just boring. Not ambitious or eclectic or even surprising. Yawn. . . . For a man known for his rambling, far-reaching riffs, in his fourth fashion season, it turned out Mr. West had nothing to say."

. . .

BUT KANYE'S WIFE'S "BREAK the Internet" photo on the cover of *Paper* would have much to say about her and the culture and race in America in the second decade of the new millennium.

Boardman had decided to do the shoot in Paris with the seventy-three-year-old French experimental fashion photographer Jean-Paul Goude, whom the magazine considered a legend. "We thought who better to pair up Kim with. We wanted something that took her to a new place that wasn't a traditional approach to a fashion magazine cover."

Long before Photoshop and digital enhancement of photos, Goude was taking oddball photos of iconic figures such as stretching the neck of his then-lover, Grace Jones. He termed his style the "French Correction," a play on the *French Connection* movie title. His work was soon exhibited in the Musée des Arts Décoratifs in Paris.

A master of photography had been assigned to shoot the narcissistic mistress of reality television and the queen of the Internet.

But that cover shot of Kim, giving very special attention to her huge ass, would spark accusations of racism—along with getting so much attention online that it appeared to break the Internet, in terms of millions and millions of hits.

Goude based his cover shot of Kim on an iconic nude photo he had taken in the mid-seventies of the skinny, small-breasted black model Carolina Beaumont, in which she is standing naked holding a champagne bottle and shooting an ejaculation-like stream of the bubbly into a champagne glass standing upright and firmly on her large, extended ass.

As the respected deejay and social observer Rich Medina asserted on his Web site, "*Paper* magazine used Kim Kardashian as a means to reincarnate [the Beaumont photo] and simultaneously appropriate Kim's possession of what's been stereotyped as Black women's physical attributes (that big ole ass) . . . for financial gain and shock value fame."

Goude, who is white, declined to be interviewed for this book. He once told *People*, "Blacks are the premise of my work." His book of photography was entitled *Jungle Fever*, and he's therefore been accused of objectifying and eroticizing black women's bodies. Goude's Beaumont and Kardashian shots have been compared to images of a black woman, Saartjie Baartman, dubbed the "Hottentot Venus," who became a "sexual freak show attraction" in Europe in the nineteenth century because of her immense Kim Kardashian–like buttocks.

With all of the black men in their lives and with their look and lifestyle, the Kardashian women—especially Kim and Khloé and even Kylie Jenner—were soon the targets of some prominent African-Americans accusing them of cultural appropriation—of lifting black style for their own purposes, financial and otherwise. The *Paper* cover, which emphasized Kim's huge ass, only added to the furor and controversy.

One later Kardashian critic was a leading activist with the controversial Black Lives Matter movement, which came to prominence because of the questionable shootings of a number of black men by white police officers across the nation. Shanelle Matthews, who handled communications for BLM, criticized Kim Kardashian for wearing cornrows—later called "boxer braids."

She asserted that Kim was misappropriating the style of African-Americans, and by doing so, was showing a lack of respect for the black community.

"Banking on blackness," Matthews declared, "is a shameful enterprise, and the Kardashians are no better than racist judges, prison officials and corporations who make money off the incarceration of black bodies." She suggested that the Kardashians knew nothing about being black, "all the while trying to be black, such as Kim showing off her huge ass in tight clothing and using black nomenclature.

"When we call out the appropriation of our beauty," continued the Black Lives Matter official, "it isn't because we are being petulant, but because the Kardashians, and so many others have no conscience about how their appropriation of our culture disempowers and disenfranchises us."

Adding to Matthews's criticism of the Kardashians' lifting of black style and culture was Sam Ennon, the founder of the Black Owned Beauty Supply Association (BOBSA), who declared that the Kardashians "want to be black so bad it hurts. It's just crazy. It's like they're trying to prove themselves. Black women are offended because they think they're going to take their black man."

While the *Paper* cover of Kim and her behind didn't actually "break the Internet"—the stunt line used to promote the now-famous cover, which became an instant collector item—the photo caught the attention of literally millions of people across the globe with access to a computer.

As Mickey Boardman noted, "The hysteria started immediately. I got an e-mail from Kim. Her subject line was 'Break the Internet,' and she wrote, 'We did it. I'm proud to be a part of it. Thank you so much.'

"At the time," said Boardman, "we thought it would be an amazing cover. We had no idea what a humongous cultural phenomenon it would be. There are a lot of celebrities who don't want to do anything too risky, but we had a feeling Kim wanted to do something wild, something iconic, and that's exactly what happened."

IN 2016, A SELF-ABSORBED Kim Kardashian, with a grandiose view of herself—an exhibitionist once described as a "poster child for the naked self-portrait"—took a four-day vacation in Mexico, and while there she shot a mind-blowing six thousand selfies, an average of fifteen hundred per day, according to a calculation made by Page Six, the colorful gossip column of the *New York Post*.

As the tabloid observed, "Kim Kardashian's narcissism has a number."

Kim responded to all the criticism, declaring, "I am empowered by my body. I am empowered by my sexuality. I am empowered by feeling comfortable in my skin. . . . The body-shaming and slut-shaming—it's like, enough is enough."

TWENTY-SEVEN

The "Misfit"

One-time Olympic decathlon champion, three times a husband, six times a father, Wheaties cereal box hero to boys and girls of all ages, and reality TV star Bruce Jenner seemed to always be surrounded by sexy women.

Never thought of as anything but masculine and straight, people who knew him well for decades, including his ex-wives and his many girlfriends, didn't give his preference for being surrounded by glamorous women a second thought. He was, they had no reason to doubt, all guy. Until a very few found out differently. Later, the entire world would know his secret: He adored being around glamorous women because he actually liked to try on their clothing and makeup and be like them, because he believed he *was* one of them.

"It was only natural that Bruce would go for fabulous babes," said a close male friend, looking back in 2016. "He was an athlete and a celebrity, and women were attracted to him, and he to them."

Then the intimate quickly added, "He still likes them. But now he's one of them. Or thinks he is. I'm still unsure. It's wait-and-see for me. I'm really mixed up about the whole thing."

When Jenner was married to Kris Houghton Kardashian for more than two financially successful decades—he gained international fame again as a member of the Kardashians' reality program—he was lost in a feminine world of makeup, lingerie, revealing club clothing, and generally sexually provocative females—his wife, his daughters, and their girlfriends. Females galore. For a straight man, it might have been heaven. For a man who considered himself a woman trapped in a man's body, it was pure hell.

Secretly, he squeezed his athlete's six-foot-two muscular form into their clothes, tried to slip his size-twelve clodhoppers into their Manolos, and tested their makeup for the right look, and just once, one of his adopted Kardashian daughters, the sex tape star Kim, walked in on him, saw him in a feminized state, and hurried away—presumably shocked and traumatized. But supposedly she kept what she saw to herself, at least at the time.

Before his very public and highly publicized coming-out as Caitlyn in April 2015—on national television with Diane Sawyer before seventeen million viewers, on the cover of *Vanity Fair* in July, looking dramatically and demurely stunning in a one-piece strapless number, and soon, naturally, with his own T-girl reality TV show, *I Am Cait*. On the same cable network as his pre-divorce family's show, Ms. Jenner was seen socializing and traveling with a transgender male-to-female (all, or in part) entourage and espousing to the world her new Caitlyn lifestyle.

But Jenner was pretty much known to some for years as a crossdresser.

When she was involved in a headline-making fatal accident on the Pacific Coast Highway not long after he declared himself a she, a private investigator, Paul Cohen, who represented one of the accident principals, was long aware of Jenner's taste for dressing up.

"There was always talk, going back years. I would see him occasionally in Malibu. He would show up at the market in Trancas and he would be wearing nail polish and makeup and eye shadow. And this was at least ten years before his transition became news," said Cohen in 2016. "I'd come home and tell my wife, 'I just saw Jenner. He looks like a girl. He's dressing like a girl.'"

After her divorce from Bruce, with whom she had two daughters, Kylie and Kendall, was finalized in 2014 on the grounds of "irreconcilable differences," Jenner's third and best known wife, Kris, publicly maintained that she never really knew what was going on in the transgender department with her husband, whom she married just days after Robert Kardashian divorced her.

But a well-connected family and business confidant said, "Bullshit! She knew—Kris *absolutely* knew. She and her team just weren't sure how it would play in Boise with her show and all of her side deals and sponsors, and all that money the Kardashians were raking in. So she went the public denial route. She played it safe. She's smart. Talking about Bruce's sexual issues could have muddied the waters. She left that to him."

IN THE EARLY EIGHTIES, around the time Bruce Jenner met the woman who became his second wife—the Tennessee beauty Linda Thompson, who was Elvis Presley's live-in lover in the King's last years—Jenner had been staying part of the time at the Playboy Mansion West because his first wife, Chrystie Crownover Scott, mother of his first two children, had walked out on him.

"Bruce became like one of the Bunnies," claimed a longtime Mansion regular and Playboy Bunny afficionado. "One night he's boogying in a tux with the girls at a dress-up party, and the next night he'd be *like* one of the girls and *all* dressed up—makeup, hosiery, high heels, the whole nine yards. I used to laugh, and just thought it was Bruce's schtick, that he was just being funny, like when Milton Berle used to come on TV in drag. I mean, come on, Bruce fucking Jenner—the

Olympics, Wheaties, a total guy's guy. Give me a fucking break. Who thought?"

Having gotten over Elvis's premature demise, Linda Thompson actually met Jenner at a meet and greet at Hugh Hefner's famed Holmby Hills party house during a charity celebrity tennis tournament. Then doing a lot of television—*Starsky & Hutch, Vegas*—it was fate for Thompson meeting Jenner there because it was her first time ever at the mansion, and she needed a man in her life.

Handsome, charming, boyish Jenner told her that he was separated, that his wife had taken their son, Burt, born just eight months earlier, and flown the coop. He had come home to find her closet—a closet whose contents he had come to know intimately—empty. In the wake of Elvis, Thompson was open for a relationship. So was Jenner, who didn't waste time. He asked if he could accompany her home from the party, and they were off and running.

She then had a roommate, a girlfriend from high school, and that first night when she saw Linda on the sofa getting to know Bruce Jenner, her teenager-like reaction was, "Oh my God, he is so hot."

Almost from the get-go, Thompson thought of Jenner as the kind of guy "I could start a family with," she acknowledged in a revelatory bestselling memoir published in 2016.

One chapter, about their turbulent life together, was candidly entitled "I Married a Woman."

For a very brief time, Jenner and his first wife, Chrystie, had a brief reconciliation. And Thompson figured it was all over for her and her handsome, manly Olympian. During his time back together with Chrystie, she got pregnant and had another child with him. But that on-and-off relationship didn't last very long.

Out of the blue, Jenner called Thompson and told her that he had good news and bad news.

The bad news was that he was a father again, this time the newborn heir was a daughter, Cassandra Lynn "Casey" Jenner.

The good news was that Chrystie "left me again!"

Jenner said they were finally going to get a divorce.

Linda Thompson was back in the game.

Years later she and Kris Kardashian Jenner would learn that they weren't the first two women to discover that they had been wed to a sexually troubled man, or as Jenner informed the world, "For all intents and purposes, I am a woman."

After Jenner went public with his gender dysphoria, the first Mrs. Bruce Jenner, from 1972 to 1981, went public herself, revealing that in their first year of marriage he had confessed his secret.

On the TV program *Good Morning America*, Chrystie said she couldn't "remember the exact words" Bruce had used in revealing his secret to her "because it was such a shock to me." Using the last name of Scott, and with a career as an interior designer in Southern California, the attractive brunette in her early sixties recalled, "He told me he wanted to be a woman, and understandably, I didn't know what to say. . . . It's so hard to wrap your head around it, particularly because he was such a manly man."

She recalled that Jenner had "never indicated anything feminine in his demeanor," and she noted, curiously, that Jenner's problem, at least at first, "wasn't really a problem" for their relationship and didn't "threaten" it. But she did leave him once, as he told Linda Thompson, and Chrystie decided to divorce him after their second unsuccessful round together. Robert Kardashian's widow, Ellen, claimed that Chrystie had once told her that Jenner was a cross-dresser who tried on her clothing and lingerie, which would be reason enough to cause marital discord.

To a weekly tabloid magazine after Jenner went public, Chrystie Scott declared, "I support him in whatever he chooses to do. I just want him to be happy." They still saw each other at family events, she said, and with their two children having families, Caitlyn Jenner was a "very proud and present grandfather." With his adult son, Burt Jenner, he's gone car hunting and racing, and his daughter, Cassandra, claimed to *People* magazine that she "supported" his big change.

It seemed that once Jenner let the cat out of the bag, everyone from her past got in on the act.

WHEN JENNER GOT INVOLVED with Linda Thompson, he was doing well. He was generating revenue from sponsors such as the raincoat manufacturer London Fog and the camera company Minolta, and he was doing commentary for NBC Sports. He was known to millions facing him at the breakfast table on the Wheaties box, he was giving lucrative motivational speeches, and as a hobby, a dangerous one, he was often seen behind the wheel of a racing car.

At one point Linda, by then known as Jenner's girlfriend, accompanied Bruce to Australia to promote a film. It was called *Can't Stop the Music.* His costars were the popular late seventies, early eighties predominately gay disco group the Village People. It was produced by the flamboyantly gay Allan Carr. But there was no hint in the film that Bruce Jenner was anything but the Bruce Jenner who the world loved and respected. And no indication that Carr had cast him because he knew his secret.

As Linda truly believed, the guy she had fallen in love with was ambitious, driven, successful, and the "ideal" all-man.

Early on, as she put it in her book, "I never really had a reason to doubt Bruce."

THEY TALKED MARRIAGE AND discussed having children, and Thompson was convinced they "shared the same basic values . . . the traditional idea of home and hearth."

To Linda, "Bruce was capable of deep passion and emotion."

In the fall of 1980, Thompson became pregnant out of wedlock with the first of the two children she would have with Jenner, whose sperm seemed to know no bounds. This one was his third. She reportedly also got a part in *The Love Boat*, a popular TV series. Jenner proposed to her near a dirt road in Malibu, and they were married on January 5, 1981, in Hawaii, when she was five months pregnant with their first son, Brandon Thompson Jenner, Bruce's third child. Life was even more perfect when they bought a "relatively modest" home in Malibu. In 1983, their second son, Brody, was born.

He was going on two years of age in early 1985 and Brandon was almost four when their father confronted their mother. She practically fell on the floor when, she claimed, he declared:

"I identify as a woman. . . . I am a woman trapped in a man's body. . . . For as long as I can remember, I've looked in the mirror and seen a masculine image staring back at me, where there should have been a feminine reflection. I have lived in the wrong skin, the wrong body, my whole life. It is a living hell for me, and I really feel that I would like to move forward with the process of becoming a woman, the woman I have always been inside."

Linda took Bruce to a therapist in 1985, hoping he would change. In sessions, he confessed to having "dressed up in his mother's and sister's clothing" when he was home alone.

For his wife, the revelations were unimaginable. As Thompson stated with irony in her memoir, "I had never been sexually attracted to women."

The most "devastating moment" came for her when he invited her to meet him in New York City, where he was making a personal appearance—as a man in a man's body. But when he opened his hotel room door, he was "dressed as Caitlyn," Thompson wrote. "Full wig. Full makeup. Heels. A nice feminine dress adorning his muscular body. And a big smile on his red lips."

During a trip to Memphis to visit Linda's parents, her mother spotted the future husband of Kris Kardashian, the future stepfather of Kardashian siblings, Kourtney, Kim, Khloé, and Rob, and the future biological father with Kris of Kylie and Kendall "posing" in front of a mirror with his genitals tucked between his legs "so that he was flat in the front."

Shocked, Jenner's mother-in-law asked her daughter, "Is Bruce queer?"

Her guilty response? "Maybe he was just being silly."

Soon Jenner began seeing a physician, getting female hormones, having electrolysis on his facial hair, and having his chest hair removed.

In the late summer of 1985, Jenner moved out and confessed that when Linda was traveling to Nashville to film her part in the TV series *Hee Haw*, he would get into women's clothes and stroll around a Beverly Hills park. When she told him he could get into trouble, he responded, "When I dress up, you can't tell that I'm Bruce Jenner."

Later, she also had the answer as to why one of her silk blouses was stretched out of shape and smeared with makeup. Running through old videotapes, she was shocked to find one in which Jenner had taped himself performing a fashion show, posing in a "glamorous" wardrobe that was his own private stash. One day a former neighbor telephoned Linda to tell her he had run into Bruce, who was all dolled up and looking pretty.

It was July, but Bruce said he was going to a Halloween party.

"Bruce had fooled not just me but the whole world," declared Linda Thompson years after their divorce.

IN 2016, WITH A MINISERIES and a documentary about the the O.J. murder case garnering much press and big ratings, one starring an actor portraying the late Kardashian patriarch, Robert; with the Kardashians' reality show still scoring huge audiences; with various Kardashians on the covers of popular celebrity and fashion magazines; and with non-stop gossip about their lives online and in print, Caitlyn Jenner's cable reality program, *I Am Cait*, was suddenly canceled by the E! network before its third season.

An E! spokesperson said: "We are incredibly proud of the two seasons of 'I Am Cait,' a groundbreaking docu-series that sparked an important and unprecedented global conversation about transgender people, their struggles and triumphs. Caitlyn and E! have mutually decided not to move forward with another season at this time. She will always remain a part of the E! family, and we look forward to continue following her journey as she appears on *Keeping Up with the Kardashians.*"

After the announcement, the former Bruce Jenner tweeted: "It's time for the next adventure. . . . thank you for the best girlfriends I could ask for!"

But Caitlyn had a bright future going forward after reality TV. She was brought on as part of the cast of season three of the award-winning TV series *Transparent*, about the life and loves of a neurotic Jewish family man, played by Jeffrey Tambor, who transitions. When the deal was announced in the spring of 2016, *The Washington Post* noted, "Two powerful influences in transgender activism are joining forces." Jill Soloway, the show's creator and the daughter of a transgender father, declared the union of Jenner and *Transparent* was a "dream come true."

The Post observed that Jenner had "become the international symbol of a transgender woman. She's been criticized along the way for how she's handled" her controversial role, but the paper pointed out that Caitlyn "aligns herself with a show that is widely considered to be sensitive and smart about the nuances of characterizing gender issues."

For a year or so, Jenner had been quietly working on a highly promoted, much-awaited memoir entitled, *The Secrets of My Life*, published in late April of 2017. But a month before the pub date, the book's big reveal made headlines: Jenner had reportedly undergone gender reassignment surgery in January 2017.

She called the surgery a "complex decision" and observed that her late penis had "no special gifts or use for me other than what I have said before, the ability to take a whiz in the wood. . . . I am also tired of tucking the damn thing in."

She would soon learn that women have the ability to take whizzes in the woods, too.

Epilogue

For all the Kardashian business acumen and successes and the immense fortune they had derived, there were a number of failures. And by the close of 2016, with the tenth anniversary of *Keeping Up with the Kardashians* incredibly looming in 2017, there were dire warning signs that the Kardashian economy was beginning to slow down.

Their reality show itself even appeared to be losing traction with viewers, who were once glued to each and every episode. In the spring of 2016 it was reported that it had the lowest ratings in its long run. The first episode of season twelve had anywhere from just over two million viewers, to just over three million, and by episode two, a half million of the Kardashians' couch potatoes had left to do other things, according to press reports.

Experts wondered whether the Kardashian phenomenon was a

bubble about to burst, despite the fact that a conservatively attired Kim, a rarity for a woman who often bared all, was on the cover of *Forbes* in July 2016, and was number forty-two on its list of the world's one hundred top-earning celebrities, with $51 million. But she was far behind Taylor Swift, who was number one with $170 million.

Because of the momager's successes with the E! reality TV show and her immense fame derived from her family's on-camera antics and all their side businesses, the Fox network had offered Kris Jenner a once-in-a-lifetime opportunity: her own talk show, or at least a test to see how she would do.

As a close family friend observed, "It's interesting that she got that deal, because Kris always, always, always watched those programs on TV, and she used to go on and on that she could be a host of any one of them—only better. She once bragged to me, 'If given a chance I could be the next Oprah. I can bullshit with the best of 'em—and people love me. They really do.' "

The Fox Television Stations Group thought so, too, or at least hoped so.

In the summer of 2013, a six-week test run was initiated. The program was called *Kris*. It was given huge publicity before it aired. Fox announced that the matriarch's daytime show would air "in select test markets" and would focus on a "daily jolt of celebrity guests, fashion and beauty trends, plus a mix of lifestyle topics—all through the distinctive and unpredictable perspective of Kris Jenner."

Naturally, Kris was thrilled.

"This is something I have wanted to do all my life so it's definitely a dream come true," she declared in a Fox-approved press release.

A survey was done asking people whether they would watch. The results were rather dismal: 12.05 percent of online voters said they were interested in watching her show. But 87.95 percent of the respondents voted, "I don't think so."

The latter group, as it turned out, was spot-on.

Kris premiered on July 15, 2013, on Fox stations in Dallas, Minneapolis, Phoenix, Los Angeles, New York, and Charlotte, North Carolina. She had a variety of B-list cohosts, but on the show's fifth airing, her infamous daughter Khloé sat with her on the set. Even the Kardashians' biggest booster and backer, Ryan Seacrest, the E! executive who discovered the Kardashians, was on one episode, playing the role of Kris's sidekick. By then Seacrest was aware that Kris needed help badly if Fox was going to green-light the show for a full season.

But after the six-week test, *Kris* disappeared from the airwaves. There were months of silence about what plans, if any, Fox had for the show. But it wasn't until a year later, in the summer of 2014, when Frank Cicha, the senior vice president and president of programming for Fox Television Stations, revealed that the show and the momager didn't work and was gone for good.

While giving kudos to Kris for working hard, Cicha voiced rare criticism in a business where one has to be diplomatic and politically correct. He told *The Hollywood Reporter*, "I think she was pretty uninteresting [on camera]. . . . That was one where [sister company] 20th Television tried to capitalize on a name. . . . When the camera was on she looked not just like a deer in the headlights, but like a deer that already got hit."

It was over for Jenner when she brought her son-in-law Kanye West on as a guest to show pictures of his baby with Kim. Cicha claimed that ratings became subpar and that some stations even got hate mail for airing *Kris*.

"When you added it up," observed the executive, "it wasn't a show that made sense for us."

It wasn't just Kris's apparent lack of talk show talent that caused *Kris* to be canceled. The celebrity weekly *Star* quoted a purported staffer as claiming, "Working with Kris was absolutely unbearable. She would show up on the set hung over and demand her beauty team to fix her up and make her look stunning."

Kris later claimed her program was not canceled. In a tweet, she firmly stated, "Rumors flying are false but glad everyone is still buzzing about our 6 week summer run!!!!"

She was even able to make failure seem a success.

A DEAL THAT SEARS had to mass-market Kim and a clothing line called the "Kardashian Kollection" also ended dismally at the end of 2014 after a four-year run.

The "Kollection" had showed up in some four hundred Sears stores in the late summer of 2011 and generated a reported $600 million by 2013 for the iconic low-brow department store chain, and added some $30 million to the Kardashian coffers. But the revenue wasn't enough, sales began trailing off, and the struggling retailer, which was closing hundreds of stores in a poor retail economy, pulled the plug. Things got so bad that at one point a Kardashian Kollection sheath dress, sticker priced at $189, was on sale for $29.99, less than the cost of a decent sweatshirt.

As the business magazine *Fortune* declared in a headline in May 2015, "Sears and the Kardashians Have Broken Up." It called the deal a "fashion collaboration of bargains and bling." The chain, it noted, "doesn't have to try to keep up with the Kardashians anymore . . . [it] flopped with customers."

DESPITE KIM KARDASHIAN WEST'S more than 90 million Instagram followers, almost 50 million Twitter devotees, and huge army of Snapchat pals, there was an even darker cloud over the Kardashian empire as their tenth anniversary on television neared.

Reports surfaced that the Kardashians' influence in print was beginning to fade. The trade publication *Women's Wear Daily* revealed that national print magazines featuring one Kardashian or another on the cover were selling less on newsstands in 2016. Examples included *Cosmopolitan*, which usually averaged little more than 531,000 in single-issue sales, but a major cover billing the Kardashians as "America's First Family" appeared with great expectations but sold only 436,500 copies. And a *Glamour* cover with Kim on it was a total disaster, selling just 164,918 copies, compared to the magazine's average of 193,108.

One online news site, reporting the fewer sales of Kardashian magazine covers, bellowed in a headline: "Is This the Collapse of the Kardashian Economy?"

By the fall of 2016, even the Kardashians' long, lucky streak of striking it rich was under a dark and questionable cloud.

Near the end of Fashion Week in Paris, where Kim and her posse were a major presence, she reported that masked gunmen had broken into her exclusive suite, tied and gagged her, and rode off on bicycles with some $11 million of her diamond jewelry that was just lying around. The media, which had built up her and her clan for years, now jumped on her true crime story like white on rice, asserting that her account was suspect.

As the respected fashion writer Robin Givhan noted, "What has bubbled up . . . is a geyser of schadenfreude, as well as a healthy dose of skepticism that the robbery truly unfolded as described." The talk in Paris, she noted, and in the U.S. media—a *New York Post* headline blared, "How Kim's Story Just Doesn't Add Up"—and in the rest of the free world was that it was all a stunt, a way to generate publicity at a time when the Kardashian economy was giving hints of tanking. But if it really did happen, if Kim's account was the whole truth and nothing but the truth, then thank heaven she was not hurt, and that insurance would cover her loss. But Givhan wrote, "Could it [the robbery] be part of the lucrative reality show that is Kardashian's life? There has been dark humor. And outright mocking."

In the wake of the heist, there were rumors, duly reported by some news organizations that were obsessed with the Kardashians, that the Kardashians' show was being suspended and that if such a catastrophe occurred it would cost Kim as much as $1 million a month. But an expert on financial matters claimed that if she positioned herself correctly in a return to social media, she could clean up again. There was lots of speculation, none of it actually panning out.

The Journalist Maureen Callahan, who had been covering the Kardashians' fame, observed in the tabloid *New York Post* that the "off-screen Kardashians seem mere avatars of their television personas, willing to manipulate anyone, contrive anything, to advance a narrative they can bounce back to the show."

And a snarky commenter on the British *Daily Mail* news Web site darkly offered the following: "It's unfortunate the robbers didn't do the world a favor and put us out of our misery."

But the Paris heist was the real deal, carried out out by a veteran gang. Kim even sued a celebrity Web site that had reported otherwise and a retraction was run.

ONE HAS TO WONDER whether the Kardashians were starting to follow in the Louboutin heels of Paris Hilton, who fell from the heights of international "It" girl fame to virtual media has-been. It could happen.

But wait.

After E! pulls the plug, which is inevitable at some point, Kris Houghton Kardashian Jenner and her crew have a plan and see a bright future. Voters, get ready to cast your ballots: The Kardashians may next be in politics.

Ever since Donald Trump entered the political arena, Kris has been "seriously talking about running for office. It's a little crazy, I know, but she keeps privately saying, 'If Mr. Weird Hair can do it, so can I. We have the same DNA,'" revealed a close source.

And a well-placed confidant recalled Kris saying over dinner while watching one of the 2016 presidential primary debates that she believed she can start what she called "a powerful and influential movement." She believes there are "millions of single moms out there" like her who, if elected, she can help to overcome adversity. One of the things on her agenda is to deal with divorce laws and benefits for single mothers and gay partners. "She really is firm," said the source, "when she says that she can 'give needy women goals and programs' based on her own life experiences, and that they can 'become rich and successful' like her. It's so odd because she even sounded like Trump when she revealed all this. Her words were on the order of, 'I can make America's moms feel great again! And everyone else, too.' "

According to this source, Kris might enter a congressional race in California or New York once *KUWTK* ends its run. "She has so much confidence," said the advisor, "that talking about the presidency some day, running for it and winning it, isn't out of the question for her. Kris always thinks big, always has."

And it could well happen, even in Kis Jenner's alternate universe where anything is possible. Aside from actor-businessman-entrepreneur-politico Trump who was elected president, just look at the celebrities who made the successful transition to politics—former Hollywood stars Ronald Reagan and Arnold Schwarzenegger, singer Sonny Bono, comedian Al Franken, and one of the few actresses, Shirley Temple Black.

Like Trump, Kris has all the right (or wrong) stuff, depending on whether one is a liker or a hater, and there are *so* many of the latter, just like with The Donald. They both come from reality television—and like Trump, Kris has an unparalleled reality TV pedigree—and neither had had any national elective political experience, which was considered an attribute in the minds of a large segment of the country, tired of the old establishment. Like Trump, who ran profitable businesses, so has Kris—clothing stores that she opened with her daughters which were successful. Like Trump, who starred in and executive produced *The Apprentice* franchise on NBC, Kris led the merry-go-round on the Kardashians' hugely successful show and spin-offs.

And there are even more similarities between the New York real estate mogul turned commander-in-chief and the momager.

Like Trump, whose Slovenian wife once posed partially nude in a European men's magazine, Kris's insanely exhibitionist second-born, Kim, is internationally infamous for publicly showing it all. Like Trump, Kris has had multiple marriages and affairs, and none of that seemed to bother voters, even some evangelicals, in the 2016 presidential race, at least until Trump was heard uttering the word "pussy" on an old video-tape that became public. That ignited a tsunami of women claiming all sorts of sexual misdeeds by the GOP presidential candidate, along with accusing him of making rude comments about women, including but not limited to Khloé Kardashian, who he allegedly called "a fat piglet" when she was in the cast of *The Celebrity Apprentice* in 2009.

"And Kris is not bothered," asserted the advisor, "by any of the Kardashian family scandals of the past. She says 'people don't give a shit and they just eat it up.'"

Kris has an immense following, and a huge voting bloc—the millions of fans of the Kardashian reality show, and the millions of consumers of her and her daughters' various brands, and like Trump, the Kardashians can show they've made jobs for Americans. And like Trump, Kris and her daughters have written bestselling books about their lives and successes.

Also like Trump, they've been involved in lawsuits and litigation. In a battle over the Kardashian sisters' cosmetics trademark—an infringement case—they had accused the major investor in their beauty brand of not compensating them or getting their approval on products prior to production. A federal judge ruled in their favor. But in another matter, the nonprofit Truth in Advertising organization charged that the Kardashians had violated Federal Trade Commission guidelines by failing to disclose that they were being paid for many social media posts for supporting products or services for which they were linked, in violation of Federal Trade Commission guidelines.

Kris and the Kardashians also have a big following among young African-American men, a bloc that eluded Trump, and have huge support among millennial women eighteen to thirty-four, and support in the transgender community—especially if Caitlyn, a staunch Republican, plays ball and stumps for her ex-wife if she, indeed, runs for elective office as she's suggested.

As self-important Kris was said to have remarked to a confidant, "I have great depth on social media. They are mine in any campaign I jump into." And like Trump, who hired the media genius and founder of Fox News, Roger Ailes, as a consultant, it's certain that Kris would use the media savvy and programming brilliance of Ryan Seacrest to help her in any race that she ever chose to enter.

In any campaign, Kris wouldn't need Donald J. Trump's support, because she has Hillary Rodham Clinton in her corner. Because of past Kardashian support, especially from Kim, Clinton was one of the few famous names who publicly showed compassion in the wake of Kim's multimillion-dollar diamond heist in Paris. "I felt really bad for her. It's horrible. I'm just glad nobody was hurt," Clinton declared just before her second presidential debate with Trump in October 2016. Of Kris's son-in-law Kanye, who left a concert when he heard about the robbery, Clinton said, "Bless his heart."

"Kris sees herself as a role model for women and girls. She sees herself as a feminist and a brand. She's an A-list international name along with being a loving and dutiful mother who turned nothing into an empire. As she told me, 'I am what America's voters need.' Kris Jenner for president," added the close advisor. "I can see it now! And can you imagine *that* first family in the White House?"

ACKNOWLEDGMENTS

Many, many people affiliated in one way or another with the Kardashians contributed to helping me piece together the true, untold story of this famous and infamous tabloid and reality TV family.

However, I must first give credit where credit is definitely due, and that is to the self-styled 'momager' herself—the brains behind the outfit—Kristen Mary 'Kris' Houghton Kardashian Jenner.

When I told an editor friend that I was planning to write a biography of the Kardashians, that I intended to go back to the beginning and probe their lives, that I would place them under a journalistic microscope and perform a forensic examination, I was strongly advised to first read a 2011 memoir that Ms. Houghton Kardashian Jenner had penned, a tome that had received great "praise" from such critics as Kim Kardashian, Rob Kardashian, Kourtney Kardashian, Khloé Kardashian, and Lamar Odom.

Indeed, their rave blurbs were on the very first page of the Kris Jenner paperback that I ordered from Amazon.

It became kind of a blueprint, a roadmap for the work ahead of me. Her assertions, claims and allegations set me on the trail to discover what was true and untrue, what was hype and what was exaggeration, and what was pure fiction. I discovered a lot of each, so thank you, Ms. Jenner, for making my job a bit easier.

Members of the Kardashians' close circle who had never before talked publicly about their relationships with the family answered hours of my probing with unquestioned honesty and remarkable candidness.

Among them, I especially want to thank Joni Migdal and Larry Kraines who practically grew up with the late Kardashian patriarch Robert Kardashian, best known today as O.J. Simpson's close friend and "mouthpiece" during the murder trial of the century. Joni was, for a time, Robert's lover, was present when Robert first met Kris, and was a close observer to their troubled union. Larry had remained lifelong friends with both Robert and Kris—though he was an eyewitness to her cheating. Still, he and his wife Joyce remained close, and Larry was even dubbed 'Uncle Larry' by the Kardashian brood.

Great thanks go to another genuine Kardashian insider, Pastor Kenn Gulliksen, who offered his candid insights during many hours of my questioning. Gulliksen was Robert Kardashian's spiritual advisor and counselor when he became a born-again Christian in the wake of a Kardashian family scandal, and also had the honor of officiating at the wedding of Kris and Robert. His honest view of Kris and his candid memories of Robert were invaluable in painting a detailed picture of their lives.

I especially want to thank Tom Kardashian—Robert's brother, Kris's ex-brother-in-law—for agreeing to be interviewed, and to talk openly and candidly for the first time about the Kardashian family. With great honesty, he revealed how he had taken the fall in the mid-1970s when the family's meatpacking business, of which Tom was an executive, came under federal investigation for bribing U.S. Department of Agriculture inspectors. He spoke with immense candor about how his arrest and plea deal left a dark cloud over him and his family for years until he received a presidential pardon.

So many others contributed their candid insights and colorful memories and anecdotes, from school chums to business associates, friends and detractors. To all of you I owe a great deal of gratitude. Most spoke on the record, but a few requested and received anonymity. You know who you are. I deeply appreciate your cooperation. This book could not have been reported and written without all of your kind cooperation.

Many thanks to: Beth Palmer, Bud Halicki, Candace Trunzo, Charles Barker, Chuck Girard, Cindy Spallino, Donna Kramer, Gable Matsumura, Happy Rue, Henry Cutrona, Jack Spradlin, Jacquie Schenz, John 'Chip' Giannettino, John Q. Kelly, Joan Zimmerman Haza, Judy Ferguson, Leslie Leach, Kurt Harding, Lani Riches, Larry Mizrahi, Larry Myers, Linda Matsuno-Parmenter, Linda Watson, Marla Ostrowksi, Matthew Tallman, Maureen Coddington, Michael Edwards, Mickey Boardman, Nate Denver, Neal Hersh, Paul Cohen, Paulette Kardashian, Phil Pennino, Phil Rodgers, Denice Shakarian Halicki, Vangie Shakarian, Richard Muse, Robert Glaser, Ron Halicki, Rose Rutkowski Cohen, Rudy Sanudo, Susan Pennino, Susan Stafford, Pat Boone, Terran Steinhart, Tony and Donna Byler, Vicki Tafelski Brickel, Vicky Thomsen, Anita Friedman, Amber Carrillo, Paul Hutcheson.

Here's hoping the readers enjoy!

SOURCES

PROLOGUE

Author interviews with Pastor Kenn Gulliksen, Happy Rue, Larry Kraines, Kris Jenner's quote "good girl" from her memoir. Description of Robert Kardashian's O.J. involvement from press accounts and TV news footage.

PART I: THE "MOMAGER"
ONE: STAY CLASSY, SAN DIEGO

Family roots based on biographical source research. Some quotes from Jenner memoir. Physical description of Robert Houghton from friends. Author interviews with Sanudo family members, Leslie Johnson Leach. Harry Shannon description from Jenner memoir. Naming of Kim Kardashian from confidential source.

TWO: SCHOOL DAYS

Author interviews with Marla Tafelski, Vicki Tafelski, Joan Zimmerman, Tom Kardashian, Larry Kraines, Kurt Harding. Details about Irving Azoff from news accounts. Some quotes from Jenner memoir. Details about relationship with Hiltons and Gabor family from author's book, "House of Hilton." Kris Jenner's idolization of Gabors from confidential source.

THREE: MEETING THE "MOB"

Details about La Costa and co-owner Merve Adelson from press accounts, Penthouse magazine investigation, and author biography of Barbara Walters, who had been married to Adelson. Account of Debbie Mungle from various sources, including friends and Jenner memoir. Research material included Clairmont High School yearbook. Interviews with Joan Zimmerman, Cheryl Wallace Weatherford, confidential source.

FOUR: HOLE IN ONE

Cesar Sanudo roots from interviews with family members and press accounts. Author interviews with Amber Carrillo, Phil Rodgers, Jack Spradlin, Carlos Sanudo, Leslie Johnson Leach, Vicky Kron Thomsen. Some quotes from Jenner memoir.

FIVE: ENTER KARDASHIAN

Author interviews with Rudy Sanudo, Jack Spradlin, Joni Migdal, Tom Kardashian, Larry Kraines, Linda Watson, confidential source. Some quotes and description from Jenner memoir, and the book *Kardashian Konfidential.*

SIX: AN AFFAIR TO REMEMBER

Cesar Sanudo golf earnings from press accounts. Some quotes and description from Jenner memoir. Author interviews with Jack Spradlin, Amber Carrillo, Rudy Sanudo, Jacqui Schenz, and confidential source.

SEVEN: COFFEE, TEA, OR ME?

Author interviews with Larry Kraines, Jack Spradlin, Cesar Sanudo family members, Cindy Spallino. Some quotes and description from Jenner memoir.

EIGHT: KARDASHIAN AND PRESLEY

Source for some Priscilla Presley history from "Child Bride," by Suzanna Finstad, and "Elvis and Me," by Presley. Author interviews with Joni Migdal, Tom Kardashian,

Susan Stafford, Larry Kraines. Joan Agajanian quotes from Finstad book. Some quotes and detail from Jenner memoir, and Linda Thompson's *A Little Thing Called Life.*

PART II: THE "MOUTHPIECE"
NINE: A CORRUPT FAMILY BUSINESS

Descriptions of Vernon from press accounts. Author interviews with Tom Kardashian on Kardasian family history, and Tom Kardashian's arrest, indictment, presidential pardon, supported by published press accounts, and U.S. Justice Department release. Author interviews with Phil Pennino, Joni Migdal, Larry Kraines.

TEN: A KARDASHIAN CHILDHOOD

Author interviews with Tom Kardashian, Larry Kraines, Linda Matsumo-Parmenter, Phil Pennino, Joni Migdal. History of California Military Academy from press accounts. Details about Dorsey High School from yearbooks and interviews with a number of alumni.

ELEVEN: JESUS AND THE KARDASHIANS

Author interviews with Pastor Kenn Gulliksen, Larry Kraines, Chuck Girard, Henry Cutrona, Joni Migdal, Tom Kardashian, Susan Stafford. Rev. Chuck Smith profile from press accounts. Details about faith healer Avak Hagopian from Los Angeles newspaper accounts and Life Magazine. Clem Davies details from press accounts. Some quotes from Jenner memoir. Pat Boone quotes from an email from his assistant to author.

TWELVE: A STEPFORD WIFE

Author interviews with Susan Stafford, Tom Kardashian, Joni Migdal, Larry Kraines, Kenn Gulliksen, Cindy Spallino. Some details and quotes from Jenner memoir. Stepford wives account from Migdal and confidential source.

THIRTEEN: WEDDING BELLS

Author interviews with Rev. Larry Myers, Tom Kardashian, Larry Kraines, Kenn Gulliksen, Cindy Spallino. Some quotes and detail from Jenner memoir. Rev. Donn Moomaw sex scandal from press accounts.

FOURTEEN: A THREE-THOUSAND-DOLLAR BELT

Some details and quotes from Jenner memoir. Author interviews with Cindy Spallino, Joni Migdal, Kenn Gulliksen, Tom Kardashian, Larry Kraines, Donna Kramer, and with a cousin who asked to remain anonymous regarding the $3,000 belt. Shelli Azoff snake anecdote from *New York Post*'s Page Six.

FIFTEEN: WHO'S YOUR DADDY?

Some details and quotes regarding the birth of Khloé from Jenner memoir. Kylie Jenner from press accounts. Author interviews with Neal Raymond Hersh, Larry Kraines, Joni Migdal, Kenn Gulliksen.

SIXTEEN: ANOTHER AFFAIR

Author interviews with Larry Kraines, Joni Migdal, Tom Kardashian. Rob Lowe background from press accounts. Todd Waterman and his mother's quotes from press accounts. Faye Resnick quotes from her book, "Nicole Brown Simpson: The Private Diary of a Life Interrupted."

SEVENTEEN: EMOTIONAL WRECK

Attorney Neal Hersh's background from press accounts. Author interviews with Hersh, Tom Kardashian, Larry Kraines, Joni Migdal, Anita Friedman. Some quotes from Jenner memoir. Garvey account from news stories.

EIGHTEEN: ENTER JENNER

Kris Kardashian meeting Bruce Jenner account from Jenner memoir. Todd Waterman quotes from press accounts. Author interviews with Joni Migdal, Larry Kraines.

NINETEEN: KISSIN' COUSINS

Author interviews with Kenn Gulliksen, Bud Halicki, Michelle Orist, Vangie Shakarian, Robert Glaser.

TWENTY: FATAL FRIENDSHIP

Author interviews with Tom Kardashian, Joni Migdal, Larry Kraines. Scene of O. J. Simpson asking Kris to make call is from Sheila Weller's book, *Raging Heart: The*

Intimate Story of the Tragic Marriage of O.J. and Nicole Brown Simpson. O. J.'s use of the N-word from TV documentary.

TWENTY-ONE: DIRE WARNINGS

Author interviews with Paulette Kardashian, Larry Kraines, Tom Kardashian, Neal Hersh, Joni Migdal. Account of Denice Shakarian Halicki's role from Lawrence Schiller's "American Tragedy: The Uncensored Story of the Simpson Defense."

TWENTY-TWO: TRAGIC TIMES

Author interviews with Joni Migdal, Kenn Gulliksen, Larry Kraines, confidential source, Vangie Shakarian.

TWENTY-THREE: LONELY FAREWELL

Author interviews with Larry Kraines, Joni Migdal, Neal Hersh, Tom Kardashian. Some quotes from Jenner memoir.

PART III: THE "MISCREANTS"
TWENTY-FOUR: "KIM KARDASHIAN, SUPERSTAR"

Kris Jenner's behind-the-scenes role in Kim's sex tape from a source who requested anonymity in interview with author. Vivid Entertainment comments from press accounts. Kris Jenner's appearance with Joan Rivers on YouTube. Some quotes from Jenner memoir. Author interviews with Larry Kraines, Tom Kardashian.

TWENTY-FIVE: IT'S REALITY

Press accounts about Bruce Jenner. Press accounts about Seacrest. Kris Jenner's memoir. *Haut Living* magazine. *The New York Times. Forbes.* Author interview with Joni Migdal.

TWENTY-SIX: A "COMPLEX" LIE

Author interviews with Nate Denver. *Complex* magazine. Author interviews with Mickey Boardman. *Paper* magazine. News reports about Odom, and men in Kardashian women's lives.

TWENTY-SEVEN: THE "MISFIT"

Author interviews with confidential source on Bruce Jenner. Author interview with Paul Cohen. Author interview with business confidant. Author interview with *Playboy* mansion source. Press reports regarding Linda Thompson, and Thompson's memoir. Press reports regarding Chrystie Scott.

EPILOGUE

Forbes and other business press accounts. Confidential sources. Press reports regarding Kris Jenner's talk show. Press reports regarding Kardashian financial business issues. Robin Givhan quote from *Washington Post*. Maureen Callahan quote from *New York Post*. Kris Jenner political talk from confidential sources.

SELECTED BIBLIOGRAPHY

Dunn, Dominick. *Justice: Crimes, Trials and Punishments*. New York: Three Rivers Press, 2001.

Edwards, Michael. *Priscilla, Elvis and Me*. New York: St. Martin's Press, 1988.

Finstad, Suzanne. *Child Bride: The Untold Story of Priscilla Beaulieu Presley*. New York: Three Rivers Press, 1997.

Jenner, Kris. *Kris Jenner and All Things Kardashian*. New York: Gallery Books, 2011.

Kardashian, Kourtney, Kim, Khloé. *Kardashian Konfidential*. New York: St. Martin's Press, 2010.

Oppenheimer, Jerry. *House of Hilton: From Conrad to Paris, A Drama of Wealth, Power and Privilege*. New York: Crown Publishers, 2006.

Presley, Priscilla Beaulieu with Sandra Harmon. *Elvis and Me*. New York: Berkley Books, 1986.

Resnick, Faye D. with Jeanne V. Bell. *Shattered: In the Eye of the Storm*. Beverly Hills, Ca.: Dove Audio, Inc., 1996.

Resnick, Faye D. with Mike Walker. *Nicole Brown Simpson: The Private Diary of a Life Interrupted*. Beverly Hills, Ca.: Dove Books, 1994.

Reynolds, Debbie and David Patrick Columbia. *Debbie: My Life*. New York: William Morrow, 1988.

Reynolds, Debbie and Dorian Hannaway. *Unsinkable: A Memoir*. New York: William Morrow, 2013.

Schiller, Lawrence and Willwerth, James. *American Tragedy: The Uncensored Story of the Simpson Defense*. New York: Random House, 1996.

Shakarian, Demos as told to John and Elizabeth Sherrill. *The Happiest People on Earth*. Old Tappan, New Jersey: Chosen Books, 1975.

Shakarian, Richard. *Still the Happiest People*. Charlotte, N.C.: LifeBridge, 2012.

Stafford, Susan. *Stop the Wheel I Want to Get Off*. 2010.

Tallman, Mathew W. *Demos Shakarian: The Life, Legacy and Vision of a Full Gospel Business Man*. Lexington, Ky.: Emeth Press, 2010.

Thompson, Linda. *A Little Thing Called Life: On Loving Elvis Presley, Bruce Jenner and Songs in Between*. New York: Dey St., 2016.

Toobin, Jeffrey. *The People v. O.J. Simpson*. New York: Random House, 1996.

Weller, Sheila. *Raging Heart: The Intimate Story of the Tragic Marriage of O.J. and Nicole Brown Simpson*. New York: Pocket Books, 1995.

Along with the aforementioned books, a number of periodicals—pop culture celebrity weeklies, online sites specializing in celebrity news and gossip, and mainstream newspapers and magazines were researched for credible stories and opinion regarding the Kardashians. Among them were: *The New York Times, The Washington Post, The Wall Street Journal, The New York Daily News, The Los Angeles Times, The Daily Mail*, and *The Guardian* and their affiliated Web sites. Also cited: *Life & Style, Radar, People, TMZ, Huffington Post, The Daily Beast, The Hollywood Reporter, US, Variety, Complex* magazine, *Paper* magazine, and *Vogue*.

INDEX